Race and Power

D0601339

If globalisation is making the world more interconnected and more homogenous, why are racist divisions deepening?

Race and Power reviews cutting-edge debates around racial politics and the culture and economy of globalisation in an accessible way for undergraduate students. Far from concluding that racism is over, the authors contend that the forces of globalisation inhabit older cultures of racial division in order to safeguard the economic interests of the privileged. Arguing that the unspoken culture of whiteness informs much that passes in the name of globalisation, the book suggests that we are witnessing a reformulation of economic relations around global racisms. Alongside these shifts in economic relations racialised identities evolve to encompass mixed heritages and mixed cultures both in personal identities and in lifestyle choices. The volume ends with an examination of the role of diasporic cultural forms in contemporary global consciousness.

Gargi Bhattacharyya is Lecturer in the Department of Cultural Studies and Sociology, University of Birmingham. **John Gabriel** is Professor of Sociology at London Guildhall University. **Stephen Small** is Associate Professor in the Department of African American Studies at the University of California, Berkeley.

Race and Power

Global racism
in the twenty-first century

Gargi Bhattacharyya,
John Gabriel and Stephen Small

London and New York

First published 2002
by Routledge
11 New Fetter Lane, London EC4P 4EE

Simultaneously published in the USA and Canada
by Routledge
29 West 35th Street, New York NY 10001

Routledge is an imprint of the Taylor & Francis Group

© 2002 Gargi Bhattacharyya, John Gabriel and Stephen Small

Typeset in Sabon by BC Typesetting, Bristol
Printed and bound in Great Britain by
St Edmundsbury Press, Bury St Edmunds, Suffolk

British Library Cataloguing in Publication Data
A catalogue record for this book is available from the British Library

Library of Congress Cataloging in Publication Data
Bhattacharyya, Gargi.
    Race and power: global racism in the twenty-first century/
Gargi Bhattacharyya, John Gabriel and Stephen Small.
        p.   cm.
    Includes bibliographical references and index.
    1. Racism. 2. Racism–Economic aspects. 3. Race relations–
Economic aspects. 4. International economic relations–Social
aspects. I. Gabriel, John. II. Small, Stephen. III. Title.

HT1521.B476 2001
305.8–dc21   2001019967

ISBN 0–415–21970–1 (hbk)
ISBN 0–415–21971–X (pbk)

Contents

Introduction

This volume seeks to develop our understanding of racialisation as an aspect of globalisation. We begin from the assumption that 'race' is constructed through a variety of social forces and that the task here is to trace how people come to be differentiated in racial terms and how this relates to shifts in global patterns of power. We argue that globalisation has transformed our conceptions of race and racism (although all too many ugly and familiar traits remain), and that what was considered to be a societal or national problem is transmuted into another symptom of our globalised existence.

This is not a textbook in the sense of offering a comprehensive overview of literature in the fields of race and ethnicity. Given the current scope of the field any such project is bound to be selective. Instead we refer to those authors whose work relates to each of the broad chapter themes of this volume. As far as key terms are concerned, we offer broad definitions but share the view held by many academic writers these days that the precise meaning of socially constructed concepts like ethnicity and 'race' as well as the different forms of racism and processes of racialisation will vary according to the context in which they are used. In the case of racialisation we adopt one of the author's distinctions between racialisation as a *process* of attributing racial differences to groups and racialisation as a *problematic* which seeks to explain those differences, barriers, etc. (Small, 1994a: 33). We use 'racism' to refer to the ideological content of such alleged differences. The latter invariably form part of a wider set of myths and logic, bound up with notions of innate inferiority and difference – what Stuart Hall has called a racist chain of meaning (1991b).

Our aim here is not to debate the pros and cons of different concepts but to contribute to the field in general through a more focused discussion of how forms of racialisation have been reconfigured through globalisation. Hence, for example, we are less interested in pitting one social division (e.g. ethnicity, race, class, gender, sexuality) against another than with exploring the ways in which these are co-constituted and reconstituted through shifts in the global order.

Within this transmutation, familiar themes are retained – and the volume focuses on these issues of identity, history and social relations, cultural production and enfranchisement. Our project is to provide a context to explain the shift in emphasis from 'old' determining ethnicities to 'new' dynamic ethnicities. In this, we are building on the suggestion that ethnicity and identity are not fixed from birth, a set of characteristics we all somehow embody, but instead take shape through a variety of changing structures. This follows Steve Fenton's point that '[ethnic categories] are not simply a direct product of shared ancestry, culture and language, but rather, also of the way ancestry is viewed, culture is constructed and language is used in the formation and modification of ethnic identities' (1999: 19).

We also reject the study of race and ethnicity as an invasive scrutiny of black people, and instead have sought to problematise whiteness. Hence our decision to make the latter the focus of the first chapter. Richard Dyer wrote about whiteness in contemporary film in the late 1980s, a period that coincided with a revival of interest in the work of black intellectuals like W.E.B. Dubois and Frantz Fanon, both of whom had written about whiteness much earlier. The settings in which whiteness was researched in the 1990s moved beyond popular representations to examine its meanings in everyday culture and identities (see e.g. Frankenberg, 1993). In our view the concept enables us to explore the origins of whiteness in the rational male subject of the Enlightenment period through the reworkings of racist myths as well as uncovering new forms of racialisation which have coincided with global developments, including the development and expansion of telecommunications and information technology. The latter have created the possibility of new, transnational allegiances and identities to emerge and make new forms of politics possible. It also allows us to turn the analytical spotlight off minority cultures (often couched in terms of problems) and focus on the ways in which privileges are maintained through the discourses of whiteness.

Like all social categories, the boundaries of whiteness shift over time and place. Groups that appear white in one context may be a racialised 'other' in another. The first chapter thus explores the ways in which whiteness has been constructed historically to include and exclude different groups, notably Irish, Jewish and Chinese ethnicities, and how these constructions were integrally bound up with ideas of class, gender and sexuality. We also examine its more recent growth as a political object amongst a number of cults, organisations and parties and consider the ways in which such allegiances take on a particular significance under new global conditions. One important cultural site for the formation and consolidation of white identities and forms of politics has been new information technologies, notably the internet. In beginning to explore the articulation of white myths and others, notably those surrounding sexuality, and to examine these in the context of new global conditions, the chapter provides an introduction to themes and issues taken up in subsequent chapters.

Chapter 2 focuses on issues of global economy, class and racialised relations with a particular emphasis on production (we discuss issues of distribution and consumption in chapter 5). This continues a long-standing debate in the field, that is, on the relationship between race and class, in which we argue that we are very far from entering the post-class era. Instead, this chapter tries to reconsider the manner in which racialisation positions people economically and makes them into particular kinds of classed agents.

Previous debates in this area have tended either to insist on the primacy of class as a social organiser or to downplay the role of class in social relations in favour of a more fluid notion of social relations made through a variety of cultural identities. This debate inevitably created a sense of absolute division between believers and betrayers, those who saw class analysis as the only method and those who saw no role for a consideration of class. The shape of this debate has continued to influence much work in the area of racialised class relations – and this has made it difficult to develop non-dogmatic ways of thinking about changing relations of race and class.

Some of the most productive and influential approaches to this dilemma have disavowed the opposition between race and class, and instead have argued that racialisation as a process inhabits class relations. This allows a consideration of the structuring force of economic relations, while also recognising that racialisation may involve an autonomous dynamic which itself reshapes class. This book tries to build on this concept of mutual determination and develop the suggestion that racialisation remakes class relations for an era with a global economy.

To this end, the chapter attempts to relocate economic analyses of racism in areas of life which are seen to typify our globalised world. In an echo of the Armageddon talk which suffuses so much social theory, the chapter takes as its key areas death, war, famine and plague. The argument is that class is seen most starkly in these areas of materiality – the hard events that determine the differential fates of different bodies. Rather than offering another all-encompassing theory, the chapter suggests methods of reintegrating economic analyses into contemporary concerns. This chapter concentrates primarily on the restructuring of global class relations and the troubled relations between rich and poor worlds, taking examples from debates around the new global division of labour, law and order, and militarism as our themes. In each case, familiar forms of racialised discourse supplement the reconstitution of class relations at their most destructive. The chapter argues that this mutual parasitism, with race and class divisions feeding each other, offers a way of understanding the interplay of race and class in an era of deepening capitalist integration. In this it anticipates and complements chapters on local economies and the manner in which racialised divisions are recreated through globalisation within rich societies.

Chapter 3 develops ideas of identity construction through a discussion of the imposed categorisation and self-identification of people of mixed origins. The conquest and colonisation of the Americas brought about fundamental transformations in the nature of sexual interactions, with large populations of mixed racialised descent developing across the entire hemisphere. These populations were largely those of Europeans, Native Americans and Africans. Some of these patterns across the Americas have given rise to notions of racial utopias (in Brazil and the Caribbean), binary systems (in the US), and intermediate categories (in South Africa). Similarly, changes in patterns of migration since the Second World War, and in the international division of labour, have brought about dramatic increases in patterns of racial intermarriage, particularly in the US. And unlike earlier generations, where coercion, brutality and rape were central to sexual inter-actions, recent patterns are characterised by individual decisions in contexts of legal freedom. They have often been articulated through prisms of free choice, individual decision-making, love and romance, and breaking down racial barriers.

The chapter goes on to describe some of these patterns and explores the conceptual, theoretical and political issues that they raise. It considers patterns in a number of locations. These patterns have occurred in different contexts and have been classified in different ways. In each of these con-texts, complex configurations of demographic, legal, political, ideological and social machinations have had decisive influences on the outcomes. Even where historically endemic patterns established during colonialism have changed, their legacies – of institutional patterns, ideas, images, ideologies – have continued to hold sway. All of these patterns have been specifically gendered, as men from diverse ethnic and racialised groups have competed for access to women as resources.

This chapter argues that while recent developments offer the potential for a critical interrogation of race and race mixture, of gender and class relations, and of nationality and identity, unless significant action is taken we are more likely to see the reaffirmation of an uncritical individualism, the denial of class advantage, the subordination of group identity and collective action to the pretext of romantic love, and an entirely untenable heralding of the end of racism. The middle sections of the book examine the continuing influence of historical factors on contemporary racisms and argue that access to resources remains a key factor in racist divisions.

Chapter 4 takes up the theme of racialised bodies and the valuing of different lives in a different arena. This chapter outlines the central role of sexuality in mythologies of race, and argues that many of the classed out-comes in the previous chapter are shaped through a language of sexual-isation. A number of recent studies have pointed to the place of sexuality in historical accounts of race-thinking and -acting. In part through the growth of feminist inquiry, accounts of racialisation have attempted to acknowledge and examine the particular dependence of race-thinking on certain myths of gender and sexuality. Chapter 4 outlines this contribution and suggests ways of taking the analysis into an understanding of the contemporary world.

The key insight of work that examines the interplay of race and sexuality has been that racism is a structure of both desire and disgust – and this fascination and repulsion construct each other to make the neurotic disease we know as racism. This idea has been repeated so often it is in danger of becoming another cliché of academic race-talk, but a resonance remains. Understandings of racism have been greatly enhanced by the realisation that racial hatred is not a straightforwardly aversive reaction – now it is possible to see the racist imaginary as an unresolved tension arising from forbidden desire.

Many of the key insights about the particular role of gender in race-thinking have come from black and Third World feminism, that feminism which develops as a critique and answer to the universalising feminism of white women of the developed world. This critique insisted that women's experience was diverse and constructed by many forces, not only through the structure of gender relations, but also through race, class, economy, international politics. This chapter reviews some debates from black and Third World feminism in order to revisit the sexualised violences of racism and understand again how and why some bodies are allotted less worth than others. The chapter ends by arguing that these sexualised violences are central to the remaking of racialised class relations in a global frame.

Chapter 5 revisits the global economy but this time with a focus on distribution and consumption. In this chapter we will explore the ways in which processes of consumption construct people as different kinds of agent. The world's racialised poor inhabit worlds severely limited in their consumption choices and often excluded from the most basic of resources. We explore the racialised politics of food production and famine including the role of global agencies like the World Trade Organisation and International Monetary Fund in the debt crisis. In the second part of the chapter we examine the impact of biotechnology and genetic modification. Such 'advances' extend the Marxist idea of 'ownership' to the organic world and to a context where the terms bio-piracy and bio-serfdom serve to characterise this new, global, racialised, class struggle.

We take the discussion of the technological adaptation of the environment one stage further through an examination of pestilence, disease and contamination. There is a certain irony in western thought and practice if we consider the role played by western adventurers in spreading disease through colonisation and how western pharmaceutical companies brought new plagues to the developing world with the introduction of so-called 'wonder drugs', and then, after all that, for western discourse to conjure fears of pollution and contamination and attribute these to the racialised poor! Such fears, of course, are lived out in western cities, with all their tensions and paradoxes. So, whilst migrants and refugees are needed to service the new global business elite and what Ghassan Hage calls 'cosmo-multiculturalism' flourishes (with or without migrants!), those fears referred to above are manifested in gated compounds, surveillance cameras, security guards, heavy policing, etc., all of which serve to allay white fears and defend white space. The revival of the city as a site of academic interest has been partly due to the rapidity and visibility of such changes in an urban context but also to the particular phenomenon of 'global cities'. Race academics (see for example Cross and Keith, 1993) have in turn explored ways in which cities have provided opportunities for reworking racist myths as well as shaping new forms of diversity and ethnic allegiances. The politics of ethnicity at a local level thus can be seen to articulate a clash, and sometimes to resonate, with wider global changes.

Chapter 6 reviews debates around the term 'diaspora' and links these discussions to more long-standing concerns about the consequences of population growth. The term 'diaspora' has infiltrated a range of debates around the idea of ethnicity. Transmuted from its origins in Jewish faith cultures, the idea of diaspora has come to symbolise the diverse experiences of many migrant peoples. This chapter revisits recent writings in the field and reassesses this debate in the light of contemporary developments such as realignments in the global political order and the rise of new configurations around ideas of faith and region.

Population movements have been a cause for intense cultural activity throughout history – both in terms of a defensive rewriting of locality and more creative reworkings of identity. Now, in the era of ecological apocalypse, the struggle to become sustainable is haunted by the constant arrival of new people. Our need to use our finite resources effectively, at both local and global levels, is in continual tension with the neediness of a growing and moving population.

In this chapter we examine this tension against wider discussions about the effects of diaspora. In particular, we review the extensive literature on consumption and the cultural production of minority and/or racialised communities. This includes an account of the emergence of new forms of 'black' cultural production in music, art, literature and film. There has been an explosion of interest in the cultural productions of diasporic communities. This has included an analysis of the cultural transformation of formerly white nations and an exploration of the mixed and hybrid formations of contemporary culture. Chapter 6 reviews this work and examines debates around the possibility and desire for 'pure' cultural forms and their relation to identities. The discussion revisits debates around 'cultural imperialism' and suggests ways of comprehending the power relations of cultural exchange which do not fall back on an untenable notion of pristine nations and identities.

We end with a brief review of the key themes of the book – and a hope that others will take up our suggestion that our changing world requires non-dogmatic and eclectic methods of understanding.

Chapter I

Changing configurations
of whiteness

> The dominant impulse of whiteness took shape around the notion of ration-
> ality of the European enlightenment, with its privileged construction of the
> transcendental white male rational subject . . . in this context whiteness was
> naturalized as a universal entity that operated as more than a mere ethnic
> positionality emerging from a particular time, the late seventeenth and
> eighteenth centuries, and a particular space, western Europe.
>
> (Kincheloe and Steinberg, 1998: 5)

In broad terms this book is concerned with exploring new, global forms of
racial privilege and the social and cultural mechanisms which secure them.
We begin with the concept of whiteness, seen as a discourse which maintains white privilege. We will develop the idea in this and subsequent chapters that whiteness works best when it remains an integral but hidden part
of the normative and social orders. However, for reasons we will explore
and which have to do with the impact of globalisation, old white imaginaries have been reworked more explicitly in response to a perceived loss of
national identity, economic security, and norms surrounding sexuality and
gender.

Traditionally race-relations discourses have focused on the cultures of
ethnic groups and patterns of discrimination as they affected black and
minority ethnic groups. The idea that 'whites' and whiteness (we shall
return to the distinction below) might themselves be important objects of
consideration was by and large overlooked in mainstream writing until the
1990s. What, then, has contributed to this shift in focus and how has it
influenced our understanding of processes of racialisation and forms of
ethnic mobilisation? In the first part of this chapter we explore some important changes which have encouraged an academic interest in whiteness and
tie these to the themes developed elsewhere in the book. Secondly we will
show how or what it means to be white and hence a bearer of white
privilege changes over time, with reference to studies of different ethnicities.
Racialised discourses cannot be seen in isolation from other discourses
which also promote dominant cultural norms, particularly those relating to

gender and sexuality. We will consider the ways in which whiteness has been bolstered through its articulation with these other discourses. Finally, we will explore the continuities and disjunctures in discourses of whiteness from benign forms of universalism and multiculturalism through the propagation of global free-market principles to self-conscious expressions of whiteness often linked to the politics of the far right.

The factors responsible for a growing interest in whiteness reflect a number of themes explored in subsequent chapters. Overall, several global developments have helped to reconfigure old patterns of ethnic relations and create new forms of racial privilege and politics. These include: economic restructuring in the West, including the demise of heavy industries, the rise of the new technologies, and the expansion of old and new service industries; the growth in significance of transnational and multinational corporations; the emergence of new global divisions of labour and, finally, the rise of 'international' agencies and global economic blocs, all of which have served to transform 'national' production forms and processes and their corresponding social relations. These relations have been racialised in a number of ways: the role assigned to migrant labour in the new service economy; the shift of production sites from inner city areas, where migrant communities have traditionally resided, to greenfield (high-technology) sites, where they traditionally have not, and finally internal patterns of migration within the Third World and the use of female labour in the production of microchips and the manufacture of designer sportswear.

The emergence of transnational political as well as economic blocs, added to demographic dislocations brought about by migration and uneven patterns of settlement, have provoked unparalleled levels of collective self-doubt and paranoia on the part of western nation-states. In turn states have sought comfort in a series of strategies – from technology-inspired forms of surveillance to politically engineered militarism; from the use of prison labour to legalised killing – all of which have served to secure white privilege, always at the expense of a set of racialised/gendered categories linked to crime, war and labour.

Globalisation has thus transformed production processes, forms of governance and social relations world-wide. The resultant crisis of national belonging, which has helped make possible the orchestration of violence and death through war as well as inspiring new forms of state repression, was never just about *national* but equally about gendered/sexual identities. The anxieties, taboos and repressed desires associated with sexuality and gender have played a significant role in the creation of new forms of racialisation and white privilege, whilst at the same time drawing on old racist fantasies. David Sibley's discussion of spatial purification is extremely useful in this context (1995: 77). Underpinning it (purification) are deep-seated paranoias concerned with defilement and pollution which have formed the basis of dominant understandings not only of racial others but of the homosexual, female and mentally ill. The above terms have played on anxieties of nation as well as more individually charged meanings. Hence the language of leaking and contamination can refer to national borders or to bodies, and the associated fears are thus experienced at a number of levels, i.e. in terms of the loss of employment and livelihood, sense of belonging as well as sexual norms.

Sibley's account illustrates the ways in which whiteness helps to refocus our gaze away from those groups invariably problematised in race-relations discourses. The concepts of race relations, racism, discrimination, prejudice, etc., have, not inevitably, but invariably, encouraged the production of a sociological knowledge of the 'victim'. Whiteness, on the contrary, problematises the perpetrators and related processes. Toni Morrison makes this point when she says that rather than look at the impact of racism on blacks it is important to examine the impact of racism on those who perpetuate it (1992: 11). However, according to June Jordan, white supremacy goes beyond racism: 'it means that God put you on the planet to rule, to dominate, and occupy the center of the national and international universe – because you're white' (1995).

Economies are racialised not just in terms of production forms and processes but also in terms of processes of distribution and consumption. If we look at racialised forms of exchange and distribution world-wide, whiteness can be seen to assert itself in numerous ways: through the instrumental role played by western governments and agencies in both the creation of and the response to the debt crisis; the 'management' of food production and distribution and famine, biotechnology and the environmental impact of the policies of western governments and multinationals on poorer parts of the world. The power of whiteness in this instance lies in its capacity to impoverish, starve, contaminate and murder, all seemingly within the bounds of legality. In exploring such global changes, this volume will revisit the notion of racialised class relations with particular reference to their material, notably bodily, dimensions.

The polarisation of wealth referred to above is not restricted to rich versus poor countries or continents. Such fissures have been reproduced in the emergence of global cities such as New York, Los Angeles, Tokyo and London, which have come to symbolise spatial and temporal transformations and compressions brought about by the movement of peoples and the growth of more refined and powerful forms of communications and information technologies. Their significance as financial centres has helped to exacerbate global inequalities of wealth as well as provide opportunities for a new low-paid service sector. As Saskia Sassen has pointed out, not all spaces and boundaries within such cities are virtual (1998). The cartography of such areas has been explored both as a site for the expression of diverse cultural forms and ethnic identities and as a rekindling of old, white, anxiety-filled imaginaries. The role of governments, corporate interests, heritage lobbies have mobilised around, redefined, institutionalised new forms of racialised white space and patterns of consumption in a politics in which minority groups are faced with a series of strategic choices and dilemmas.

The significance of communities marked by race and ethnicity (whiteness, we argue, has in part thrived on its ability to remain ethnically unmarked) has been transformed as a result of struggles for colonial independence, post-colonial forms of interdependence *and* dependence. At the same time, new forms of politics have emerged, in part inspired by migrations and the formation of new diasporan communities and in part by the increasingly significant role played by corporate communications empires and their ever more sophisticated technologies. Out of these conditions a new and exciting politics of representation has emerged in which cultural producers, entrepreneurs and community organisations of hitherto marginal or excluded ethnicities have produced complex and diverse forms of cultural expression whilst at the same time challenging dominant white imaginaries. The latter have been fuelled by anxieties induced by numerical decline and by a media-fed message that anti-discrimination laws, quotas, etc., have turned whites into a class of underprivileged victims.

Our argument developed in this book is that such anxieties are misplaced. Globalisation has reconfigured social relations and there have been some losers as a result, but whiteness in its new global guise remains powerfully intact. Some of the old codes associated with privilege may have been questioned (e.g. around language and dress) but many of the mechanisms of white privilege (e.g. social networks) remain (P. Williams, 1997). Hence we are concerned with whiteness less in its extreme political manifestations than with its role in securing privilege through seemingly neutral discourses. June Jordan has acknowledged the role of common-sense rhetoric in the discourse of whiteness rather than just in the crude outpourings of groups like The Aryan Nation or the British National Party (1995). In the words of Nelson Rodriguez, 'whiteness is "so there everywhere" that we rarely question its spaces, logics, or assumptions' (1998: 50).

The shifting terrain of the white imaginary

Studies of the historical construction of whiteness have focused on different media and cultural forms as well as 'white' ethnic groups themselves. 'White' culture is represented in terms of traditions, core values and key historical moments selected and channelled through its key institutions and very much reflecting what Barnor Hesse refers to as 'white amnesia' (1997: 92). For example, research has shown how the fictional literary canon has been created in ways which relate closely to the formation of both white masculinity and white femininity in nineteenth-century England. As Said asserts,

> by the 1840s the English novel had achieved eminence as the aesthetic form and as a major intellectual voice, so to speak, in English society . . .

[Novelists like Jane Austen, George Eliot and Mrs Gaskell] shaped the idea of England . . . and part of such an idea was the relationship between home and abroad.

(Said, 1993: 85)

In novels of the imperial period, this relationship between home and abroad was rooted in relations between 'whites' (whose whiteness remained assumed and understood) and 'others'. For example, Jane Eyre's character was premised on a knowledge of the slave-owning plantocracy and the racial theories which supported it. Her status was also significantly tied to the death of Bertha, Rochester's Jamaican wife, who set fire to herself (and the house) in order that 'Jane Eyre might become the feminist individualist heroine of British fiction' (cited in R. Young, 1990: 165). Women like the Brontës were thus very much products of their imperial times. Whilst they transgressed in terms of their traditional feminine roles they did so, nevertheless, as white women. In *Mansfield Park*, the stability and prosperity associated with home is made possible because of what is happening abroad, namely on Thomas Bertram's slave plantation in Antigua. The latter is 'mysteriously necessary to the poise and beauty of *Mansfield Park*' (Said, 1993: 69).

Toni Morrison elaborates some of these themes in her analysis of early American literature and the constitution of white masculinity. In the following she sees the development of white male settler ideology in relationship to the 'other':

I want to suggest that these concerns – autonomy, authority, newness and difference, absolute power – not only become the major themes and presumptions of American literature, but that each one is made possible by, shaped by, activated by a complex awareness and employment of a constituted Africanism.

(1992: 44)

Romantic fiction provided early American writers with a means of conquering fear through their imaginations, by expressing deep-seated anxieties 'of being outcast, of failing, of powerlessness, their fear of boundarylessness, of nature unbridled and crouched for attack; their fear of the absence of civilisation, in short the terror of human freedom' (ibid.: 37). Its narrative themes were built around the search for self-validation and struggles with the 'natural world'. In literature, whiteness became the ex-nominated synonym for self-realisation through conquest, civilisation and enlightenment and the antonym of unbridled nature, savagery and darkness. In this context, racialised discourse became a metaphorical device for concealing forms of social degeneration and conflict potentially far more threatening than the racialised accounts around which the narratives were invariably spun (ibid.: 63).

The ascendancy of whiteness in these accounts is thus associated with the rise of capitalism, modernity and the nation-state, and the cultural capital which coincided with such developments. Although it is invariably linked to white western subjects, who came to represent the embodiment of humanity and reason, whiteness is not simply an ontological state. It is an imaginary. In Aaron Gresson's words, 'whiteness is not limited to physical characteristics like hair texture, skin hues, nose shape, lip and hip size, and the like. Whiteness is about the position that the category of "White people" happens to occupy in people's minds' (cited in Semali, 1998: 183).

Whiteness thus clearly emerged in an old global order marked by the rise of the western rational subject and his imperial project. Our purpose in this chapter is to illustrate the ways in which the forms and boundaries of whiteness have shifted over time, ultimately with a view to mapping its terrain under a more recent set of global conditions. The historical contingency of whiteness implied here has a number of features which will form the basis of the sections which follow. Firstly, groups defined as 'white' in one era may be racially marked in another. The emphasis on whiteness thus should not imply that forms of racialisation are reducible, universally accepted categories of 'white' and 'black'. Hence, it is possible for groups to appear white at one time and not at another. It is also possible for groups widely perceived as 'white' to be defined in racialised terms. There are no hard-and-fast rules here. Secondly, discourses of white privilege do not stand alone; they depend on other discourses and identifications for their appeal, gender (masculinity/femininity), class and sexuality being the most obvious. Finally, although whiteness stands for privilege in general, it is by no means internally coherent and can be manifest or coded in a range of seemingly contradictory political discourses.

According to Toni Morrison the discourse of whiteness is never static because it is always defined in relationship to 'otherness' and that historical/political circumstance insists that both (whiteness and otherness) are flexible enough to accommodate different groups at different times. One of the best-documented examples of the changing subjects and objects of white discourse is that of the Irish. Noel Ignatiev's book *How the Irish became White* (1995) illustrates both the transience of racial categories and the co-existence of contradictory sets of interpellations. Ignatiev, David Roediger and Theodore Allen have documented the shifts in status accorded to the Irish in the US in the nineteenth century. Prior to that the Irish were known as 'niggers turned inside out', an idea compounded by strong ties between the Irish and African-American communities in some northern cities. According to Roediger, 'for some time there were strong signs that the Irish might not fully embrace white supremacy' (1991: 134). In consequence their white/citizenship status was by no means assured under the terms of the Naturalisation Act 1790 (ibid.: 41).

During the course of the nineteenth century a number of factors together served to redefine the Irish in the order of racial privilege. The first was a series of political alliances which brought the Irish closer to white southern interests: the Catholic Church and its media, for example, 'at best . . . muted defences, and at worst racist defences, of slavery' (ibid.: 138). Furthermore, Jackson's Democratic Party offered the prospect of alliance with the southern planter class in return for an inclusive status within the idea of a white republic. The alliance increasingly compromised those Irish soldiers fighting on the side of the Union in the civil war who saw their position as jeopardising their alliance with the pro-slavery planter class (Ignatiev, op. cit.). Christine Sleeter refers to this alliance between the Irish and the southern planters as part of a process of 'white racial bonding' (1996: 261), the upshot of which facilitated the 'whitening of the Irish' and their 'assimilation' into mainstream US culture. In the aftermath of the civil war, economic restructuring also provided the Irish in the US with opportunities for upward mobility. Industrialisation created a new manual sector in the north in which the Irish played a prominent role. For example, roads, canals and textiles became labour-market niches for Irish labour. Political alliances once again proved important in securing positions in city bureaucracies, including the newly established police forces.

As well as political and economic factors in the drawing and redrawing of racialised boundaries, the role of the print media in the formation of the Irish as a 'white' constituency was also significant. For example, during the civil war, the New York *Caucasian* attacked abolition in the interests of the white working class (Allen, 1994: 143). The *Working Man's Advocate*, too, argued that African-Americans were better off being plantation slaves than competing on equal terms with white labour in the north. The *Irish Citizen* constituted whiteness in relationship not only to African-Americans, stating that 'we want white people to enrich the country, not mongolians to degrade and disgrace it' (9 July 1870, cited in Lee, 1996: 196).

Overall, political and economic factors, combined with the views expressed by cultural institutions including the Catholic Church and the print media, culminated for the Irish in what Roediger refers to as an 'imperative to define themselves as white' (op. cit.: 137) and to 'treasure their whiteness as entitling them to both political rights and to jobs' (ibid.: 136). The whitening of the Irish in the ways suggested by Ignatiev and Roediger does not rule out its co-existence alongside continuing forms of anti-Irish racism, including the New England custom of burning an effigy of the Pope on Guy Fawkes day and the 'Blood Tubs' used to 'dip' the Irish, not to mention the indicative comments of an Oxford academic who proposed that 'the best remedy for whatever is amiss in America would be if every Irishman should kill a negro and be hanged for it' (cited in Jamieson, 1992: 79).

The history of Irish relations with England adds an interesting dimension to the study of changing forms of racialisation and the historical contingency of whiteness. Theodore Allen explores the shift from what he calls racial to national oppression in the late eighteenth century. Initially colonial dominance was secured legally and ideologically through the enactment of the penal laws which banned literacy, curtailed property rights and dismantled family ties amongst the Catholic community (1994: 81ff.). The shift away from what Allen refers to as this religio-racism to an oppression based on nationality was made for expedient reasons as the English became aware of the need for a domestic (in this case Catholic) bourgeoisie to act as a colonial buffer. However, far from dying out altogether those old racial imaginaries were reworked in the context of Irish emigration to England in the nineteenth century and again in the context of political conflict in the twentieth century.

Ironically whilst the Irish were forming political alliances with white interests in the US, they were the object of very different forms of racialisation in England in the latter part of the nineteenth century. According to Mary Hickman (1995b: 78), the Irish were subject to police brutality, and the object of divide-and-rule tactics on the part of the state, which at the time was intent on preventing an alliance between Chartists and Irish nationalists (ibid.: 78). The 'paddy joke' was part of the cultural armoury designed to fragment groups whose common working-class interests might otherwise have been seen as uniting them. In exploring the significance of the paddy joke Phil Cohen writes,

> his 'congenital stupidity' is . . . symbolised by his proverbial absence of family planning. His catholic tastes (in food and drink) are another sign that he does not fit in . . . it is in and through the figure of the paddy that racist theories of intelligence and moral degeneration were linked and relayed through popular culture to become common sense.
> (Cohen, 1988: 74–5)

Even racist theories themselves appeared in the popular press, admittedly laced with humour for more immediate consumption. For example, in 1862 a cartoon appeared in *Punch* with the title 'the missing link: a creature manifestly between the gorilla and the negro' (cited in Pieterse, 1992: 214). This kind of spurious science was supported by ideas of the 'wild Irishmen' and the 'monstrous Celtic Caliban capable of any crime known to man or beast' (Curtis, 1971: 29).

What such studies of the Irish in the US and England suggest is that racial markings have shifted in response to changing historical and political conditions. The dilemmas facing groups whose whiteness has always appeared conditional is an important part of understanding forms of ethnic mobilisation and broader cultural strategies. Jewish as well as Irish communities have been forced to address at times the costs and benefits of concealing and/or mobilising around ethnic difference. The price of 'ethnic concealment' may be denial and a loss of self and communal forms of identification, and may not always work, particularly in periods of national 'crisis', for example the discriminatory use of the Prevention of Terrorism

Act (Hillyard, 1993) or popular anti-Irish racism in the wake of bombing campaigns in mainland Britain. The repertoire of images, jokes and stories from the nineteenth century have been reworked and retold with relative ease in the columns of the tabloid press in Britain (see Curtis, 1971, 1984). Likewise, efforts to assimilate into the mainstream British community have not prevented institutionalised discrimination in such areas as housing, employment and health (Hickman, 1995b). What have been concealed are the levels of discrimination (ibid.).

The relational and historically contingent role of the white imaginary is well illustrated in the case of Christianity and Judaism. Medieval anti-Semitism served to unite Christendom at a time (during and after the Crusades) that Christianity was under threat from both Islam and Judaism (Trachtenberg, 1993: 11). Sartre describes the significance of anti-Semitism in relationship to the construction of white Christian identity thus:

> the Christian, the Aryan, feels his body in a special way . . . the messages and appeals that his body sends him come with certain co-efficients of ideality, and are always more or less symbolic of vital values . . . the nonchalant or the elegant . . . the grace of women . . . and to these values are naturally linked some anti-values.
>
> (1962: 120)

However, anti-Semitism not only expressed the racialisation of religion but in the nineteenth century accommodated some of the specious claims of so-called scientific/biological racism. According to Sander Gilman (1991: 172), for example, the view that Jews were black-skinned was widely held from the seventeenth to the nineteenth centuries. Moreover this was linked to the idea that Jews physiologically resembled Africans. In the words of Robert Knox, 'the African character of the Jew, his muzzle shaped mouth . . . the whole physiognomy, when swarthy, as it often is, has an African look' (cited ibid.: 174). Other physical markings gained in significance. The nose was one such marker, the significance of which was confirmed by development of plastic surgery or rhinoplasty in the early twentieth century. The nose also had sexual connotations according to psychoanalysts of the period. Hence, according to Freud and Fleiss, the nose was analogous to the genitalia, and their prognosis for sexual dysfunction was nose surgery (ibid.: 188). Anti-Semitism was of course rife in Europe during this period, from the Dreyfus Affair in France to the police role and press coverage of the 'Ripper' murders in Whitechapel in London, and the establishment of anti-aliens organisations in England supported by the popular press of the time (S. Taylor, 1993: 174) and culminating in the Aliens Act 1905 aimed implicitly but decidedly at Jewish immigration. According to Robert Miles, the Act 'was formulated at a time when a negative, racialised, representation of Jews was widely reproduced . . . the formal definition of "undesirable immigrant" in the Act was understood in the everyday world to refer to Jews' (1993: 145).

The popular press in England continued to bolster anti-Semitism well into the twentieth century. During the 1930s the *Sunday Pictorial* described a possible influx of Jewish refugees escaping fascism in mainland Europe in terms of a babble of waving palms at an eastern bazaar and as a threat to the English countryside (cited in Kushner, 1989: 127). In a similar vein, local newspapers like the *Hackney Gazette* openly supported discrimination against Jewish tenants (ibid.: 59). Moreover, of the role of Jews in the so-called black economy, Tony Kushner writes that 'the identification continued, present in radio plays, house of commons, popular literature, comics . . . major attacks on Jewish involvement in black marketing in papers ranging from *Time and Tide* and *The Daily Mirror* to *The Spectator*' (ibid.: 120).

Likewise in the US, the media played a strategic role in redefining white and not just Protestant national identity in the aftermath of the civil war. For example, according to the *Boston Investigator*, Jews were denounced as 'about the worst people of whom we have any account' and 'a troublesome people to live in proximity with' (cited in Dinnerstein, 1994: 31). Moreover, Baltimore's three Catholic newspapers during the last decade of the nineteenth and early part of the twentieth centuries reveal anti-Semitism in their editorial columns. And of course, there was the not insignificant role played by Henry Ford in propagating anti-Semitism both through his pronouncements (e.g. 'The Jew is a mere huckster who doesn't want to produce, but to make something out of what somebody else produces', cited in ibid.: 81) and in his own *Dearborn Independent* which published, amongst other anti-Semitic pieces, the forged protocols of the Elders of Zion. Elsewhere the views of eugenicists were flourishing on both sides of the Atlantic. Intelligence tests in the US were used to demonstrate the feeblemindedness of all but the Protestant descendants of north-west Europe with the result that 'racism fused with eugenics in scientific circles, and the eugenics circles overlapped with the nativism of white protestant elites' (Brodkin, 1998: 29).

Since the 1940s anti-Semitism has been less explicit and, some would argue, no longer defines national identity in contrast to Jewishness; rather the latter is now integrally bound up with mainstream notions of what it is to be American (Dinnerstein, 1994). As in the case of the Irish this has not meant the elimination of racial markers altogether and it certainly does not preclude their re-emergence in the future. Karen Brodkin, for example, cites evidence of the personally held anti-Semitic views of Richard Nixon and George Bush 'and its prevalence in both their administrations indicates its persistence in the Protestant elite' (1998: 37). Likewise, Dinnerstein cites the role of anti-Semitism in extreme right-wing organisations, as well as its more subtle presence in mainstream culture in the form of the 1980s 'Jewish American Princess' slur, as examples of anti-Semitism's continuing capacity to resurface within dominant, white Protestant culture (op. cit.: 136).

Race and sex

A recurrent theme in this book is the way in which reworked and new forms of racialisation articulate with other discourses. We are particularly interested in the ways in which global class relations have been the object of processes of racialisation. Yet we also argue that racialised relations are simultaneously constituted in terms of sexuality and gender and that the material, bodily consequences of such discursive investments should form a significant part of our analysis. This relates to a further point, that these discourses do more than co-exist. They strengthen each other's grip on popular consciousness and cement social divisions across a range of axes. Cora Kaplan makes this point when she urges us not to think of race and gender in a hierarchical structure 'reciprocally constituting each other through a kind of narrative invocation, a set of associative terms in a chain of meaning' (cited in Lewis, 1996: 15).

A number of writers draw loosely on psychoanalysis in order to explore the roots of racialised discourses in the unconscious. For example, Zillah Eisenstein (1996) seeks to establish links between the multiple and fluid hate crimes characteristic of the last years of the twentieth century. Hatred, she argues, embodies fear, and racial and sexual markers are the mechanisms through which we 'see', 'speak' and/or 'deny' fear. But it is fear of the unbridled self, not the other, which is at the root of racism, homophobia, etc. The practice of mapping identities onto different bodies, be they white female, Jewish male, black female or black male, says more about the dysfunctionality of those doing the mapping than about those being mapped. According to Gilman, 'The "white *man's* burden" thus becomes his sexuality and its control, and it is this which is transferred into the need to control the sexuality of the Other, the Other as sexualized female' (1991: 194, emphasis in original).

The analysis of whiteness takes an interesting turn here. The object now is not just to assert, sanction and explain privilege but to police and control the behaviour and values of the albeit shifting category of 'white people'. In other words, constructions of otherness, in deploying ideas of sexuality and gender, thus became repositories for a contradictory set of white desires and fears. For example, Young describes how black women and lower-class white women in the nineteenth century were positioned as objects of transgression and denial as part of the process of constructing traits associated with both white middle-class femininity (chaste, passive, dependent, etc.) and masculinity (independent, strong, brave, etc.) (L. Young, 1996: 161). The popular media proved significant cultural mechanisms through which such ideas took hold. In Young's words,

Newspapers, popular entertainment, postcards and comics in the first decade of the twentieth century constantly reinforced the idea of war as glamorous, character building and fascinating: an activity which occurred in far-off exotic places . . . These images and fantasies were inextricably linked to conceptualisations of masculinity, and the idea of what constitutes masculinity was a key site for confrontations springing from racial conflict.

(1996: 60)

The notorious case of Jack the Ripper is worth mentioning here since it serves to illustrate the ways in which gender, sexuality and class were articulated with anti-Semitism. The tale of 'the Ripper' is well known and the subject of numerous books, films and waxworks objects. In 1888 the police issued a cartoon-type caricature of a man alleged to have carried out the murders of six prostitutes in London's East End. The image was clearly meant to establish his Jewish, east European origins. The image worked because it played on precisely those fears and repressed desires of white masculinity referred to above.

Hence the press at the time reported that 'the criminal was a sexual maniac of a virulent type . . . and . . . that he and his people were low-class Jews' (cited in Gilman, op. cit.: 115). Such reporting exacerbated tensions within London's East End and fuelled attacks on the local Jewish community. However, what gave the case added resonance was the link it was able to establish between deviant racialised sexuality and fallen white femininity. Dominant police/press discourses thus served both to regulate whiteness and secure racial/gendered/classed hierarchies at the expense of Jewish masculinity and white lower-class femininity. Such constructions were not new, even then. As Gilman points out, the Jew–prostitute connection can be traced back to the image of Moll Hackabout, the 'Jew's mistress' in Hogarth's *Harlot's Progress*, as well as resurfacing in Marcel Proust's *Remembrance of Times Past* (ibid.: 120). The point is that such stories are available to be retold and adapted at different times.

A century later, a case involving many of the ingredients of that of the Ripper emerged in the world's media. O.J. Simpson was a US football quarter-back legend in his time but who had remained one of white America's favourite adopted sons, sustained by his regular appearances on TV commercials and small parts in Hollywood films. Remained, that is, until he was accused of the murder of his wife Nicole Brown Simpson and her friend, Ronald Goldman. O.J. quickly became a 'black criminal', *Time* magazine even 'blackened' the police photoshot of Simpson, thereby allaying any doubts as to his 'real' racial status. The mugshot image of Simpson not only came to symbolise the latest incarnation of black criminality. It also came to stand for the threat of black male sexuality and the corresponding vulnerability of white femininity reflected in the bloodied images of Nicole Simpson (Fiske, 1994: xvii). Old photographs of the Simpson family shot in happier times and reproduced in the media only served to remind viewers of the inherent instability and dysfunctionality of interracial relationships (ibid.).

Despite *Time*'s best efforts to establish O.J.'s black credentials, for the first part of the trial at least O.J. remained a middle-class celebrity. It was only with the release of the Fuhrman tapes in which the said police officer talked on tape of giving blacks a good beating that the racial gloves came off on both sides. Set against a backdrop of the court decision to acquit the Los Angeles police officers responsible for beating Rodney King and the subsequent riots, the case became increasingly polarised in racial terms. On the one hand many African-Americans celebrated the jury's verdict of 'not guilty' which they saw as a condemnation of Mark Fuhrman and a defence of Rodney King as much as it had to do with the innocence or otherwise of O.J. Simpson. Many whites, on the other hand, were outraged by the verdict on the grounds that the case against Simpson was proven and as such the court effectively denied the interests of (white) victims of (black) domestic violence.

Although such taboos surrounding interracial sex have been around for over four centuries, they received a boost in the late nineteenth and twentieth centuries with the emergence of the eugenics movement. The latter, with its emphasis on 'in-group purity' and the consequences of 'diluting' inherited qualities through mixing with 'out-groups', gave those taboos a rational, pseudo-scientific gloss as well as justifying an array of racisms including genocidal forms of politics such as those witnessed in Germany in the 1930s. Eugenics used such terms as 'disease', 'plague', 'infection' both metaphorically and literally to construct a common-sense discourse around 'class, gender, "race", sexuality, and mental ability' (Young, op. cit.: 51). Interestingly, although the movement proved a source of inspiration for the extreme right in both western Europe and the US, its early sympathisers included members of the Labour reformist Fabian Society, for example Sydney and Beatrice Webb, and early feminist campaigners for contraception, such as Marie Stopes. The fact that such views have always had the capacity to extend across the political spectrum in this way relates to a distinction made by Kovel in his psychohistory of whiteness (1988) between dominative racists who are explicit and intentional and aversive racists whose racism only surfaces when put to the test. The former might include Aryan extremists while the latter might include liberals who privately hope that interracial partnerships happen to someone else's children. We shall return to such continuities below.

The racialisation of the Chinese communities in England and the US in the late nineteenth and early twentieth centuries illustrates forms of racialisation which emerged against a backdrop of colonial wars and massacres prosecuted by the English at the centre of which was the trade in opium (Kiernan, 1972). Those Chinese labourers who were brought in to work on the railroads and in the construction industry in the US in the nineteenth century were the object of scare stories not dissimilar to those described above. For example, in 1854 the *New York Daily Tribune* alleged that the Chinese and the 'oriental' were 'uncivilised, unclean, filthy beyond all conception, without any of the higher domestic or social relations; lustful and sensual in their dispositions; *every* female is a prostitute, and of the basest order . . . Clannish in nature, pagan in religion they know not the virtues of honesty, integrity or good faith' (cited in Lee, 1996: 184, emphasis in original). The significance of white fears in underpinning such outbursts is underlined by the deployment of the trope of 'inundation' which Lee describes thus: 'the phobia of drowning in an unclean and alien fluid is invoked . . . the fear of contamination, the terror of being made unclean by the filthy and sick' (ibid.: 187). 'Dirt' invoked fears of the decay and submergence of white culture in a tide of 'waste' (ibid.: 188). Such ideas provided the ideological basis for legislation both restricting immigration (the 1882 Exclusion Act) and banning intermarriage, neither of which was repealed until the 1940s (ibid.: 197).

Although the economic role of Chinese immigrants in England reflected past links with ports and seafaring rather than new forms of transport and construction, popular press reactions were by no means dissimilar. For example, the *Sunday Chronicle* talked about Liverpool as a 'yellow town not fitted to be part of civilized white society' (cited in Clegg, 1994: 9). In 1906, the *Weekly Courier* ran a headline 'YELLOW PERIL: PUBLIC INDIGNATION INCREASING', and in 1911, *London Magazine* wrote 'beneath its calm and dingy exterior there stir the same dark passions, instincts and racial tendencies which cause this mystic yellow people to be so misunderstood, feared and hated' (cited in Lee, op. cit.: 200). Ideas of contamination and the dangers of interracial sex were also prevalent in press reports of the time. For example, the *Courier* ran an article under the headline 'TAINTING THE RACE' in which interracial mixing was described in the following terms: 'the result of such unions [between Chinese and English women] is found in swarms of half-bred children to be seen in the district . . . [moreover] it is not only degraded women who mate with these men' (ibid.: 211). The aim here has not been to provide an exhaustive account of the racialisation of the Chinese community but to illlustate the ways in which discourses of sexuality and gender were used to bolster those of race against a background of old-style white colonialism.

Disjunctures and continuities

In this section we explore the heterogeneity of discourses of whiteness but also their similarities. Kovel's distinction between dominative and aversive racists emphasises an important difference but not at the expense of the fact that both types are racist. On the one hand whiteness in the West is most self-consciously expressed in far-right political organisations and movements. In the US, for example, the military defeat in Vietnam, the widespread prevalence of a gun culture, an 'anti-big government' tradition, Christian fundamentalism and feminism have all been cited as factors responsible for a crisis of white masculinity and the emergence of white supremacist groups based on militias and/or Christian fundamentalism. In England, on the other hand, the situation has been somewhat different with networks based on football clubs and music, a historically specific relationship to Ireland, debates about electoral versus confrontational politics and the demography of local areas all playing their part. Furthermore, the anxieties and fears of such groups on both sides of the Atlantic have been fuelled by a sense of capitulation to global forces: the onset of new forms of telecommunications and information technologies, economic restructuring, class/political fragmentation and the emergence of new global power blocs. An important argument developed here and elsewhere in this book is that contrary to such concerns these changes are less of a threat to, and more of a realignment of, white masculinity, which has often been quick to take advantage of new global conditions.

For example, the internet has provided opportunities for organisations and parties of the far right to form alliances, exchange ideas, collectively mobilise and sell their products world-wide on a scale not possible prior to the IT revolution. The growth of a distinct genre of white supremacist music is a case in point. Internet technology has not only provided a global market for white supremacist merchandise including music and T-shirts but also access to publications. The growth of a particularly aggressive racist *and* global version of white masculinity, though not the direct result of technological developments, has certainly benefited from such advances.

The above discussion illustrates the more brutal, uncoded versions of whiteness. Somewhere nearer the 'centre' or mainstream of the political spectrum and even towards its more liberal, progressive end whiteness manifests itself in more coded forms, in ways which parallel Kovel's aversive racism which only appears when put to the test. Arguably, the more white sensibilities are tested in response to such factors as migration, new forms of cultural representation and difference, and anti-racist politics, the more likely coded whiteness whatever its political hue will increasingly decode itself. However, since we are talking about a reconfiguration of whiteness rather than its dismantling, the so-called crisis which is invariably expressed in terms of white men may only reflect a period of adjustment to a new set of conditions. Moreover, whiteness is implicit in a range of discourses which either conceal their true colours altogether (for example, discourses of markets and free trade) or even more paradoxically conceal their whiteness beneath a discourse of multiculturalism and human rights. Moreover, there are risks associated with more explicit, self-conscious expressions of whiteness. The more the seemingly universal discourses of the centre (e.g. liberalism, the rule of law, free markets) reveal their ethnic particularity, the less 'universal' they appear. In so doing they undermine a key source of their legitimacy, that is, their apparent ethnic neutrality.

The relationship between more coded and more explicit discourses of whiteness has been encapsulated in David Duke's career in US politics (from Democrat to KKK to Republican state senator) which not only serves to indicate the transitions possible within a single political lifetime, but more interestingly the ways in which political issues associated with white supremacism in one decade reappear in mainstream platforms in the next. So, for example, Duke's recommendations on immigration, affirmative action and welfare were dismissed as extremist rhetoric of the lunatic fringe in the 1980s only to become part of the mainstream political agenda in the 1990s. Although he himself ultimately failed to fully realise his goal of bridging in Barkun's words the cultic/mainstream divide, others have taken up such issues in their campaigns and legislative programmes. The success of such campaigns has relied on their articulation by respectable politicians and, equally important, by black spokespeople whose physical presence enhances their apparent universal and neutral appeal. The seemingly diverse appeal of an issue is no guarantee against its exclusionary and discriminatory effects.

Popular culture has also provided an important conduit through which both distinct and congruent forms of white masculinity have been constituted as Fred Pfeil's study, *White Guys* (1995), has confirmed. Both the *Lethal Weapon* (Dir. Richard Donner, 1987, 1989, 1992) and *Die Hard* films (Dir. John McTiernan, 1988, 1995, and Renny Harlin's *Die Hard 2*, 1990) worked around themes of lost innocence, irrelevant/redundant 'old world' values and skills, and political and institutional corruption and/or incompetence. According to Donna Haraway, whilst films like *Rambo II* and *Top Gun* assert male violence, they simultaneously undermine men's claims to authority, what she has called the 'paradoxical intensification and erosion of gender itself' (cited in Pfeil, 1995: 27–8).

In Gibson's terms (1994), such representational forms were bound up with a wider political and economic context, namely the military defeat of the US in Vietnam as well as the collapse of the manual-labour sector and the changing role of women in western economies (1994: 28). Another cinematic expression of white masculinity in the 1980s was the iconic figure of Arnold Schwarzenegger, whose 'new'/'old' white working man invited his audiences to respond to both his Aryan/super-human physical presence and to his 'ridiculous implacability, obscene violence, and hulking insensitivity with a sneer that then permits the qualities sneered at to be embraced and enjoyed' (ibid.: 31).

Rock music, too, has had its fair share of white male icons from Elvis Presley, Mick Jagger, Bruce Springsteen to Axel Rose. Whilst they straddle various musical tastes, traditions and youth cultures, these musicians also reflect a broader normative allegiance. Springsteen has been particularly interesting because he has in part sought an affinity with white working-class culture, both lyrically, in tracks like 'The River' and 'Born to Run', and in his own physically buffed appearance. According to Pfeil, Springsteen's success has been achieved through his ability to bottle his aggression (but not so as to hide it completely), his attachment to national symbols (e.g. the American flag) and his reliance on 'white' musical influences (notably rockabilly and country-western). His music thus gained a wider appeal even extending to those (e.g. Ronald Reagan) with whom at an individual level Springsteen disagreed politically.

To suggest that there is a continuum at work in the context of Hollywood film and western popular music is not meant to imply that *Born in the USA* and tracks such as 'Barbecue in Bostock' are equivalent or that John McClane in the *Die Hard* films or Riggs in the *Lethal Weapon* trilogy is a mere fictional incarnation of Timothy McVeigh or David Lane. The point here is to suggest that at some level there is a core set of values and motivations underpinning what are widely different and often contradictory actions.

What this also suggests is that whiteness is by no means necessarily linked with something intentionally malign. The point here is that it is expressed and reinforced more by routine, everyday culture than the conspiracies of the militias or Combat 18. At root whiteness has been about maintaining traditions, representing culture (necessarily selectively) and anchoring identities. The problem with such forms of whiteness, 'innocent' as they appear, has been their exclusivity and the inevitable hierarchies of representation and access which result. Such are the unspoken, unconscious, yet privileging effects of whiteness in spheres of both cultural production and consumption, which we will discuss again in subsequent chapters.

Whiteness: themes and characteristics

Much of this book is concerned with mapping new forms of racialisation in the light of global changes. The alleged crisis of whiteness and in particular of white masculinity is not so much a crisis as a reconfiguration of forms of white dominance and the means of securing white privilege in a new era. In concluding this chapter, we will summarise some of the main themes and issues to emerge from our discussion of the concept of whiteness.

We have used whiteness not so much to refer to a set of cultural characteristics (Thanksgiving, pubs, morris dancing, etc.) as a discourse which effectively secures privileges and forms of exclusion. Fiske refers to this as a strategic deployment of power or the space from which a variety of positions can be taken (1994: 42). The emergence of whiteness has been traced back to conditions in the eighteenth century, namely the overthrow of the feudal religious orders in the West and the emergence of modern capitalism and the western bourgeois democratic nation-state. Under such conditions emerged the rational white subject with his capacity to define and regulate the subjectivity of others and to turn individuals into objects of information and thus amenable to constant scrutiny. Whiteness, therefore, cannot be understood outside of the discursive, regulatory and technological means at its disposal to position itself through others (Foucault, 1972). New global networks of media technologies and inter-related systems of communication thus provide potential mechanisms for new forms of regulation and repression as we shall explore in chapter 5. This is not surprising given the military's role in the development of many of these new technologies and their subsequent use as interconnected data bases for both surveillance and the storing of information on personal finance/debt, criminal records, etc. (Thompson, 1995: 134). Increasingly, new legislation requires employers, especially those in the public sector, in the judicial system and in finance, to monitor the citizenship status and credentials and other relevant information available from the growing data banks of personal records.

We have argued in this chapter that discourses of whiteness rely more on concealing white privileges under the guise of allegedly ethnically neutral discourses than overtly proclaiming their ethnic allegiance. The tactics of concealment include 'ex-nomination', that is to say where the power of whiteness exists precisely in its capacity not to be named; 'naturalization', through which whiteness establishes itself as the self-evident norm or bench-mark by which others are defined and inevitably seen as deficient; and finally 'universalisation', where a discourse is apparently able to speak for everyone but in fact represents the views and interests of a privileged minority (Fiske, op. cit.: 43). In Dyer's words, 'whiteness is often revealed as emptiness, absence, denial or even a kind of death' (ibid.: 44). W.E.B. Dubois uses Americanisation to refer to a similar process when he writes,

> What the powerful and privileged mean by Americanization is the determination to make the English New England stock dominant in the United States . . . it is but a renewal of the Anglo-Saxon cult; the worship of the Nordic totem, the disfranchisement of Negro, Jew, Irishman, Italian, Hungarian, Asiatic and South Sea islander – the world rule of the Nordic white through brute force.
>
> (cited in Sundquist, 1996: 384)

In the first of her Reith lectures, Patricia Williams put it another way when she said that one of the privileges of whiteness was to appear 'unraced' (1997).

Another reason why whiteness is able to keep itself hidden is because it works through other discourses. David Sibley has made some persuasive connections between the 'body sexual' and the 'body politic' in which terms of images of defilement, degeneration and contamination dominate the discourses of both (1995). Likewise, Barnor Hesse analyses the 'white' underpinnings of racial harassment with reference to the significance of body imagery in racialised constructions of city spaces. He writes, 'in the context of racial harassment the body of the other is viewed as a surface of inscription for the shrunken visibility of a white appropriation of the city' (1997: 98). Threats of city spaces being overrun, that is (of being) 'violated' and 'penetrated', make racial harassment the 'inevitable paranoiac anticipation of those events' (ibid.: 99).

Implicit in the above is an appeal to psychoanalytic discourses to unravel the complex processes entailed in the construction of whiteness. Most commonly the psychological basis of whiteness has been attributed to deep-seated insecurities, anxieties and fears which are then expressed in numerous, neurosis-driven expressions of whiteness. The aim of racialised forms of surveillance would be to allay white fears through the ability to know without being known (ibid.). But whiteness is not just rooted in fear; it also elicits fear. This is powerfully evoked in the writings of Frantz Fanon and W.E.B. Dubois who both have much to say about whiteness through their own consciousness of blackness. In *Black Skin, White Masks*, Frantz Fanon describes his reaction to being shouted at by a young white boy with the words, 'Look at the nigger . . . Mama, a Negro', and how such comments 'imprisoned him' and 'sealed him into that crushing objecthood' (1986: 113 ff.). As a result, he argued, 'the white world, the only honourable one, barred me from all participation' (ibid.). For Fanon whiteness meant subjectivities defined both through and by others as well as the internalisation of guilt. However, whiteness is more than induced guilt, according to Fanon. It is also corrupt and dehumanising, as he implies when he writes, 'when whites feel they have become too mechanised they turn to men of colour for human sustenance' (ibid.: 129). Writing earlier in the century, Dubois also noted that whiteness not only positioned blacks but positioned whites in constraining ways. The latter were thus forced to live out their racist subjectivities and in so doing they were imprisoned in their own whiteness.

We argue that there exists a complex relationship between 'being white', 'acting white' and whiteness as a discourse which transcends embodied whiteness. Whilst it is self-evident that white skin has brought 'disproportionate access to that power base' (Fiske, op. cit.: 49), it is also true that whiteness is echoed and materialised by groups not necessarily defined as white. Our discussions of Irishness and Jewishness also illustrate the ways in which whiteness is socially constructed and deconstructed according to different historical circumstances.

It follows from this last point that whiteness is not a monolith and that the boundaries of exclusion and privilege vary historically. They also vary according to other social relations, including gender. Vron Ware (1992) has explored the specificities of discourses of white femininity. For example, during the colonial period white women were seen as conduits of the race (ibid.: 37), thus fitting neatly into notions of pure stock and contamination espoused by eugenicists. White women were seen as particularly vulnerable and hence in need of protection (ibid.: 8–9). This belief reached fever pitch, according to Ware, in the aftermath of the so-called 'Indian Mutiny' of

1857 with the fear of sexual assault becoming a powerful indicator of wider control of the colonies (ibid.: 38).

Likewise, John Hartigan's ethnographic study of Detroit distinguishes three forms of whiteness, those associated with the 'hillbilly', 'gentrifier' and 'racist', each defined according to class, neighbourhood, sense of history and relationship to the city (1999). Ruth Frankenberg also disaggregated whiteness into three 'white' perspectives: colour evasion and colour cognisance (each with its own internal differences), both of which were a reaction to a third perspective, essentialised racism (1993: ch. 6). These authors have not only recognised the diversity of whiteness. They have argued that whiteness cannot be defined in terms of a set of fixed ethnic characteristics but is something which can only be defined relationally and historically. Like blackness, it is not about biological differences per se but about the cultural meanings/social constructions often, although not always, associated with skin differences. Blackness and whiteness in this sense are political concepts and just as Stuart Hall said he did not think of himself as black until the 1970s so others might only now be seeing themselves as white. Frankenberg captures the changing and diverse attachments to different ethnicity depending on time and place, by her use of the terms 'social and political salience' (Frankenberg, op. cit.: 214–15).

Although there are differences within whiteness we have also argued that there are strong continuities too, particularly when viewed across the western political spectrum. Whilst few would deny the differences when it comes to actions and outcomes, the underlying core dimension of whiteness is its capacity to secure white privilege. This has been varyingly achieved by violent and more subtle means (for a fuller discussion of the differences and continuities between 'white pride', 'normative' and 'progressive' forms of whiteness see Gabriel, 1998).

Whiteness has been undermined by what has been referred to as a politics of representation. Stuart Hall distinguishes this from the relations of representation which is more concerned with issues of bias, positive and negative images, and access to media institutions. The 'politics of representation' has been more concerned with the production of diverse forms of representation which in effect challenge stereotypical, essentialised notions of black identity or monolithic versions of black culture, and even the notion of black itself (Hall, 1992a: 253). Such politics are to be found in all spheres of representation, including film (see e.g. Shohat and Stam, 1994; Diawara, 1993; Bhattacharyya and Gabriel, 1994), photography (see e.g. Ten 8, Gilroy, 1993b), television, press, radio (see e.g. Riggins, 1992), art (see e.g. Gilroy, 1993a; Jordan and Weedon, 1995: Part IV; the journal *Third Text*), music (e.g. Dines and Humez, 1995; Gilroy, 1993b; Dent, 1992; Wallace, 1990) and literature (e.g. Birch, 1994; Cobham and Collins, 1990). Apart from constituting forms of cultural expression in their own right, this new 'phase' as Hall describes the politics of representation, whatever its aim, has become an all-important corrective to the attempts within whiteness to define, subsume and appropriate other ethnicities in its own terms.

Conditions varyingly captured by Stuart Hall as the 'global post-modern' or by Cornel West as the 'new politics of difference' have increasingly drawn attention to whiteness, if not called it into question, both epistemologically (i.e. as a knowledge) and as an ontology (i.e. a state of being). Such conditions, we argue throughout this book, have economic and political as well as cultural dimensions and have invariably coalesced in overt terms around renewed assertions of national and ethnic identity. Meanwhile, seemingly more neutral universal discourses disguise their ethnic allegiance in, for example, the rhetoric of free trade and international law and order, and even in discourses of human rights and multiculturalism, where we might expect to find oppositional voices.

Chapter 2

New forms of racialisation in the global economy

Accounts of globalisation tend to fall into two camps. On the one side there are those who argue that we are witnessing at the turn of the twenty-first century a qualitative shift in the structures of international capital (see Ohmae, 1995). On the other there are those who argue, with equal venom, that this new era of globalisation is nothing new at all, that it is the same old story of capitalist exploitation, intensified and extended, but in essence the same (see Harvey, 1989). The two sides keep on slugging it out over this unanswerable conundrum, not only for the love of social-science truth, but also because they believe that what is at stake is our ability to change the world.

In this world of focus groups and post-Marxist angst, it can be difficult to remember that in some traditions the quality of your analysis is seen to have direct consequences for the effectivity of your politics. Of course, this has had its tensions – not least that the people doing the doing have been largely remote from the people doing the thinking, theorising, explaining. However, the broad assumption that a proper understanding of the workings of the world economy at least, if not the world in all its varied formations, was necessary to a proper plan of action and understanding of local political processes – and, most importantly, that what you chose to do would spring from what you understood – continues to shape much debate about class, economy and global relations. Now, as discussions of globalisation become more wide-ranging, we see this assumption in writing across the political spectrum – from both those who see the spread of capitalism as the universal route to freedom and those who see the overthrow of capitalism as the only hope for humanity. What remains common to all is the question of historical specificity – what is so new about this new world order?

> Much of this rather spurious debate arises from a confusion of globalisation with its precursor movements, namely internationalisation (as in the increasing interwovenness of national economies through international trade) and transnationalisation (as in the increasing organisation of production on a cross-border basis by multinational

organisations). Thus, for example, economic globalisation is often perceived as a process in which distinct national economies, and therefore
domestic strategies of national economic management, are increasingly
irrelevant.

(Hoogvelt, 1997: 114)

The debate has been about the newness of globalisation – have we seen this
before or is something quite new taking place? Clearly, accounts of the
racialisation of social relations have argued for some time that the interconnectedness of the globe – whether this be economic, cultural or political –
has shaped the local (Hall, 1991a; Goldberg, 1993). It is hard to think of a
racism which does not refer to a wider foreign world, if only in its fantasy
structures – even hating your neighbours is normally articulated as a belief
about where you and they come from and, therefore, belong.

What is at issue, then, is the nature of the global connections we are
describing. As the extract above explains, the longer growth of international
trade and multinational companies has rendered familiar the idea and
experience of a highly interconnected globe, at the level of economy at
least. Which leaves the strange phenomenon of globalisation, with all its
attendant hype and angst, still unexplained. There is nothing new here in
the spread of connection – we have all lived in a world economy for some
time. What is new, perhaps, is the intensity of these connections.

The expansive phase of capitalism was characterised by the *extension*
of the fundamentals of economic activity, namely trade and productive
investment, ever further into more and more areas of the globe; that
phase has now been superseded by a phase of *deepening, but not
widening capitalist integration.*

(Hoogvelt, op. cit.: 115)

Whatever conclusions we draw from the debate about globalisation, few
would disagree that something is happening to social organisation on a
global scale. The task here is to identify the impact of this new world on
our experiences of racialisation and the material outcomes of racism.

The first part of this chapter reviews some more recent contributions to
our understanding of racialised relations in a global economy, before
reflecting on a key debate implicit in much of this writing, that of the
relationship between race and class. The third section explores the race/
class link within somewhat different contexts through looking at the ways
in which racialised production processes have been tied to discourses of
both law and order (with reference to prison labour) and militarism and
war. The overall focus of this chapter is on racialised production relations,
though we note that the latter cannot be understood without reference to
social relations of class and gender. We will explore other aspects of the
racialised economy in chapter 5, notably in relation to both patterns of

consumption (and non-consumption) and unequal forms of distribution and exchange.

Global economic change and racialised labour

In Scott Lash and John Urry's view globalisation has indeed prompted a qualitative shift in economic relations towards a state of 'disorganised capitalism' (1987). The latter is characterised by: the circulation of capital, commodities and money over a greater distance and at greater velocity than before within a framework which is increasingly international as opposed to national; the collapse of smokestack industries in the western world and the displacement of mass production by small-batch, lean production; the increasing role of multinationals as stateless corporations; the shift of manufacturing industry from the West to newly industrialised economies; feminisation and racialisation of work as part of an expansion of part-time, temporary, non-unionised employment; maintenance of approximately half the national economies reliant on the export of one or two commodities and/or raw materials; continuing inequalities that arise from the concentration of wealth in two dozen or so nations and two hundred or so multinationals; global migration of labour on the basis of investment decisions of multinationals or government policies; and, finally, the growth in significance of international agencies like the International Monetary Fund, the World Trade Organisation and the World Bank. The strategic role played by the World Trade Organisation in particular has been witnessed in its attempts to support multinational food-producers like Del Monte against the interests of the small banana-producers in the Caribbean.

The growing significance of intellectual property and information is at the heart of the new global economy. The Third World owns 1 per cent of world patents, a figure which obscures the extent to which the western corporations appropriate traditional Third World knowledge with regard to medicines and agricultural products only to patent and market them as if the knowledge originated in the West (Kundnani, 1998/9: 67). Global media corporations work hand in hand with multinational companies to the mutual advantage of both. The case of Michael Jordan's sponsorship of Nike sportswear is a case in point. The significance of his celebrity sponsorship was felt not only in an exponential increase in Nike profits but in the enhanced popularity of basketball in the US and in the viewing ratings for Rupert Murdoch and Ted Turner's media empires (see LaFeber, 2000).

The fragmentation of the production process (which formerly took place under one factory roof) has resulted in a globe-wide assembly line for some products, what Harvey calls spatial displacement of production. One aspect of this has been the sub-contracting of stages in the production cycle to smaller businesses. This has enabled large multinationals to minimise the consequences of a fall-off in demand and/or to respond quickly to changes in demand. Franchised enterprises thus have to be flexible both in terms of labour and product range in order to meet the needs of their multinational partners. 'Downsizing', as this process of contracting out has become known, has spawned a revival of old-fashioned sites and forms of production like sweatshops and homeworking. In addition to these, new forms of organisation have emerged like call centres which provide a centralised enquiry/response service for industries as diverse as power, transport and communications. Together this highly eclectic mix of forms within advanced western economies (Harvey, op. cit.: 187) would appear to lend support to the notion of disorganised capitalism, i.e. an economy no longer predominantly concerned with manufacture or predominantly organised around factory-based systems of mass production. The point here is to explore specific points where race and class intersect, where capital inhabits and mobilises around discourses of race and gender.

Migrant labour has been a crucial historical ingredient in the formation of both colonial-Fordist and now post-Fordist capitalism. The triangular trading relationship between western Europe, West Africa and the Americas brought slaves to the sugar, coffee and cotton plantations of the Caribbean and southern states of the US, in exchange for the raw materials which were shipped back to Europe for manufacture in the burgeoning factories and sold on to markets including those in West Africa in exchange for a further supply of slaves (King, 1995: 12). Patterns of migration have been shaped by economic conditions (for example in Ireland in the nineteenth century) and political circumstances. The latter have included migration which has resulted from persecution, for example in Russia at the turn of the century, and that which has arisen from relations between the old empires and their colonial territories forged in past centuries. The arrival of SS *Empire Windrush* in 1948 from the Caribbean set in train a succession of post Second World War migrations from Pakistan and India in the 1960s and Bangladesh and East Africa in the 1970s.

Under conditions of mass production, migrant labour was drawn to the heavy, smokestack industries associated with iron and steel and the production of tools, machines and component parts for a whole range of industries, including construction, shipbuilding, automobiles and clothing. The collapse of these industries and the rise of sunbelt cities and high-technology 'valleys' like silicon and corridors like the M4 in England (noted for research and development of computer hardware and software technologies) had profound effects on labour and, in the case of more recent refugee communities, they continued to settle in the inner cities. In contrast, the demand for labour in the high-technology industries was met by a predominantly indigenous white workforce and, particularly in the US, by a cadre of highly skilled professionals primarily from south-east Asia. Older immigrants and those of older immigrant origin were thus further marginalised in the workforce as industries moved out of the inner cities and located overseas or in the case of new information /communications industries in the new suburbs.

The transformation and expansion of the service sector has been a defining characteristic of disorganised capitalism and one with varying consequences for different groups in the labour market. Service industries have been a feature of western economies since the early days of industrialisation, but their range has extended beyond retail, transport and administration to include social and health services and leisure as well as services like insurance banking and accountancy and those emanating from information technologies (Lash and Urry, 1987: 196). The impact of this disorganised capitalism has been a dualist pattern according to Lash and Urry: the expansion of highly paid, professional and managerial employment which attracts a predominantly white workforce at one end and the 'McDonaldization' of low-paid service work at the other (a term used by Ritzer, 1993, to refer to the organisation of work around the key principles of efficiency, calculability, predictability and control, although as Ritzer points out these are never actually realised). Racialised labour, women and young people have been recruited to this sector not just because they have been relatively cheap, but also because of specific cultural factors, for example the importance companies attach to ideas of image – age, dress, speech – and/or the demand for 'emotional labour' invariably associated with women (Lash and Urry, op. cit.: 201–2).

In the West the expansion of the service sector and the downgrading of jobs have increased opportunities for female low-wage, racialised immigrant/migrant labour. The downgrading of the manufacturing sector has coincided with demands both in high-tech industries where there are low-wage assembly-line jobs and in the older industries which have been re-organised around non-unionised work, as well as sweatshops and industrial homework (ibid.: 121). It should not be forgotten that high-income gentrification also has produced its own peculiar demand for a low-wage sector including waitresses, nannies, maintenance staff and cleaners (see N. Smith, 1996).

The twin processes of offshore production and immigration have also provided new opportunities for the incorporation of Third World women into the labour market (Sassen, 1998: 113). The shift towards export manufacturing in less developed countries has seen a rapid growth in the numbers of female workers in electronics, garments, textiles, toys and footwear and a corresponding decline in the proportion of women in the service sector (ibid.: 114–15). Indonesian workers who, in 1996, made 70 million pairs of Nike trainers, were earning just over $2 a day in the course of which they were forced to work six hours overtime and were subject to beatings and sexual harassment (LaFeber, op. cit.: 147). Whilst some of these industries appear more traditional in terms of the form of organisation of work, e.g. sweatshops, there is little doubt that such production plays an integral role in global capitalism's latest phase (Sassen, op. cit.). These developments in turn are the result of the tendency for capital to relocate in regions which can attract a cheap, non-unionised labour supply for its labour-intensive production processes.

Alongside the expansion of export manufacturing has been the migration of women to the US and other western countries, often from precisely those regions of export manufacturing (ibid.: 116–17). The high turnover of labour in this sector, linked to the 'mental and physical fatigue associated with these jobs' (ibid.: 119), has created a pool of unemployed who having migrated to the city and become westernised are less keen to return to their community of origin. The fact is that these western firms give workers 'access to information and a sense of familiarity with the sense of destination' (ibid.: 119–20) which has made emigration to the US a more practicable option (ibid.: 119).

The informalisation of the economy is an important feature of the changes discussed above which have had a corresponding significance for racialised labour. According to Sassen, immigrants have taken advantage of processes of informalisation rather than created them (ibid.: 154). Informalisation, according to Sassen, has taken place as a result of the economic restructuring discussed above and prompted by the inequality of both earnings amongst consumers and profit-making capabilities amongst firms in different sectors of the economy (ibid.). Instead of attributing the emergence of the informal economy to immigration, Sassen argues that it is an inevitable outgrowth of advanced capitalism (ibid.: 155). In other words economic restructuring, changing market conditions, patterns of investment, etc., were responsible for the emergence of the informal economy. Immigrants provided one potential source of labour within these new conditions but did not cause informalisation of the economy. 'Informal' in this sense means lacking regulations to do with health and safety measures, holiday entitlement, overtime rates and other rights associated with trade-union membership.

Refugees and asylum seekers who have fled civil wars, dictatorships and/or 'ethnic cleansing' have been easy prey for unscrupulous employers seeking to avoid the costs of running a business in the formal economy. Multinational and transnational companies have been attracted to locations where there is a 'hire and fire' work culture and where the less evidence of health-care and pension schemes and redundancy packages the better. Deregulated work conditions have thus attracted both an immigrant or migrant workforce and one which is invariably gendered. For example, in parts of south-east Asia, including Tokyo, manufacturing industries, notably metal and plastic processing and textiles as well as high-tech industries, have heavily relied on the use of female labour amongst illegal immigrants (ibid.: 113).

The role of national governments, whilst eclipsed by that of global agencies like the WTO and agreements like GATT, should not be forgotten in these developments. Alliances between military regimes in Nigeria, Burma and Indonesia and multinational oil companies have been instrumental in securing corporate interests at the expense of local peoples and the environment. In Burma, for example, 25,000 people were displaced to make way for the installation of gas pipelines whilst local forced labour was used to build roads and military barracks (CARF, 1998: 3).

Race and class

Before we are swept away by the hyperbole of globalising rhetoric, it is worth remembering that internationalising forces have shaped all our worlds for some time. The history of 'race' as an ugly concept that justifies and perpetuates ugly social relations can be told as the history by which Europe becomes international in the most unpleasant of ways. In the broadest of broad-sweep accounts, the European world gains ascendancy through a violent ability to shape the global. The ability to industrialise, expand, become modern and to consume comes to Europeans and their descendants through the expropriation of resources and labour from other parts of the world. This long period of gloom also gives rise to ideas of race and racialisation – and it is in this era of European ascendancy that the unlucky fate of suffering colonisation, genocide or enslavement is argued to be an outcome of the lesser attributes of a biologically distinct group (see Chomsky, 1993).

The global economy which is constructed from this violent history is one marked as much by coercion as it is by trade. The long era of this coercion ensures that some parts of the world benefit from the materials, cheap or free labour and ready markets of other areas – and uneven development comes to be the main story of international capitalism.

There are long-standing accounts of this process which place the colonised, enslaved, underdeveloped and dark-skinned world in the role of perpetually exploited proletarians in relation to the resource-stealing white and western world (Robinson, 1983; E. Williams, 1964). In this version of the world, the global working class are of colour, and not by accident. Rather, capitalist expansion has depended so heavily on mythologies of race and their attendant violences that the double project of racial and economic subjugation is a constitutive aspect of this expansion.

This is an important argument throughout this chapter. Instead of struggling to link the discrete structures of race and class, this account views race and class as always inextricably connected, two moments in the same structuration. The task is to suggest methods of describing this relation in specific instances.

In order to explore the workings of racialised class relations and the formation of classed races in our time, let us take a lead from other accounts of class. The following categories characterise some key approaches to the study of class formation.

- Class as a location in a system of production.
- Class as shorthand to name differential access to resources.
- Class as a system of status and prestige.
- Class as an indicator of a person's ability to sustain and protect their physical well-being.

The discussion which follows takes these categories as a guide to analysing class relations in contemporary events. However, rather than focus upon models of hierarchy or productive relations which fit our new circumstances badly, this chapter will attempt to reinsert a consideration of class into more obviously contemporary agendas and to suggest that these phenomena represent a tangible deepening of capitalist integration.

Economics, racialisation and globalisation

Debate about the social consequences of racial division has a long-standing interest in the relation between race and class. This relation has been identified as the key to understanding both the iniquities of racist outcomes and the complexity of class relations. The debate has started from the assumption that society is stratified, that class and race offer two competing conceptions of this stratification, and that one or other must be primary in the relation. Although the arguments between opposing views in this dialogue have not always been edifying, they have been marked by a serious attempt to make sense of inequality within national societies.

The discourses of globalisation can seem to erode or supersede the languages of both race and class. Class evaporates to be replaced with either the dreamy fiction of a universal middle class sharing the products of late capitalist consumerism or the uncertainties of economic exchanges that are so transitory that the lived identities of class can never form. In one version of the new globalisation, race is all there is – after the Cold War and its more easily narrated binary oppositions, now we find ourselves in the scary uncertainties of increasingly fragmented ethnic conflicts. In this context, apparently, previous accounts of racism are no longer appropriate or useful – because what we are experiencing is a time when everyone is fighting each other, not another replication of a structural inequality or some other tired old analysis of oppressor and oppressed, doer and done to.

At the same time, there is more and more talk about the body and its central role in all our social identities and experiences. Much of this work has grown out of the debates around feminism and sexuality and an increasing recognition that embodiment is itself a complex social process rather than a natural occurrence. More than ever, we are realising that the rendering of flesh into bodies entails many different accounts of value. The debates about race and class and their interrelation have filled volumes and caused falling-outs and considerable unhappiness to many. Various commentators have argued that:

- 'Race' is an ideological construction and therefore has no analytic value. By implication, everything comes down to class (Miles, 1982, 1984, 1993; Guillaumin, 1988).
- 'Race' has its own history and dynamic, and the resistance of racialised peoples is a more accurate model of social change for the contemporary world than a class-based analysis from the nineteenth century (Gilroy, 1987).
- 'Race' and class are independent entities, yet their histories are intertwined. Racism is a strategy of capitalism which splits the working class, creates hierarchies of privilege among waged workers and ensures an industrial reserve army of less-enfranchised labour (Sivanandan, 1990).

This volume is informed by the insights of all these approaches. Race is a fiction, yet it has its own history. Economy shapes our lives, yet class is not a static concept across history. The history of capitalist expansion and development reveals the interrelation of race and class as separate but mutually reinforcing entities, yet the mechanism of this relation remains mysterious. Rather than propose an all-encompassing be-all-and-end-all answer to the conundrum of this relation, this chapter examines some instances of the intersection of class and race. The informing assumption of this work is that economy shapes our lives and our life chances, whoever and wherever we are. This economic determination continues to stratify, exploit and divide people, as it always has – and in this process, capital occupies and mobilises whatever myths of race, barbarism and unworthiness it can. What follows is an attempt to understand the interplay of race and class in a number of key settings and to argue that a non-dogmatic attention to the workings of racism and class exploitation as producers of material outcomes is essential to an understanding of the globalised economy.

Without revisiting the unhappy period of this earlier battle, it is worth remembering that the virulence of this debate stemmed from the belief that getting this theoretical point right will lead to real political effects in the world. Ellen Meiksins Wood sums up many elements of the debate with her questions about what comes after class:

> The questions can be posed this way: if not the abolition of class, then what other objective? If not class interest, what other motive force? If not class identity and cohesion, what other collective identity or principle of unity? And underlying these programmatic questions, more fundamental historical ones: if not class relations, what other structure of domination lies at the heart of social and political power? More basic still: if not the relations of production and exploitation, what other social relations are at the foundation of human social

organization and historical process? If not the material conditions for sustaining existence itself, what is the 'bottom line'?

If the objective of socialism *is* the abolition of class, for whom is this likely to be a real objective, grounded in their own life-situation, and not simply an abstract good? If not those who are directly subject to capitalist exploitation, who is likely to have the social capacity to achieve it, if not those who are strategically placed at the heart of capitalist production and exploitation? Who is likely to have the potential to constitute a collective agent in the struggle for socialism?

(1986: 91)

Any retreat from class as analytic concept or organising rallying cry signals a retreat from these questions. At the heart of this account is a question about how we conceptualise social change. For Meiksins Wood, social relations are structured through the forces of economy proper, our old friends the relations of production. Economy forms people as classed agents – not racialised or gendered agents – and this agency impacts on economic relations as the route to wider social change. Only the working class has this strategic role – at once essential to the productive process and with nothing to lose from its disruption. Other people may suffer on the grounds of race, gender, sexuality, religion or some other factor – but their suffering does not constitute this key strategic role. Only workers have the power to alter their conditions of living through instigating this widespread social change. Give up on the primacy of class and you give up on this possibility. While this is no excuse for bad behaviour, it is at least an explanation for the tone of these exchanges.

However, there is another way of approaching the debate. While many of the arguments were about the nature of agency – who can make history? – there was also a wish to construct better analyses. Everyone acknowledged that the fictional construction 'race' was tied to certain material outcomes. This tie was not static or universal – but 'race' was socially significant precisely because some material trajectory could be traced through it.

In the remaining sections of this chapter, we explore some areas in which the scary and tangible materialities of contemporary racialisation can be felt. Rather than organising our discussion around the metatheory of the class/race dichotomy and then seeking to illustrate this with suitable examples, the chapter seeks to describe and make sense of some of the world's horrors, notably those with a racial twist. The starting assumption is that agency is always a contextual matter – there is no universal answer. What you can do will always depend on where you are, who you are and how these various contingencies fit together. What matters is remembering that things can still be done and that trying to understand the world is part of this process.

One ongoing debate is whether racism affects material outcomes or whether it is another order of experience. At its worst, this debate can seem to suggest that if race is not class, if race is not collapsible into the apparently more measurable disadvantages of class, then racism is almost nothing at all. Without material indicators, racism can seem to be no more than a variety of hurt feelings. In the wake of the Macpherson Report, an inquiry into the murder of Stephen Lawrence, a young black man murdered on the streets of London in 1993, popular understandings of racism have changed and now in Britain there is a more widespread acknowledgement of pervasive racist violence. Yet even this very different order of material outcome is explained in relation to access to resources. The institutional racism which has been exposed and unpicked in the aftermath of the Lawrence inquiry is identified as a widespread lack of entitlement – poor access to services, discrimination in employment and education – as well as harassment and attack by official and amateur actors, police and freelance racists alike. We are left with a situation where it becomes difficult to understand structural racism except as an aspect or variation of economic disadvantage. The less obviously instrumental manifestations of racist violence are once again consigned to the realm of inexplicable madness. Racism can come to be seen as two distinct brands – the unfortunate but non-violent discrimination of institutions and the random psychosis of racist attacks which yield no material advantage. Too narrow a focus on access to resources can imply that one brand has nothing to do with the other. Instead this chapter seeks to chart the connections between resource issues and direct as well as indirect violence.

Most discussions assume that class is read through economy manifested as material outcomes. This is what material indicators are taken to be – what you have, what you consume, income and expenditure (Wright, 1997). However, it is difficult to code all material indicators of racial disadvantage as outcomes of class or economy in this way. The material of the body is so vulnerable in such a variety of ways that not all that happens can be articulated through the idea of class proper. If we take material effects as being split into two broad categories of violence and deprivation, with violence including all active attacks on the body and deprivation accounting for the varied manner in which access to resources and opportunity is limited, then our argument is that deprivation can be coded as an economic phenomenon. Of course, violence and deprivation can go hand in hand – and the later discussion will give some examples of this. However, the discussion here will focus on the processes by which certain bodies are allotted certain values and their access to physical comfort is shaped by this allocation of value. The detail of this process still occurs through the mysterious relation of 'race' and class and will include such old bugbears as relations of production, stratification and social status. However, the discussion here will take the ability to obtain physical comfort (with all the culturally various conceptions this entails) as a marker of economic empowerment in various locations.

In the remaining sections, we want to reconsider ideas of the body as the vehicle of value production. This discussion of valued and unvalued or undervalued bodies and the lives they lead takes place within the wider framework of debates around globalisation. To a large extent, discussion of the new shapes of the global has focused on the economic ramifications and, by implication at least, on our ideas of class.

Mortality and inequality

When we consider the differential capacities of people to safeguard the physical well-being and safety of their loved ones and themselves, ultimately we are looking at people's ability to enhance life and forestall death. The consideration of various forms of economic disempowerment through racialisation is always an account of the ongoing battle with mortality. This is the death which doesn't level but comes too early to the poor the world over and which creeps into the experiences of the living to steal the pleasures of being alive. What follows is a discussion of the new arenas in which economic exploitation steals the lifeblood of the living and pushes the racialised poor into early death.

The most familiar discourses around class can lead us to see only the workplace as the locus of analysis. The wage is the key to social relations and the place in which it is haggled over is the site of social change. Without wishing to distract from the importance of a continuing attention to workplace politics, we need to remember that the world is still awash with people who do not experience work as a money relation. These are people who suffer the worst ravages of class, and yet do not fall within the remit of class analysis. This chapter seeks to remind the reader of the disposable people of our times and to chart the connections between the varied forms of modern-day slavery.

Although the uncertainties of globalised living alarm the rich world and reshape social relations in accordance with this fear, for the poor world the disruption cuts deeper still. Another much discussed aspect of our newly globalised world is the damaging effect this has on the most vulnerable sections of the world's population. We could read this as another aspect of the deepening of global relations – countries which have long been tied to the economic imperatives of former and/or current occupiers find themselves unable to offer the frisky flexible economies required by the new rules of global trading. Instead, a reworking of the old colonial relations takes place – and now the poor world again provides the most dangerous and least valued services to the rich. Of course this is a continuation of the long history of European expansion and domination via the drug trade (Plant, 1999).

Others have written of the deepening of the informal economy which goes alongside the development of global structures (Castells, 1997). This can be understood on two levels – within nations, a parallel economy of unrecorded work, illegitimate goods and crime grows through the exploitation of the vulnerability of certain groups, most predictably the migrant and/or racialised; at a global level, certain nations become locked into the trade of illegitimate goods and services, again through the vulnerability of their citizens and the overall weakness of their economies. Castells explains:

> What is new is the deep penetration, and eventual destabilization, of national states in a variety of contexts under the influence of trans-national crime. While drug traffic is the most significant industrial sector in the new criminal economy, all kinds of illicit traffics come together in this shadow system that extends its reach and power over the world: weapons, technology, radioactive materials, art treasures, human beings, human organs, killers for hire, and smuggling of every profitable item from anywhere to anywhere are connected through the mother of all crimes – money laundering. Without it, the criminal economy would neither be global nor very profitable.
>
> (Ibid.: 259)

Therefore, the globalised economy creates conditions which appear to confirm the excessive fear of crime in the rich world. Some places seem to be overrun by sexwork and the drug trade, some groups of people seem to work only in the illegitimate sector. To the anxious eye of western affluence, the threat can appear all too tangible – a spreading disorder which promises to overrun the West with its worst fears of reverse colonisation. As a result the war-on-drugs racket opens as an endless and unaccountable drain on public resources – and maintains the infrastructure for other supposedly just wars.[1]

The prison-industrial complex

Within the rich nations, racialised minorities have tended to suffer the most privation in times of economic hardship. The pattern of this deprivation in the era of globalisation has been described as the formation of a new underclass, a concept which has initiated much debate. The concept of the underclass has been used to pathologise a section of the (largely urban) poor and to suggest that their bad luck and economic hardship spring from some aspect of their culture, identity or lifestyle. The underclass are seen to be within the working class, yet not working or not working enough or not working legally; poor, yet not deserving; disempowered, yet still dangerous. The discussion of the term 'underclass', in recent times, has been tied to debates about the efficacy of welfare. In particular, the underclass, if it exists, is argued as referring to those who cannot be helped by existing social policy. In fact, key proponents of the underclass thesis argue that welfare itself exacerbates the problems of the hapless underclass – making them ever more dependent, unmotivated, unable to develop life skills or to sustain stable families (Murray, 1994; Herrnstein and Murray, 1994). As Goldberg explains, this debate contains a hard-to-miss racial message:

> the notion of *the Underclass* explicitly erases the exclusionary experiences of racisms from social science analysis while silently enthroning the demeaning impact of race-based insinuations and considerations. It distinguishes the especially impoverished from the ordinary poor while aggregating together those whose conditions of experience in various ways – in terms of race, gender, and class – may be quite different. It thus promotes a single policy solution for perhaps very different difficulties and social problems people find themselves facing.
>
> In a society whose advantages and opportunities are racially ordered, a concept like *the Underclass* will almost inevitably assume racial connotation.
>
> (1993: 172–3)

As the term 'underclass' has become a not-so-covert reference to the racialised poor, a number of racist associations have emerged. Throughout this debate, the idea of an underclass has shown its close affiliation to the rhetoric of law and order – fears of the underclass are often indistinguishable from fears of crime. This section seeks to map the relations between this restructured economic landscape and criminal justice systems across the rich world which work to contain the problems of the so-called underclass by placing them within an ever-growing prison population. We want to suggest that the penal system comes to play a new and enhanced role in our new world order for old-fashioned economic reasons, and that what we are witnessing is the development of a prison-industrial complex. Angela Davis coins this phrase to describe the reorganisation of governmental business around the structure of the penal system.

> All this work, which used to be the primary province of government, is now also performed by private corporations, whose links to government in the field of what is euphemistically called 'corrections' reveal dangerous resonances with the military industrial complex.
>
> (1998: 146)

Plenty has been written about the racialised fantasies of law-and-order debates across the western world and beyond (see Hall *et al.*, 1978; Gooding-Williams, 1993). However, this work has tended to concentrate on the formation of effective social mythologies – the concern is to find out why some stories can shape the world and people's lives. The shift which comes with the concept of the prison-industrial complex is one which places myths of criminality in real economic structures and mechanisms. What Davis is suggesting is not that racism can make you poor and being poor can make you steal, but that correctional systems are themselves a business and their escalating growth reveals a will to profit, not respect for the law.

Davis allows that this process operates through ideology and itself offers another prop to a wider collective delusion about the nature of order, justice and criminality. The prison-industrial complex emerges as a response to another crisis of legitimacy – what we are witnessing is a process whereby the experience of disenfranchisement, economic instability and material hardship of too many in the quickly disintegrating developed world is recoded into a fear of crime and disorder. From here, it is a short step to reignite those ever-present racist under-and-over currents and to perceive that it is the racial other, not global capital, which is ruining our lives.

'Coloured bodies are the main raw material in this vast experiment to disappear the major social problems of our time' (Davis and Gordon, op. cit.: 147): this is an old-fashioned refrain of much black Marxism or Marxist black politics – racism is a veil for the real exploitative relations of capital and it serves to distract people from their real enemies. A racialised obsession with crime is no different in this regard and people substitute a concern about the security of their homes for a more frightening and harder-to-articulate concern about, for example, the security of their livelihoods.

> This is the ideological work that the prison performs; it relieves us of the responsibility of seriously engaging with the problems of late capitalism, of transnational capitalism. The naturalisation of black and brown people as criminals also erects ideological barriers to an understanding of the connections between late-twentieth-century structural racism and the globalisation of capital.
>
> (Ibid.: 148)

Davis is claiming that prisons work to disallow effective political organisation against the racist effects of globalisation. The prison-industrial complex provides a veil for and distraction from this process of new global racisms and exploitations and does the important ideological work of rallying dissent away from social relations and onto the monstrous spectacle of crime. However, alongside this ideological work, the prison-industrial complex also performs some hard economic business. Behind the cover story of punishment and rehabilitation, prisoners have become another source of the new breed of unfree labour. The precise impact of unpaid labour in any economic system has long been a source of dispute. From debates around domestic labour to arguments about the Atlantic slave trade or the work-to-death regimes of Nazi concentration camps, it has been difficult to assign hard values to stolen labour. Too often, contemporary commentaries fall back into denunciations of absolute evil and make no connections between these thefts and violences and the more everyday instrumentality of the pursuit of profit.

Instead of this division, we want here to chart the relation between the ugliest forms of racism and bigotry and economic instrumentality. In particular, we want to suggest that the era of globalisation has given rise to new forms of unfree labour, a manner of exploitation which once again trades on the differential values allotted to different people through racialised culture.

A number of highly respectable agencies have echoed this concern that the cheap labour demanded by global markets is too often obtained through coercion, including the coercion of prison labour. Although the concern about forced work is more often heard as a concern about the human-rights abuses of backward cultures and economies, for example, the abuse of prison labour in China's rush to economic expansion,[2] our point here is that these abuses are more widespread than is often acknowledged. The following description is only one example.

> The operation is part of Badger State Industries, Wisconsin's prison industries program, which employs about 600 of Wisconsin's 10,000 inmates to produce everything from coffee cups to furniture – and, of course, license plates. Last year, Badger State earned $1.2 million in profits on $15.4 million in sales by peddling its products to state and local government agencies. To protect manufacturers and labor from unfair competition, Wisconsin places restrictions on the selling of prison-made goods to the private sector. But that's about to change. The new state budget includes a scheme to make prison facilities and labor available to commercial enterprises. This, says Gov. Tommy Thompson, will help pay for the costs of housing the escalating prison population and provide prisoners with a work ethic. What Thompson didn't mention was that the legislation will embed prison industries in the private sector, which in other states has led to a downward pressure on wages and to lost jobs for Joe and Jill Taxpayer.
>
> (Elbow, 1995)

Under the guise of rehabilitation, prison work performs the oldest management tricks in the book – undercuts wages, exploits the most constrained workforce imaginable and, through this, disrupts the organisation of workers on the outside. While there are some suggestions that the spread of prison work into more sectors of the economy is an attempt to finance the increasing costs of an escalating prison population, the sums don't add up here. The costs of supervising prison work programmes eat up any possible surplus that could pay for the prison system. Instead, and as usual, the only winners are the companies who get cheap and docile labour and the prestige of appearing to contribute to the social good. Using prison work is a way of competing in the global marketplace, as prisoners themselves identify:

'It's positive that you can make some money before you get out and stuff,' says Dale Austin, an upholstery sewer at Oakhill who is serving a 10-year sentence for burglary. But it also takes away a lot of jobs from people on the streets. Austin, who says he buys books on politics with the money he earns, sees a grand scheme in bringing private business into prisons.

'They're gonna open up more industries and build more prisons. And the more industries you got in prisons takes away from people's jobs on the streets. And it takes away from the cost of sending businesses overseas.' The object, says Austin, is to lower domestic labor costs. 'They get lower labor costs right here in, like, a little Third World country,' he says, referring to Oakhill.

(Ibid.)

We are not suggesting that this is all part of some masterplan to incarcerate and exploit the global poor – all this can happen, sadly, without any particular plan or order being in place. Instead, we are suggesting that the outcome of an intersection between a long history of racialising crime, an increased sense of risk in the rich world and the development of a global economy which values cheap labour as an efficiency gain is a situation in which the forced labour of prisoners in rich (and not so rich) economies mirrors the differently coerced labour of other places. The pursuit of profit in new circumstances adapts to the constraints and possibilities of this conjuncture – and the social monster of crime provides the much desired cheap and obedient labour.

A variety of indicators show that unpaid and barely paid work is growing in the global economy. Despite the belief that the market economy, including the international market whatever its shortcomings, transforms everyone into waged labour sooner or later, other evidence suggests that the era of globalisation is also the time of a new slavery. In a problematic and much discussed book, Kevin Bales describes the plight of these 'disposable people'. Bales outlines a number of features which distinguish his conception of the new slavery:

Old slavery	*New slavery*
Legal ownership asserted	Legal ownership avoided
High purchase cost	Very low purchase cost
Low profits	Very high profits
Shortage of potential slaves	Surplus of potential slaves
Long-term relationship	Short-term relationship
Slaves maintained	Slaves disposable
Ethnic differences important	Ethnic differences not important

(Bales, 1999: 15)

Bales's work is difficult to read. He chooses key sites of new slavery – predictably locations in the poor world, despite repeated reminders that slaves are everywhere – and then builds an account of the system of enslavement around the stories of the enslaved. The catalogue of horrors – beatings, starvation, sexual abuse, endless labour, people worked to death – makes for hard reading. However, despite the promise to explain the new slavery as an economic system, there is little here that examines the new slavery as a symptom of globalisation. Too much of the local accounts rely on a version of the backward-culture thesis, so that some societies are alleged to be more open to the growth of slavery because of their cultural beliefs. While the constant reminder that some people are enslaved because it makes other people rich punctuates the work, there is little indication of the circumstances which make this more possible now.

However, even from our cursory discussion, we can identify some features of Bales's list which fit our template of a globalised economy. Bales is describing a world in which human labour has become far too plentiful and thus devalued. Although many will take issue with this, he also describes Atlantic slavery, the trade in African people by Europeans, as another order of slavery. This he calls the old slavery, and without for a minute disputing its brutality, Bales suggests that this old slavery, for all its cruelty, did not regard slaves as disposable people. The old slavery, according to Bales, represented a system in which slaveholders viewed slaves as expensive investments to be maintained. The high price of slaves meant that slaveholders wanted to assert legal ownership of their property, to keep slaves alive and to maintain the relation of ownership with any children of their slaves. Now, Bales argues, the enslaveable poor are so plentiful that slaves are no longer expensive items to purchase. It is no longer profitable to spend money to maintain slaves over any length of time – more money can be made by disposing of them and obtaining new slaves in their place.

While there are various problems with Bales's account and his distinction between old and new slaveries, not least the tendency to elide the distinctions between coercion, ownership and the ability to exploit economic desperation, there remains something compelling about the larger suggestion that the globalised economy profits from unfree labour. The most mainstream accounts of globalisation identify the increased mobility of capital as a central feature of this new deepening of international capitalism (see Castells, 1996). Workers lose many of their bargaining positions in this process and find themselves in a global price war to cut wage costs (see Aronowitz and Cutler, 1998; Martin and Schumann, 1997). As the world becomes increasingly filled with desperate people trying to keep themselves and their families alive, employers who can move their business to ever cheaper labour have few ties to their employees. Those who rely on cheaper labour coming to them do not need to develop longer-term relationships with workers who are so easily replaceable – it is easier and more profitable to prey on the desperation of a new migrant or other vulnerable person. Whether or not we deem these events part of a new slavery, globalisation has made human beings even more expendable in the pursuit of profit.

The key point to remember here is that the globalisation of the economy – that deepening of capitalist relations which changes the face of everyone's business – depresses the wages of most people in the world. Even in the rich world, even in times of economic growth, real wages have fallen:

> It is true that between 1973 and 1994 per capita GNP in the United States grew by a full third in real terms. At the same time, for the three-quarters of the working population that have no managerial or supervisory responsibility, average gross wages fell by 19 per cent – to just 258 dollars a week. And that is only the statistical average. For the bottom third of the pyramid, the drop in pay was more dramatic still: these millions of the population now earn 25 per cent less than they did twenty years ago.
>
> (Martin and Schumann, op. cit.: 118)

In the rest of the less-affluent-than-America world, everyone feels the pressure of capital flight towards cheaper labour. Even havens of cheap work fear that somewhere else, less developed, more desperate, will undercut their wages and steal their jobs (see ibid.: 101, 146).

The prison-industrial complex develops alongside this global change in working relations, so that just when levels of poverty begin to escalate uncontrollably everywhere, the poor themselves become the problem. Incarcerating a large proportion of the poor population diverts attention from economic hardship, creates another stratum of work in the criminal justice business and disciplines the unruly poor of the rich world in such a manner as to make them hyper-profitable once more. In prison, work becomes transformed again into a privilege and a therapy, an education and a pleasure – and these other values compensate for the lack of adequate or fair financial rewards. Instead, the everyday cash values of production and exchange go into the pocket of the philanthropic entrepreneur. Increasingly, prison work produces products which enter the mainstream market – at once rendering law and order profitable and undercutting the wages of (organised) labour on the outside. In this way, the criminal justice system serves as another mechanism for remaking class relations and reproducing racialised divisions among workers.

Legislated death

A discussion of the prison-industrial complex in the US and beyond leads bloodily and inevitably into a deliberation on the death penalty. As explained earlier, this chapter is concerned to outline the workings of racialised class relations as a system of allotting differential values to human beings. The suggestion is that all the processes which relegate some people to a status of being more expendable, more disposable and easier to kill or let die are also part of the structures of class.

In the introduction to *Live from Death Row*, John Edgar Wideman writes about his amazement at finding in 1981 that 'My country, the United States of America, ranked third among the nations of the world in the percentage of its citizens it imprisoned. Only Russia and South Africa surpassed us' (cited in Abu-Jamal, 1996: xxvi). He goes on to remark that the governments of Russia and South Africa fell to internal revolutions which would not accept repression over reform. Of course, the optimistic implication is that the US cannot sustain this repressive apparatus indefinitely. What is missed out of this remark is an understanding of how people become agents in relation to different repressive structures. One of the attractions of the prison-industrial complex is precisely the use of forced labour in a system which greatly limits resistance and provides few opportunities for organised opposition.

The state-sanctioned killing of people, and particularly men, of colour – whether through the official procedures of the death penalty or the more covert activity of police and prison guards – serves as a disciplinary mechanism in the wider complex. Rather than an unhappy accident, the all too frequent killings in the name of law and order can be seen as a necessary warning in a larger system. Killings confirm the stories of ruthless enemies of society (even when these enemies are unarmed, unwell, outnumbered) – but also keep people scared, showing that righteous defence can be ruthless too, another incentive to be obedient and law-abiding and to have nothing to do with the absolute other of racialised criminality.

It is no longer a secret or a surprise that the death penalty in rich nations kills racialised minorities, not white folks. When we place this legislated killing alongside the amateur night operations of deaths in custody and police and prison brutalisation of minorities across rich and poor economies, the class/race promise of law and order becomes all too apparent. Lesser peoples will be exterminated, because this is for the good of society (see Amnesty International, 1999; Australian Government Publishing Service, 1991; Bhattacharyya, 1998).

Across the developed world, the world which remains relatively rich for a number of its inhabitants, the hype around law and order serves a similar range of dubious purposes. Everywhere the same patterns emerge – greater rifts between rich and poor, an entrenchment of the informal and illicit economies, greater insecurity for both the wealthy and the wealthless. Alongside these shifts away from the dream of prosperity for all comes a fresh resurgence of racialisation of minorities. As economic divisions harden, the old will to biologise class difference re-emerges, opportunistically attached to the particular histories of each location. The over-arching narrative that appears everywhere is the one that suggests that a propensity to criminality and a predisposition towards poverty are intertwined characteristics, both determined by blood or culture, but never by history or social structure.

Alongside the legitimated killings of the death penalty, the racialised pursuit of law and order has brought death to many other people of colour. The new ravages of transnational capital have entrenched the suffering of the global poor and put paid to older dreams of progress and good living for all. Now the world's have-nots are stuck in the role of dangerous criminals – and must pay the consequences for their wayward lack of resources.

Law and order is the parallel narrative which makes the iniquities of globalised national economies palatable and liveable. This is the story which squares the circle for us in this time, as in others, and the means by which strange contradictions are reconciled. Once we have accepted the world as a place of criminal danger where resources must be directed to protecting the haves from the have-nots, we have begun to accept that poverty will not be eradicated by social reform or economic growth. We no longer look to welfare to keep us safe – the assorted and varied war against crime is our only hope.

The military and the monetary

While the various outcomes of the globalised economy do not strictly conform to descriptions of a location in the relations of production, we want to remember that that position at the edge of formal economies, where the very poor and very desperate and too often racialised slip in and out of (barely) paid employment, is also a class location. The experience of having extremely limited access to resources, little social standing or recognition, and an inability to sustain and protect the basic well-being of yourself and your loved ones should be recognised as an outcome of class relations.

Of course, the sticking point here is that, unlike the mythic working class who will organise to save us all, here the possibility of agency and resistance is constrained. This deadly hyper-exploitation works by breaking the will of labour. By denying political recognition to work and foreclosing the possibility of organisation through workplaces, employers seem to refute that central promise of left victory-wallahs, that labour is irreplaceable. The next section reviews another aspect of the disposability of ordinary people in the new world order.

The twentieth century was marked by an unprecedented linking of national economies to military build-up and armed conflict. Unlike previous models of the war state, which explained boundary expansion as a historically precise imperative, the twentieth century introduced the concept of militarisation as a route to overall prosperity. In a less attractive mirror of the welfare state, the endless task of preparing for war guarantees a certain level of economic activity in the national economy. For the richer western nations in particular, militarism serves as a valuable component of strategies for maintaining prosperity. This relation to the military, which, dangerously, can never contemplate any possibility of lasting peace, is famously christened the military-industrial complex (see Regan, 1995). The process of its formation reveals the rise to influence of the military even in democratic states at peace and highlights the dubious but essential role of the arms industry in western affluence.

After the militarisation in the name of peace of the Cold War years, the world has entered an era in which the components of global influence are no longer easily identifiable. Whereas the Cold War caused the proliferation of military hardware and military conflict, all in the name of peace in our time, the demise of the Soviet Union has unsettled the basis of the US war economy. Why build the army if there is no threat from communism? And without the dangers of the Soviet imperial project, why do the world's poor need to be persuaded of the pleasures of democracy and freedom through the barrel of a gun? Throughout the Cold War, for major players and lesser breeds of poodle such as Britain, the growth and consolidation of military capability were justified through a rhetoric of defence. We want peace, but they want war – to maintain peace we must be ready for war. The doublespeak of 1945–89 shaped the lives of us all, throughout the globe. Military power gave certain nations a key role in the maintenance of global peace.

However, in the aftermath of 1989, military power became another thing altogether. Now the US had no devil-twin counterpart, against whom stockpiling could be matched. Instead, maintaining military might had to be justified in itself – and the justification was the need to meddle, not the need to defend. This shift, despite its considerable appeal to many in the West, has contributed to a decline in resources for military spending.

> As the Cold War drew to a close from the mid-1980s, military spending around the world began to fall. Domestic arms markets contracted and the size of the global trade in weapons, military equipment and related technology began a steep decline. The international arms market not only shrank, but its character and dynamics also began to change dramatically.
>
> (Cornish, 1995: 1; see also Cooper, 1997: 105)

Without a phantom enemy to arm against, the basis for the military-industrial complex in the West becomes uncertain. In the absence of previous fictions of spheres of influence, arms trading ceases to bow to any form of regulation and the international arms market reveals again its commercial orientation. Without the cartoon enemies of former eras, militarisation increasingly appears as another process of endless accumu-lation – not a rational strategy of defence, but an irrepressible machinery to perpetuate conflict. Even in the rich world, where the threat of domestic crime allows a militarisation of civilian life under the promise of law enforcement, the actual military is losing ground in the popular imagination.

In fact, the confusion about the role of military power in world domi-nance has its seeds in earlier and more confident military endeavours.

> Vietnam exposed for all the world to see the impotence of misapplied military power and the military bankruptcy that went with it. The end result was a gargantuan military machine in shambles: the officer corps demoralized, the enlisted men exploited, and the armed forces as a whole confused and bewildered about their mission. In despera-tion, some parts of the military flirt with counterinsurgency (a euphe-mism for counterrevolution) as the military's principal goal for the future. Such a mission creates trends and proposals that logically lead to the advocacy of military supremacy over civilian authority.
>
> (Koistinen, 1980: 19)

Common sense holds that Vietnam is the lesson which dissuades the US and others from meddling in the business of other nations. This, apparently, is the wound in the psyche of expansionist policy, the humiliation which alters the conception of national pride and steals public support away from military endeavour (see Engelhardt, 1995). However great the evidence to the contrary, the popular line is that the US learned better than trying to help ingrates, and post-Vietnam America is minding its own busi-ness and looking after number one. Foreign policy is a low priority, unless there is a US trade interest (so what's new?). Voters no longer value military spending or see the point of maintaining the armed forces – less through a new-found respect for the sovereignty of other nations, and more through an irritation that 'our' lives and resources are not appreciated by those we purport to protect and save.

In fact, of course, the shift has been from overt military attack to the more disguised manoeuvres of counter-insurgency. Since Vietnam, the hand of the US has been present in untold numbers of local struggles – arming and training, funding and fighting – all in the interests of freedom and democracy.

> The American view of guerilla war was simply that all such wars were partisan in nature; all had support from an external sponsoring power and all were backed, at least implicitly, by an over-the-border presence of a regular army. Any seemingly domestic insurgent movement was either externally sponsored or was soon captured by an external sponsor. Additionally, guerilla war was seen as the early warning sign

of an impending conventional cross-border attack from a hostile, Soviet-dominated state.

(Cable, 1986: 5)

Even after Vietnam, the hotter aspects of the Cold War continued to ravage the lives of the poor world. The domestic struggles of former colonies quickly took on international dimensions, with larger rivalries played on and through the bodies of other peoples. The end result for the poor world has been a combination of social structures cut through with battle scars and an inability to make space to chart national destinies – western military intervention has played a key role in keeping the colonial in neo-colonialism. However, even this covert war by proxy with the evil forces of communism can no longer justify militarisation without end. Now, at last, there have been indications that the ordinary people of the rich world, and the US in particular, are not interested in being the world's policemen (Chanley, 1999). Belatedly, some aspect of the Vietnam lesson is being learned – even if only as a response to economic hardship.

> [T]he idea that the nation can and should play world policeman must be abandoned, and military solutions to what are essentially social, political, ideological, and economic issues must be foregone. This is not to propose a new form of isolationism or 'fortress America', as Cold War hawks are so eager to charge. Instead, it means a foreign policy of sane and reasonable priorities for the world's major power, reasonable priorities that stand somewhere between attempting to ignore the world and attempting to mold the world in the American image.
>
> (Koistinen, 1980: 124)

The impact of the global economy on US living standards, as discussed above, has made the role of global guardian and its accompanying resource cost far less attractive. Sadly, it seems that the US response to this dis-illusionment has been to railroad other rich nations into supporting US agendas for global policing. Now US intervention is once again an overt business, carried on in the name of NATO or the UN or, we may as well understand, right-thinking people everywhere. We are entering an era in which, perversely, powerful nations engage in overt and costly military aggression with the seeming indifference or at most irritation of their own populations.

One glaring irony of our era of globalisation is that, for the rich world at least, the rest of the world appears increasingly distant and remote. Unlike the heady self-congratulation of previous imperial education, where learn-ing about the various subjugated nations of the white man's domain became part of his burden, now global dominance is marked by having no need to know about anyone else (Giroux, 1996).

While the populations of powerful nations, and of the US in particular, can be irritated into supporting intervention at the suggestion that lesser others have no respect or obedience, the idea that the world's well-being is the responsibility of the rich and powerful is harder to sell. However, this has been the core lie at the heart of the new militarism – that the powerful have a paternalistic duty of military intervention. In the remainder of this section, we will consider the manner in which western populations consent to their role in this new militarism, despite reservations, and the effect this has upon ethnicised divisions.

The machinery of total war

Other commentators have long remarked that the process of endless militarisation for peace is in fact a process of disciplining civil society (Chomsky, 1989: 199). While we have seen that the much vaunted peace of the post-1945 era is at least questionable and partial, it remains the case that the idea that military might was necessary in order to sustain an always fragile peace has played a powerful role in the politics of the West. The rich world has come to organise its resource allocation in such a way as to allow for a constant preparation for war.

> The perpetuation of war is what I call Pure War, war which isn't acted out in repetition, but in infinite preparation. Only this infinite preparation, the advent of logistics, also entails the non-development of society in the sense of civilian consumption.
>
> (Virilio and Lotringer, 1997: 92)

This state of pure war is another version of the military-industrial complex which Eisenhower came to decry. An economy which devotes substantial resources to the avoidance of war through militarisation creates the same powerful interest group of the professional military and arms traders as an economy which is engaged perpetually in armed conflict. In some regards the infinite preparation may call for greater resources, as the threat we are guarding against defies quantification. What remains in question is the extent to which the pursuit of war, either through battle or infinite preparation, can maintain prosperity.

The long reign of the new right (now at an end, apparently) saw an intensification of military spending across the rich world. The various and varyingly smart technologies of recent warfare have their antecedents in this era of high-profile investment. While welfare provision was eroded and varieties of monetarism ensured increasing levels of unemployment, the ability to conduct war with the most sophisticated of weaponry was considered a key priority for the free world (E.P. Thompson, 1985). At the same time, the law-and-order agendas discussed above became central tenets of mainstream electoral politics. This, in turn, precipitated a growing militarisation of civilian police forces – and the boundaries of acceptable and expected policing practice have stretched accordingly.

> It's no longer exo-colonization (the age of extending world conquest), but the age of intensiveness and endocolonization. One now colonizes only one's own population. One underdevelops one's own civilian economy.
>
> (Virilio and Lotringer, op. cit.: 95)

This echoes the idea that globalisation intensifies a network which was formed in a previous era – deepening rather than extending the reach of capital. Although other evidence suggests that it is not 'only' one's own population which is colonised now, the broader idea that the machinery of empire is now a technique of domestic government fits the experience of many places.

> The threat's hypothetical and completely phantasmic nature in the doctrine of national security contributes toward the disintegration of territory – and not only of territory. In the name of security, in the name of protection, everything is undone, deregulated: economic relations, social relations, sexual relations, relations of money and power. We end up in a state of defeat, without there ever having been a war.
>
> (Ibid.: 104)

In the rich world, the entrenchment of old inequalities and the rise of new forms of impoverishment, uncertainty and economic insecurity are all reframed as necessary hardships in the pursuit of national security. Debates about sovereignty collapse the languages of economy and military, so that holding our own territory means preparing to fight on all fronts, as a national economy and as a military state. Instead of the endless safety and prosperity of a post Cold War equilibrium, the inhabitants of the rich world find that the threat of war continues to steal their resources and make them afraid.

New wars and humanitarian intervention

Instead of the promised shift into total peace and global harmony, the end of the Cold War and the subsequent and still not decided reworking of international relations has brought new and different conflicts and a greater sense of global insecurity. Kaldor (1999) has argued that globalisation and the power vacuum left after the demise of the Soviet Union have given rise to a new form of armed conflict, what she terms 'new wars'. She describes the characteristics of new wars as the politics of identity, the decentralisation of violence and the globalised war economy. In this telling, the politics of identity refers to the mobilisation around ethnic, racial or religious identity in order to claim state power. Kaldor sees this politics as in contrast to politics of ideas which mobilise around forward-looking and inclusive projects such as individual rights or democracy or a modern nation or socialism. While there is an acknowledgement of the abuses in the name of these inclusive projects, she argues that the impulse to build better futures and to include all who support this project is distinct from an identity politics that looks with nostalgia to a lost past and excludes others on the basis of an imagined essence. Although we may question this absolute division and suggest that in the case of conflicts around faith in particular, it is impossible to distinguish identity from forward-looking political project, the observation that the world is riven with ethnicised and violent conflict is hard to deny (on the complexities of religious politics, see Bhatt, 1997).

The decentralisation of violence refers to a number of related issues. The first is the shift from using battles to gain territory to borrowing the tactics of guerrilla and counter-insurgency warfare to avoid battle and gain territory through political control of the population. Kaldor distinguishes this from theories of liberatory guerrilla warfare which seek to win over the local population to co-operation and support. Instead, she sees new wars as carrying out an extension of the battle-avoidance of counter-insurgency tactics, so that areas are destabilised by widespread terror against the civilian population and territory is gained through population expulsion. The second is the decentralisation of military forces from vertically organised hierarchical armies to disparate alliances of a variety of fighting forces, spanning the divide between legitimate and illegal. The third is the spread of conflict zones into civilian life and the expansion of conflict into neighbouring areas.

The globalised war economy refers to the opposite of the military-industrial complex or the state of pure war – we could think of this as the war economy of the poor world. Kaldor explains that here, as opposed to a centralised and totalising war economy, few people participate in war, unemployment is high, the economy is very dependent on external resources and the infrastructure of the domestic economy is damaged by war. Kaldor argues that this leads to fighting units financing themselves through crime or external assistance (which itself may be criminal). She argues, 'All of these sources can only be sustained through continued violence so that a war logic is built into the functioning of the economy' (Kaldor, 1999: 9). In this way, regions become locked into a cycle of war which is hard to break.

Overall, Kaldor describes a world of escalating armed conflict – more fighting, less accountability, and ethnic cleansing as the new logic of warfare. Sadly, the picture she paints is familiar and convincing – it is hard to deny the nature and frequency of recent armed conflicts. What is less convincing in this account is the depiction of the global framework, a depiction in which the West is almost absent, little more than a bemused spectator of the barbarity of others. However, as we have argued, the intensification of global integration has made the world more interdependent as well as more incomprehensibly separate. There is some recognition of this in the discussion of the supply of arms.

> The end of the Cold War and of related conflicts like Afghanistan or South Africa greatly increased the availability of surplus weapons. In some cases, wars are fought with weapons raided from Cold War stockpiles; such is largely the case in Bosnia-Herzegovina. In other cases, redundant soldiers sell their weapons on the black market, or small-scale producers (as in Pakistan) copy their designs. In addition, arms enterprises which have lost state markets seek new sources of demand. Certain conflicts, for example Kashmir, took on a new character as a result of the influx of arms, in this case a spill over from the conflict in Afghanistan. The new wars could be viewed as a form of military waste-disposal – a way of using up unwanted surplus arms generated by the Cold War, the biggest military build-up in history.
>
> (Kaldor, 1999: 96)

What is missed in this account is the extent to which the Cold War led to military build-up in many regions of the globe, with plenty of conflict by proxy between the West and East. In the aftermath of the Cold War, the world is realigning around the power blocs created through these former imperial patronages. Even the most local struggle must have an eye to the international community and the response of the West – global influence requires this international recognition, whether of an ally or an enemy.

In the light of this, international bodies are discussing their role. In particular, there are suggestions that international law should be reworked to place less emphasis on state sovereignty and more on international norms. Kaldor also argues that many of the most conflict-ridden zones of the world are not states, and therefore have no right to the legal protection of sovereignty. Instead, she advocates a move towards cosmopolitan law enforcement – international intervention to safeguard local populations. In this, Kaldor echoes a larger theme in international debate, 'a trend towards seeing certain humanitarian and legal norms inescapably bound up with conceptions of national interest' (Roberts, 1999: 120).

The national interests in question are those of the affluent world, those able to mobilise international bodies and intervene in other regions, and to some extent this recognition is also an outcome of global integration. Now the conflicts and abuses of other regions may become issues of national interest to the West through the connections of diasporic communities, the dispersals of economic interest or the uncertainties of re-forming global alliances. When these national interests override respect for the sovereignty of another state, international law is no longer a check on the aggression of the powerful. The outcomes of this situation can range from the 'humanitarian war' of NATO bombing in Kosovo and Serbia, to the 'war against international terrorism' of US bombings in Sudan and Afghanistan. Whatever our views on particular conflicts, it is hard not to regard the overall shift as one towards greater and unstoppable power for rich nations, which may interpret their national interests as they wish.

Uneven globalisation

An attention to recent warfare shows that the uncertainty of international relations has consolidated the power of the US and its allies and thrown up new power factions in many regions. We are witnessing the development of a global system with one unaccountable global power, but many, equally unaccountable, local forces. At both global and local levels, the outcome is a more open recourse to armed intervention. We can think of this as an aspect of uneven globalisation.

> Uneven globalization is best conceived as a dialectical process, stimulating integration as well as fragmentation, universalism as well as particularism, and cultural differentiation as well as homogenization.
> (Holm and Sorensen, 1995: 6)

This is the larger argument of this chapter, and the book, that globalisation both unifies and differentiates, and that in this process, ethnic divisions are remade. In many places, we see the follow-on conflicts of the Cold War and the scramble for regional ascendancy rearticulated as ethnic conflicts.

> What emerges from these analyses is not a grand vision of globalized, peaceful societies but great diversity, not only between North and South but also among and within the different regions and countries of the world. New zones of peace and new zones of conflict exist alongside each other, all in the same 'World Order'.
> (Ibid.: 15)

Alongside this diversity, we see the US emerge as unassailable arbiter of international human rights and the legitimacy of military intervention. Although the ultimate benefits of the recent conflict in Kosovo are yet to be realised, the spectre of a fearless US flanked by an obedient UK, using military tactics against international terrorism or for just causes, anywhere in the globe, pretty much at will, does not bode well for most of the world's poor. Even the most benign reading which regards military intervention as well-meaning leaves open the question of how these excursions will be paid for.

The shift in global relations which allows one nation to act unchallenged is the same shift which, allegedly, has laid the nation-state to rest. A major aspect of debates around globalisation has been the suggestion that nations are no longer key players in world politics. Instead, globalised capital operates through nation-states only when convenient and resistant nations find that their sovereignty is all too easily overturned. The move towards pure war, coupled with the absolute power of new global policemen, leaves the global poor open to violent attack at the whim of their aggressors. Without the check of threatened escalation, military intervention becomes even more expedient a strategy – little more than a back-up to the economic coercion already in place. Of course, the poor of the world have suffered the consequences of war for profit for ever. What alters in our time is the extent to which participation in the global market on the terms of the rich can be enforced through military intervention.

What is at issue here is not that there are wrongs in the world, or even that there is such a thing as a just war. What is at issue is the extent to which the nation-state, oppressive old queen of high modernity, can purport to offer any shelter to her subjects against the incursions of globalising forces. The new militarism shows us that, when the stakes get high enough, national boundaries and sovereignty offer no protection at all.

With so many cracks in the fiction of the nation, and balkanisation as the new story of how the polity is formed, armed conflict is increasingly seen as a matter of ethnicity. This reworking of nations is another aspect of the coming to global power of the truncheon-wielding US. As the global economy hails regions in groupings other than that of nation, conflict and loyalty are increasingly organised along non-national lines. We see divisions within former nations spinning out of control, affinities growing across or astride former borders and an all-round destabilising of what we understand by sovereignty. It is into this changing territory that the global policeman steps – making the whole fragmenting and conflict-ridden world into his backyard.

Slow and quick deaths

So far we have considered the manner in which some bodies become disposable – easily replaceable forced labour, or phantasmic enemy to be destroyed at home and abroad. Our contention is that this occurs through an array of industrial complexes – prisons and criminal justice to discipline an unruly populace and provide a little union-busting labour, militarisation of security at home and abroad to, again, discipline that unruly populace, maintain a power elite and, most importantly, enable the smooth workings of 'free trade'. The violence of these processes is made possible through the mythologies of race – these disposable, criminal creatures, dying from sanctions and bombings, endlessly threatening and yet less developed, are not like us. The fear that we will become like them keeps us in line, while the belief that we are not allows horrors in our name. In a globalised world where everything seems scarce apart from labour, these are some of the ways that class and race are remade together. In chapter 5 we consider recent debates around hunger and disease – and suggest that these experiences also form a part of class/race structures.

Conclusion

This chapter has explored new forms of racialisation in a reconfigured global economy. On the one hand, our discussion has focused on shifts in labour, capital, sites of production (including outsourcing) and the emergence of new industries and their accompanying forms of racialisation. We have reviewed evidence of the emergence of new global divisions of labour offering highly paid jobs in information technologies, financial and business services on the one hand, and low-paid, low-technology work at the other end of the service sector.

In contrast, the relocation and emergence of new forms of manufacturing industry have created both job losses in some parts of the western world as capital sought newer, cheaper labour elsewhere and new job opportunities in growing urban centres in the Third World. Such developments have coincided with migratory movements, in part international exacerbated by war and conflict, but also internal prompted by rural poverty and job opportunities in the towns. The mapping of new employment patterns shows them to be racialised, gendered and mainly involving poor people. Migration itself is of course not confined to the poorer classes, and we return to the phenomenon of what Featherstone (1995) calls a third class, or at least their consumption patterns, in chapter 6.

We have also looked at production in terms of the view that human bodies are expendable, either used directly in its service or dispensed with, i.e. killed, as a result of extraneous production pressures. The use of prison labour has become an increasingly popular alternative in the search for cheap, captive labour. Its role not only serves production and profit imperatives but also forges links between discourses on the economy and those on law and order.

The so-called new world order has thrown up new political alignments including new forms of global policing, yet many of the old military-industrial pressures have remained intact. Such forces have been consistent in propagating war and/or the prospect of war in order to find global buyers for their arsenal of products. The cost of resultant international and internal conflicts has been witnessed in terms of human death tolls and human displacement, the latter providing a cheap and vulnerable pool of workers for the newly expanding service economies of the West.

We have argued that these various locations in the processes of production and service delivery reveal the dynamics of race, class and gender in the new global economy. Through these unequal relations, racism continues to enable the hyper-exploitation of some groups of people. In chapter 5, we will argue that these productive relations are supplemented by a parallel structure of unequal consumption and distribution. While the world is reshaped by global forces, older structures of race and class continue to determine the quality of everyday life.

Notes

1 For discussion of the war on drugs and its costs, see http: //www.drugwar.com and http: //www.drugsense.org/wodclock.htm
2 See http: //www.oxfam.org.uk/

Chapter 3

Race mixture and people of mixed origins in western societies

European conquest and colonisation of Africa and the Americas, and of vast territories in Asia, over the last 500 years have caused fundamental transformations in the nature of sexual interactions between populations that had remained relatively separated for centuries, with large populations of mixed racialised descent developing across all these territories. The populations indigenous to these territories themselves comprised widely different ethnic and phenotypical variations, but Europeans largely represented them as distinctive 'racial types'. The patterns that unfolded across these continents reveal marked differences. Patterns across the Americas have been called multicoloured systems, even 'racial utopias' (in Brazil and the Caribbean) (Whitten and Torres, 1992). The US has a largely binary system in which anyone with a trace of African ancestry has come to be regarded by whites as 'black'. There grew intermediate categories in southern Africa (for example, South Africa and Zimbabwe). Highly complex patterns also developed across Asia, for example, in India and in Malaysia (J.F. Davis, 1991). People of mixed origins have occupied a different status in different countries. We are most familiar with what has happened in the Caribbean and South America where people of mixed origins occupied a higher status than blacks, especially in South America where class and colour play important roles in the negotiation of status. Or with South Africa in which they occupied an intermediate status between whites and blacks. Mexico has its own system in which the offspring occupy a nominally higher status than either group – the mestizos, as they are called, or the 'cosmic race'. While most literature has been written on systems that refer to children of black/white couples, similar types of systems apply to other groups, for example, to Japanese/white children in Japan, to Vietnamese/white children in Vietnam (see Spickard, 1989). In more recent decades, dramatic changes in the patterns of international migration, and in the international division of labour, have brought about significant increases in patterns of racialised interaction, in the numbers of people dating and marrying across racialised boundaries and identities, and in the numbers of people of mixed racialised descent.

In this chapter we use the framework of the racialisation problematic to explore two sets of related issues concerning people descended from populations that are regarded as distinct 'races' (that is, groups usually called 'mixed-race'). The first set of issues concerns the numbers, ancestries and identities of people of mixed descent. The second set of issues concerns the images and language used to describe 'race mixture' and people of mixed descent, as they are reproduced across a range of institutions in contemporary western society. What we want to emphasise is the ways in which issues to do with notions of 'race' are inextricable from issues that have no apparent necessary connection to 'race', issues such as class, nationality, gender and sexual desire. We describe some of these patterns, and explore some of the conceptual, theoretical and political issues which they raise. The primary focus is on the US and England. In each of these contexts, complex configurations of demographic, legal, political, ideological and social machinations have had decisive influences on the outcomes. And even where historically endemic patterns established during colonialism have changed, their legacies – of institutional patterns, ideas, images, ideologies – have continued to have decisive impacts. All of these patterns, of course, have been specifically gendered, as men from diverse ethnic and racialised groups have competed for access to women as resources. What we show is that the growth of populations of mixed descent, both racialised and ethnic, and the greater vocalisation by them of their concerns and priorities, pose enormous and necessary challenges to ideas of racialised purity and identity, and highlight in more explicit ways than previously the arbitrariness of racialised identities and boundaries, as well as the factors that shape such boundaries. If developed further, many of the arguments offered by groups campaigning for greater recognition of mixed identities promise to bring about a fundamental transformation of the ways in which racialised identities are defined and articulated. At the same time, the pervasive discourses and images of 'race mixture' and people of mixed descent in various institutions demonstrate how ideas of 'race' remain deeply embedded in the social fabric of contemporary society. Each of these sets of forces owes much to history.

Today in the US patterns are very different from in the past. The laws against 'miscegenation' ended in the 1960s, and rates of dating and marriage across racialised identities, as well as the numbers of people of mixed origins, have gone up dramatically. The range and nature of images about such relationships are far more pervasive across the media, especially on television, and in the press. The partners and children of such relationships are far more vocal than ever before, and play a far greater role in the creation and dissemination of images. Nor are such images confined to children of black/white relationships, as they were in the past, but rather cover all groups – including those with black and Asian ancestry, Asian and white ancestry, Latino and Anglo ancestry, and Native American and white ancestry. And unlike earlier generations, where coercion, brutality and rape – much of it with the force of law, and the power of politicians behind it – were central to sexual interactions that transgressed racialised group boundaries, recent patterns are characterised by the exercise of individual rights in contexts of legal freedom. Overwhelmingly, the individuals involved articulate their decisions through prisms of free choice, individual decision-making, love and romance, and breaking down racialised barriers (Root, 1992, 1996; Funderburg, 1994).

But before we announce the end of racism, start promoting a 'colour-blind' society and begin singing 'coffee-coloured children' we should reflect on the scope and limits of these changes.[1] While much has changed there is a lot that remains problematic. Racisms and racialised hostility still keep racialised groups apart, including segregation in employment, housing and neighbourhoods, and inequality in income, occupations, education and social interactions. There remain pervasive stereotypes of women of colour which continue to debase and violate them. Dating and marriage remain overwhelmingly between people within the same racialised and ethnic groups, and where patterns transgress racialised identities they are highly regional, and highly specific to certain groups. And the language used to describe such relationships, and the children of them, remains premised on antiquated and untenable assumptions. Images and notions of 'race mixture' are used by a range of different institutional domains. And even among academics, where the analysis should be clearer, more critical, problems remain pervasive, with troublesome language, concepts and theories, for example, exchange theory (Tucker and Mitchell-Kernan, 1995).

While many recent developments offer the potential for a critical interrogation of race and race mixture, of gender and class relations, and of nationality and identity, on their own they are less likely to lead to substantial improvements, and more likely to lead to the reaffirmation of an uncritical individualism, the denial of class advantage, the subordination of group identity and collective action to the pretext of romantic love and an entirely untenable heralding of the end of racism. There have been substantial changes but they are insufficient on their own for us to be convinced that they will have expansive effects on national patterns of dating and marriage, or on the types of images that prevail, or lead to fundamental changes in the way academic analysis is undertaken. We need to recognise the problems of racialised hostility and discrimination, and of racist stereotypes, as well as the real problems that many people of mixed origins continue to face. At the same time we need to recognise the broader structural and ideological factors that sustain many of these problems – demography, inequality, stereotypes. We suggest that one way to do this is to develop a more satisfactory conceptual language and theoretical framework, which would entail recognition that sexual relationships across racialised identities are perennial and central, not recent and peripheral, and that populations of mixed origins have always been around.

Historical background

If the first thing Columbus did when he arrived in what was later named the Caribbean was praise God and then ask for gold, then what shortly followed was a request for women, who were then sexually abused. Other colonists did exactly the same, including Cortes (Trexler, 1995). Populations of Europeans and Africans, Native Americans and Asians, interacted throughout the metropolis and the colonies (Forbes, 1993). The patterns across the Americas have been called multicoloured systems, even racial utopias (in Brazil and the Caribbean). In the major characterisations, blacks of mixed origins are represented as having benefited from rich white fathers, preferential work responsibilities, better living standards, greater access to legal freedom and better patterns of social mobility once legally free (Cohen and Greene, 1972). Many of these characterisations are certainly true, particularly for South America, but one of us has shown for the Anglo territories that people of mixed origins operated under far greater constraints than usually acknowledged (Small, 1994b). We must challenge the major images of blacks of mixed origins under slavery because they are based on a small, unrepresentative sample, and from evidence largely compiled by whites. It is true that many blacks of mixed origins enjoyed real advantages, but only in favourable circumstances, that is, where they had a wealthy white father, and benefited from stereotypes that prevented their working in the fields. But most blacks of mixed origins were not in those circumstances – they usually had a poor white father (who often abandoned them), or had no white father at all; they usually remained enslaved and working in the fields, or if in the house they were subject to hostile circumstances from the master–enslaver and mistress–enslaver. Many suffered unique atrocities, including rape and the physical and psychological pain of incest (Small, 2001b). In these circumstances blacks of mixed origins and blacks (presumed to be unmixed) related to one another by family, community, a common predicament and similar goals, worked together, lived and ate together, played and socialised together, and worked for political and cultural advancement. We will only learn more about this when we begin to pose broader and different questions, and collect more varied evidence, than those that have dominated the agendas of academics thus far. Clearing up these historical issues will not lead to immediate change in action – but as educators we have a responsibility to provide a full appreciation of all the facts.

As patterns of sexual interaction unfolded, the attitudes of powerful white men towards 'race mixture' were clearly stated and almost invariably hostile. Under colonialism and slavery, laws were introduced to prohibit 'amalgamation', and to prosecute those that practised it; after the Civil War, laws were introduced against 'miscegenation'; white politicians deprecated it, while presidents condoned lynching; films avoided scenes of intimacy across racialised groups, according to a Hollywood code aimed especially at blacks and whites; professors and medical doctors offered scientific evidence that 'race mixture' contaminated Europeans, biologically and culturally, and gave rise to a population of mixed origins that was physically inferior and psychologically unstable. Literature generally provided the creative analogues of such views. At the same time, the vigour with which white men opposed 'miscegenation' officially, especially for men of colour, was exceeded only by the fervour with which they practised it privately.

By the end of legal slavery in the US there were around 500,000 people of mixed origins across the nation, including many that had been legally free for decades (J.W. Williamson, 1995). This population continued to grow and to interact with those who appeared to have no non-African ancestry, and many became leaders, activists and successful entrepreneurs in the black community. Today, the African-American population reveals a distinctive array of phenotypical (especially skin colour) variations, and themes of difference within the African-American population are widespread in black popular culture, including literature, film, art and photography.

The growth of a population of mixed origins in the UK, especially in England, reflects how the specific circumstances of power, economics and demography shape outcomes. Historically, England has always had a small population of colour – Africans that arrived after the American War of Independence, or as the accompanying enslaved persons and servants of West Indies merchants returning to the UK; Indians as students, or as sailors. Estimates suggest a maximum of 15,000 in the 1770s (Fryer, 1984; Myers, 1996). This population remained small, and by the nineteenth century included prominent blacks such as William Davidson, Robert Wedderburn and, towards the end of the century, Samuel Coleridge-Taylor who became a famous composer and conductor. Less common were women of mixed origins, the most notable being Mary Seacole who was involved in the Crimean War and became known as the black Florence Nightingale. The 1911 Census reported 9,189 people from the West Indies in Britain, the vast majority of whom would have been black or mixed (Tizard and Phoenix, 1993). The population continued to remain small, and even by the 1940s, when West Indian servicemen arrived in Britain – along with thousands of African-American military personnel – it numbered no more than a few thousand (Walvin, 1973). Among the people of colour that arrived there were very few women. This demographic imbalance was a major factor in the particular pattern of dating and marriage that occurred between whites and people of colour – while tiny in number such relationships were overwhelmingly between men of colour and white women.

A population of children of mixed origins grew up, especially in the port towns where people of colour lived – London, Cardiff, Liverpool and Bristol. People of mixed origins were the subject of both liberal and racist attention, a particularly prominent example being the report by the Liverpool University Settlement in the early 1900s (Christian, 1997). This report painted a hostile picture of these relationships, suggesting that the white women involved in them were degenerates or prostitutes, the black men licentious and criminal and the children social misfits (Rich, 1996). Few people of mixed origins were successful, and their experiences generally were adverse, with almost no evidence of the levels of success and privilege that many of their counterparts enjoyed in the Caribbean and the US. Despite this, members of the black communities, along with white mothers, worked to alleviate the discrimination their children faced, and sought to instil in them respect and self-esteem (Sherwood, 1994).

Several factors have remained consistent in this historical experience: black people have faced relentless racialised hostility (discrimination, abuse, violence, attacks) and have been stigmatised and constrained by multiple racialised ideologies; successive governments have encouraged and manipulated white fears of black people, for purposes of electoral success; and black people have sustained communities of resistance, particularly via their diasporic links and identification. Black people thus remain systematically disadvantaged, but their resolve to survive and succeed has never deserted them. At the same time, transgressive relationships have involved primarily black men and white women and were largely consensual (a situation at variance with that in the US where historically such relationships were between white men and black women, usually involving coercion, most frequently involving rape). People of mixed origins never were the beneficiaries of the preferential treatment usually attributed to them in the Caribbean and the US, and with parents that were relatively powerless due to racism (against black men) and sexism (against working-class white women) they remained largely disadvantaged and stigmatised: a population more frequently pitied than applauded.

Transgressive relationships and people of mixed origins

Rates of marriage in the US are lower than in the past. People tend to marry at a later age and the marriages do not last as long, with divorce rates as high as 50 per cent. But among those who marry, marriage across racialised groups is on the rise, with the highest rates occurring among Asians, Native Americans and Hispanics, all of whom have rates of marriage to members of a different racialised group of over 50 per cent. Women in these groups are far more likely to marry across racialised groups – usually to a white man. The percentage of blacks married to non-blacks has also steadily risen, and while the rates are lower (in the 1990s, 3 per cent of blacks who married, married a non-black), they constitute the highest absolute numbers (blacks amounted to 48 per cent of all people of colour in 1990). This will change shortly as Latinos become the largest minority group in the country – as early as 2005 by some estimates.

Marriages across racialised groups occur least often in the south, and most often on the West Coast. Rates are as high as 10 per cent in California, with some cities (Los Angeles and the San Francisco Bay Area) around 20 per cent. Similarly, cities like New York, Chicago, Denver, Seattle have rates several times higher than the national average. No state beats Hawaii, which has a rate of 85 per cent for marriages across racialised groups. Such marriages are more common among the middle class, particularly those with a university education, are far higher among younger people, and far more likely, by definition, when it comes to people of mixed descent. Today, the higher the educational level of those getting married, the more likely the marriage to last, without regard to racialised group identity. The highest rates of marriage are for Asian-American women who marry non-Asian men (usually whites). Patterns are equally high among Native Americans and Chicanas. For blacks it is the men rather than the women who marry outside their racialised group – 3.6 per cent of men compared to 1.2 per cent of women. While black women display the lowest rate for any racialised gender category, their numbers have doubled in the last five years and are likely to continue rising faster than other groups given the shortage of economically active black men, and the lower rates of economic disparities between black women and black men. These patterns indicate that women refuse to submit any longer to the dictates of men over the nature and expression of their sexual choices. And marriage is only the tip of the iceberg. Far more dating occurs than marriage – it involves less pressure, is more fleeting and is motivated by different factors – and all the evidence suggests it continues to increase. Surveys reveal increasingly larger numbers that have dated across racialised groups, or who say they would consider doing so. In a recent survey at least 30 per cent of the population said they would do so, with dramatic variations among racialised categories (90 per cent of 'Hispanics', 60 per cent of blacks and 47 per cent of whites) (*USA Today*, 1997).

These numbers, of course, are reflected in the growing size of the population with multiple racialised ancestry. In the 1990 Census almost 10 million people checked the 'other' box, a number widely believed to be an undercount of actual numbers. We know that large proportions of the American population are mixed, though millions choose to deny that mixture, or are unaware of it, for a variety of reasons, particularly the salience of the distinction between white and 'non-white', and the dominance of 'hypo-descent' in their lives.

In Britain in 1988–90 around 53 per cent of Caribbean men aged 16–24, and 36 per cent of those aged 25–44, who were married or cohabiting had a partner who was a white woman (Modood *et al.*, 1997: 77, Table 1). At the same time, 36 per cent of Caribbean women aged 16–24, and 29 per cent aged 25–44, who were married or cohabiting had a partner who was a white man (ibid.: 78, Table 2). In 1994 there were about 14 million couples in Britain, of whom 13.77 million were men and women of the same ethnic

group. There were over 200,000 couples involved in mixed-ethnic relationships (Douglas, 1999: 16). Among the category 'black-other' over 50 per
cent of men, and almost 50 per cent of women, had white partners (Phoenix
and Owen, 1996: 120). By the mid-1990s, 'as many as half British born
Caribbean men and a third of women, had chosen a white partner' and
'for two out of five children (39 per cent) with a Caribbean mother or
father, their other parent was white' (Modood et al., op. cit.: 27). This
indicates the comparatively higher levels of transgressive relationships in
Britain, and offers a compelling reason for believing that such relationships
are bound to continue, and that the numbers of people of mixed racialised
origins are bound to grow.[2] But at the same time, it should be remembered
that over 99 per cent of white men and women who lived with a partner
had a white partner (ibid.).

The 1991 Census revealed that amongst a population of almost
55 million, there were at least 228,504 people who identified themselves as
being of mixed origins (where this meant having a white parent and a
parent that was either black (African, or Caribbean or mixed) or Asian
(Indian, Pakistani or Bangladeshi). Among this group there were 54,569
identified as 'black/white', and 61,874 identified as 'Asian/white'. These
individuals totalled a tiny 0.5 per cent of the entire British population, but
at the same time numbered around 8 per cent of the 'ethnic minority' population of the nation (Phoenix and Owen, op. cit.). It is clear that this is an
understatement of the numbers of people of mixed origins, for it speaks
only of those who cross the primary racialised identities of blacks and
Asians, and because there were other categories in the Census that involved
mixed people but the questions were asked in a way that makes it unclear
whether the individuals identified have any African, African-Caribbean or
Asian ancestry (see the explanation in Phoenix and Owen, op. cit.: 121).
As compared with people of colour generally in Britain people of mixed
racialised origins are younger and were more likely to have been born in
Britain. As will be seen, they are far more likely to be involved in a mixed
relationship when they come of age.

Between 1983 and 1991 a series of surveys by the British Social Attitudes
Survey provides data on attitudes towards transgressive sexual relationships. Asked if they would object to a close relative marrying someone of
Asian or West Indian origin, about 50 per cent of white Britons said
that they would mind 'either a lot or a little', but their rates declined from
54 per cent in 1983, to 43 per cent in 1991 (Phoenix and Owen, op. cit.:
116). In 1991 a poll conducted by the *Independent on Sunday* asked
whether people should marry only those within their own ethnic group.
Some 31 per cent of whites, 17 per cent of blacks and 39 per cent of
Asians agreed (Phoenix and Owen, op. cit.: 116). It is clear that the difference in attitude of Asians reflects issues of culture, in particular religion, to
a far higher degree than issues of race.

Evidence from several series of interviews conducted throughout the 1990s reveals the complex experiences of people of mixed origins of all ages, in their relationships with their white families, especially their white mothers, and the white and black communities, and in their range of expressed identities (Tizard and Phoenix, 1993; Goodwin, 1994; Parker, 1995; Ifekwunigwe, 1999). Some of these studies pay detailed attention to the attitudes of children of mixed Asian and white parentage, indicating how patterns among them often vary. Contrary to the popular stereotype of blacks of mixed origins widespread in the black community, and frequently reproduced in the white press, blacks of mixed origins do not invariably look down on blacks and regard themselves as white. In contrast their views are highly varied, depending on the context in which they grew up (family, community, neighbourhood, schooling) and their own physical appearance and cultural experience. Tizard and Phoenix found that the most common pattern among teenagers was to claim both identities. This was also common among older people. Claire Harvey, 35 years old, reports: 'I'm both mixed and Black and I embrace all my sides' (Douglas, op. cit.: 18). And Lucille, 34: 'I identify myself as Black for political reasons. In this society you have to identify your affiliations but that doesn't stop me expressing my individuality as a mixed race woman . . . I'm very comfortable with who I am – a Black woman of mixed parentage' (ibid.). One of the respondents in Ifekwunigwe's study in Bristol reported, 'I think at the end of the day, White society has never accepted me. They've seen me as a contamination to their stock. Diseased person, and even worse than havin' two Black parents, worse than even that. If you come to extermination, we would probably go first. Nazi Germany, that's the sort of vibe I get off white people' (Ifekwunigwe, op. cit.: 8). Blacks of mixed origins experience racism from whites and from blacks, and experience discrimination from both because they are mixed (Phoenix and Owen, op. cit.: 129).

By the end of the 1990s Asian/white relationships were still less frequent than black/white relationships, but the number of children of mixed Asian/white origins is larger than the number of black/white origins. This is because the Asian population is twice the size of the black population in Britain and will soon also outstrip the number of people of mixed black/white ancestry. At the same time, the Asian population is far more indigenous than ever before, and has a higher class profile than blacks – Asians are far more likely to graduate from university and to secure professional occupations than are blacks. These facts will also ensure that the numbers of relationships and marriages across racialised identities will increase, as will the numbers of children born to these relationships. To a far greater degree than children of black/white relationships, these children highlight issues of culture, religion and language, for example, as the older generation resists the dilution of its culture through assimilation. Battles over gender and generation will continue, with the fathers, Asian or white, of women involved in these relationships taking far more strident action to constrain them than they take against their male children. There has been evidence of significant family conflict occurring, and of ostracism of family members (usually offspring) who become involved in such relationships. Without the same historical incidence of Asian/white as of black/white relationships, it remains to be seen how patterns among the former will unfold.

Contemporary problems in the US and the UK

These studies clearly demonstrate substantial improvements in attitudes as compared with the past. However, when we take into account some of the structural features of contemporary contexts, we can see that persistent problems remain. Across the US patterns of segregation remain remarkably high, as do patterns of inequality. Americans continue to grow up in neigh-bourhoods, attend schools and socialise with other Americans of the same racialised identity or ethnic group (Massey and Denton, 1993). Whites still own more wealth, earn more income, hold better jobs and achieve higher educational levels than do black Americans (Oliver and Shapiro, 1995). Racist hostility – discrimination, abuse and attacks – remain endemic. Discrimination at work and in school is common. Blacks and other groups of colour continue to face victimisation by the police. Verbal abuse is common (Small, 2001b). Globalisation, particularly at the economic level, continues to exacerbate the problems that working people of colour face (Torres *et al.*, 1999; Small, 1999). Contemporary western societies are still the foundation for the promotion of pernicious stereotypes and racist images of people of colour in general, and women of colour in particular (Kaplan, 1997; Torres, 1998). Demeaning and villifying, sexually objectify-ing images of women of colour are pervasive in the media. Black women continue to be presented as prostitutes, strippers, welfare mothers, sexual objects. Latinas are also portrayed sexually (note the obsession with Jennifer Lopez's backside), and Asian women are seen as sensual and sub-servient – eager to please, exotic, erotic (Oboler, 1995; C.E. Rodriguez, 1997). These images play a central role in shaping attitudes across racialised groups, and remain a central factor in motivating white men to pursue relationships with women of colour.

Patterns of marriage and dating are extremely concentrated and highly segregated. Over 97 per cent of marriages are still between members of the same racialised group, and this in a nation where people of colour amount to around 25 per cent of the population. Even in California, the state with the highest rates of marriage across racialised groups, they constitute only around 10 per cent of all marriages. If we exclude four states – distant Hawaii, and mainland California, New York and Florida – marriages across racialised identities are about as common today as they were in the southern US at the start of the century (Perlmann, 1997). Continuing housing, educational and occupational segregation, and the prevalence of stereotypes, will sustain such patterns. Besides, notions and images of 'race mixture' have a far greater currency in a much wider range of American institutions than is suggested by the numbers – as we demonstrate in the following sections.

Although far less strident than in the US, racialised inequality, segregation and discrimination are equally entrenched in England (Small, 1994a). Communities of colour remain relatively segregated from whites, they occupy inferior housing, tend to do less well-paying jobs, and face abuse and hostility of various kinds (Solomos and Back, 1996). Women of colour still figure prominently in the images of prostitutes, sluts, 'scrubbers' and tramps in Britain (O'Connell-Davidson, 1998). Try to make a telephone call in any of a thousand telephone boxes in Earls Court, Charing Cross, King's Cross or south London and you'll see postcard adverts for 'Buxom black women' and 'Exotic Asian girls'. The topless pictures of young women and girls that adorn page 3 of the *Sun* contribute to this. The numbers involved in dating and marriage across racialised groups is far higher in Britain than in the US (as we demonstrated in the statistics above) but it is far from commensurate with the demographics of the nation (Parker and Song, 2001). The partners to such relationships, and their children, continue to face hostility and verbal abuse (Alibhai-Brown and Montague, 1992; Ifekwunigwe, op. cit.).

In both countries, then, given the high correlation between socio-economic status and marriage across racialised identities, the continuing patterns of segregation and the dissemination of demeaning stereotypes, these harsh facts of racialised inequality mean that patterns of sexual relations across racialised groups are highly likely to continue to remain low for some time, more so in the US than in Britain.

Besides, if larger numbers and far more frequent discussion of people of 'mixed race' promise to resolve a number of problems, then they have also made far more explicit than before a range of problems that have been historically entrenched and suppressed. People of mixed origins proclaim that many of the problems they face come from blacks as well as whites; and they demand identities that challenge the traditionally established identities (that is, they no longer accept that their only option is to embrace an identity associated with the subordinated group of colour, black or Asian). The proliferation of identities associated with people of multiple origins, racialised, ethnic, religious – what the postmodernists have called the fragmentation of identities – and the growth of new ethnicities poses many threats to relationships which were previously cemented on the pre-mise of suppressing differences of this kind. Identity politics is important today and the old-fashioned identities of nation, class, gender, religion, ethnicity compete with the new-fangled ones of 'mixed-race', global identities, multiple identities. Increasingly larger numbers of people are claiming multiple identities, and the right to change identities at will. Debate around 'mixed-race' identity threatens to burst fragile coalitions; as well as prevent new ones from forming.

The growing numbers of people descended from more than one racialised group constitute another chapter in the compendium of complexities that threaten to tear at the fabric of social alliances and coalitions. These patterns, perhaps less immediate in their threat, not as obvious in their potential devastation, are no less ominous in their ability, if left unaddressed, to overwhelm the alliances and coalitions that have been built so far, and to prevent the development of new coalitions. For example, the 'mixed-race movement', as it is called, illuminates other issues, other divisions, other fractures, which we have too long overlooked in our attempts to build coalitions. In the US the issues are in the larger public domain in debates about the Census category, with organizations such as the National Association for the Advancement of Colored People, the Urban League and La Raza taking a stance in opposition to a 'mixed-race' category in the Census. We have also seen enough accusations of privilege and preference, self-interest, betrayal and treachery to suspect that more is yet to come. In the UK accusations about successful blacks who marry whites for status, and people of mixed origins who reject 'black' identities, and accuse blacks of hostility and victimisation are common (Modood *et al.*, 1997). For example, throughout the 1980s and 1990s, Bernie Grant, MP for Tottenham, was criticised because his partner was white. Grant said that hostility to his relationship has been expressed but not frequently. He added it 'hasn't got the same steam in Britain, it's yet another American import that's failed' (Goodwin, 1994: 8). Oona King continues to be criticised gratuitously because she is of mixed origins (black and Jewish). Underneath these issues, then, are antipathies and antagonisms of a more serious kind, likely to erupt if left unchecked. And already sufficiently robust to prevent alliances between people who have much in common in their more fundamental social and political goals.

Identity formation for people of mixed origins follows similar vectors to identity formation for blacks (presumed to be unmixed), but can often become more convoluted, some of the variables being more intricate, and with other kinds of social pressures to take into account. Once again context is critical, as Mark Christian has shown in his consideration of South Africa, Jamaica and Britain (1997). Partners and children in relationships that cross racialised group boundaries have to negotiate between both sets of families, and their opposition to the relationship; they have to circumvent stereotypes about the sexual motivations of black men with white women, and what that says about black men's attitudes towards black women, often including their mothers; they have to negotiate how the white women in such relationships are seen as social outcasts at best, prostitutes usually, and the presumption that something must be wrong with them if they want a black boyfriend. There are also the nasty names, the offensive stereotypes, the expectations that one must prove how black one is; as in 'half-caste' and 'half-breed', which presume biological degeneracy, the questioning of one's political commitment. The history of people of mixed origins in Liverpool, and Britain's other seaports, provides sufficient evidence of the trauma that has frequently been an inescapable component of a mixed identity in Britain. For example, people in Liverpool have hurtful memories of travelling to Bootle, or Scotland Road, or Halewood, to meet white uncles and aunts. That these issues have persisted in recent decades is strikingly obvious, as 'coffee-coloured children' attests. It is a creatively brilliant example of the vortex of racialised identity for people of mixed origins in England. Similarly there are innumerable examples of the determination to prevail, to insist on one's priorities and, as one of us has said elsewhere, to refuse a victim mentality even if victimised. It would be so easy if they could, as so many people have so effortlessly urged, simply be black. But that's not the case, never has been, almost certainly never will be.

In these complex processes kinship is an indispensable factor in the matrix that shapes identity. For blacks of mixed origins it is even more so. The black family can be the focus of criticism, some times with good reason – especially over domestic violence. But also it is in the family that we find strength and reinvigoration. Many studies show that the family is a major site for shaping identity, particularly for people of mixed origins, along with community, friends and the media. Little surprise that kids raised with white mothers in all-white neighbourhoods, estranged from their fathers, and/or from other black family members, might be ambivalent or openly hostile towards black identity. Little surprise, too, that kids raised in a black or mixed neighbourhood, with the black and white parent present, and sustained contact with other black family members, are less ambivalent. This means that blacks of mixed origins, like blacks, Asians, whites, in fact any group, will continue to embrace a diversity of identities, cultural traits, political values. I doubt that we'll be able to avoid this as a fact. Instead, we might more profitably figure out how to get people, blacks and non-blacks, to embrace a sense of community that goes beyond the excesses of individualist selfishness.

Nor is the academy in either nation free from such problems. Academic analysis of race mixture and people of mixed origins continues to deploy an antiquated conceptual language, or to piggy-back on such language. Analysts continue to talk about 'mulattoes' and 'race mixture' as if they are neutrally descriptive and real phenomena, rather than intrinsically negative concepts that are emotionally charged (J.W. Williamson, 1995; Zack, 1993). Even where new language has been introduced, it is often severely flawed (Spencer, 1997). One of the most prominent features of the growing numbers of people of mixed descent is their rejection of the stereotypical and derogatory names, like 'half-breed', 'half-caste', 'mulatto', or 'Oreo' and 'Coconut', which deride both blacks and blacks of mixed origins for being 'black on the outside, white on the inside' in terms of their attitudes and values. People of mixed origins, and their parents, have struggled and continue to struggle to identify themselves with appropriate names and labels which are not hostile (Ifekwunigwe, op. cit.). A whole series of new names have been developed, especially in the US, including 'bi-racial', 'multiracial' 'AmerAsian', 'Afroasian', 'Hapa'. The word 'mono-racial' is used for people presumed to have parents with the same racialised ancestry (Root, 1996: ix–xi). In England many of the same names are used, along with a few others. But the idea of 'bi-racial' suggests that there are original races, and the person is the offspring of two of them. The term 'multiracial' suggests that a person has origins in at least three different races. Overall, whatever gains are made in ameliorating the harshness of previous terms, the language that continues to be used reifies notions of race, and perpetuates the idea that race has a real existence outside its socially constructed meaning.

In many of these contemporary problems, the influence of the past dances on the present, particularly as reflected in the premises underlying discussions of race, and in the images of race mixture, and people of mixed origins. They provide an uncritical portrayal of preferential treatment in the past and present; they privilege lighter-skinned women over darker-skinned women. The past is also responsible for the language of race mixture that we have inherited. While most of our attention must focus on the present, no successful resolution of today's problems can come about until we have a thorough reappraisal of the influences from the past.

The discursive terrains of 'race mixture' in contemporary societies

Diverse and divergent discourses of 'race mixture' and of people of mixed origins are spread across the entire range of contemporary US and UK society. At one extreme are discourses that preach separation as a principle (for example, those associated with white supremacist groups). At the other end are those which promote sexual integration as a principle (for example, the 'mixed-race movement'). Occupying spaces in between are a range of others including those in the media, and in the romance and sex industry. A common theme across these discourses is that they reveal institutional actors who appropriate, reproduce or create images for their own purposes. And they do so largely by reproducing images that are predicated upon the antiquated notions of race purity and mixture. These images are pervasive, entrenched and difficult to dislodge.

Very few national or prominent local politicians, or key social agencies, make statements about 'race mixture' or people of mixed origins in the US or Britain. Despite this, the expression of attitudes towards 'race mixture' and people of mixed origins is pervasive in US and British society, attitudes that are articulated using the varied idioms of distinctive discursive terrains. Discursive terrains are social idioms (or ways of talking) based on expected and accepted principles that provide the context for interpreting and evaluating social concerns. Discursive terrains have distinctive features that serve as conceptual corridors through which 'race mixture' is defined and understood. They also invoke the criteria by which 'race mixture' is to be approached and evaluated. These discourses draw upon long-established ideas and notions and use a language and vocabulary that has shared collective meanings. While such discourses are not restricted to specific institutional sites, nevertheless it is possible to identify several that have unique vectors in particular institutional sites. We call these sites 'social domains', and they are characterised by institutional structures, particular social constituencies and elaborate modes of articulation. When we examine these domains and terrains we find explicit and detailed articulations of 'race mixture' and hybridity, articulations which reflect and infect public and individual discourses and beliefs. We want to suggest that they are irreconcilable with one another.

At one extreme are white supremacist groups, and their followers who expound a discourse of race purity. The main language of this articulation is good old-fashioned racism, that is, biological truth, race purity, mongrelisation, and cultural and intellectual decay. The motivation is physical, mental and cultural purity, the ascendancy of the white race, and to avoid pollution and contamination. Advocates see themselves as the 'real leaders' of the white race in a constituency largely comprising good-for-nothing white men, intellectual and educational failures, those who were near-misses politically, as well as a whole array of marginals driven to extremes. The goals are preservation of racial purity and civilisation, and taking over the White House and government. The designated methods are legal, extra-legal and illegal; laws against the wanton irresponsibility of dating and marriage across racialised groups, the explusion of immigrants of colour and the extermination of inferiors, along with a general perpetration of violence and terror. Information is disseminated via newsletters, marches and websites. Today, many supremacists refer to the Bible for rationalisation, one website entitled 'God's Order affirmed in Love Reference Library for Reconstructing a National Identity for Christian Whites' firmly opposed to race mixing because it ends up 'destroying the races as God created them'. Another seeks authority in science arguing that 'hybridized recombinations of racial-genetic traits actually reduce, and are destructive of, biological racial diversity to the extent that they replace or deplete the parent racial stocks'.

At the other extreme is the 'Mixed Race Movement' in which a discourse of individualism and personal rights is prevalent. Central to this domain are articulations of the inveterate US principles of individualism, free choice, the rule of law, avoidance of persecution and the rights of representation for those that pay taxation. The motivations underlying this discourse are acknowledgement, respect, identity, inclusion and participation in the body politic. The primary constituency is people of mixed origins themselves, especially middle-class, college-educated ones, and their families, especially white mothers. The goals are inclusion of people of mixed heritage in all government agencies, especially the Census, so that a far more nuanced appreciation of racialised diversity can be acknowledged, and the implications of such nuances for the health and welfare of these people can be addressed. The designated methods are research and evidence, lectures and publications, especially biographies, lobbying of governments, dissemination of information on suffering. The designated audience is primarily the government, educators and policy-makers.

Motivated by the 'always painful contradictions' of mixed heritage, the rigidity of racialised classifications and the rule of hypodescent, the movement comprises a set of organisations, institutions, marches and demonstrations, support groups, families and individuals who have produced books, articles, journals and newsletters. While people of mixed heritage are prominent here, it is their parents who were the primary force behind the establishment of the movement. Groups include the Association of Multi-Ethnic Americans, RACE (Reclassify All Children Equally), HAPA Issues Forum, I-Pride, Interracial Network and the Interracial Family Alliance. The movement is heavily shaped by class, most of those involved possessing elite educational qualifications and professional jobs, and an inordinate number originating in elite universities, including Harvard, Yale, Wesleyan, Brown and the University of California, Berkeley. Nakashima identifies three goals for the Mixed Race Movement: to seek inclusion and legitimacy in existing 'racial/ethnic communities'; to shape a common identity and agenda in 'new multiracial community'; or to dismantle the 'dominant racial identity in a community of humanity'. She prefers to see these as different approaches, different dimensions of the movement, rather than as divisions (1996). The introduction of a category in the Census is seen as a primary way to begin to achieve many of these goals. The movement claims that the Census will reveal the inadequacies of current racial identifications, will provide more accurate numbers of people of multiple heritage, will affirm an identity of multiple heritage and provide access to resources. A 'check all identities' category was introduced in the Census 2000, largely as a result of the movement's activities. But while this can be claimed as a success, the movement has made explicit many antipathies and antagonisms which have for so long remained implicit. A number of organisations like the National Association for the Advancement of Colored People oppose the Census category and see it as both a distraction and a dilution of the collective power of people of colour. They advocate the integration of the races, sexual mingling, representation in the singles columns, as a priority. Brown University's mixed-race group at one time required all its members to be dating across racialised categories.

These two discourses represent extremes – the Mixed Race Movement advocates 'race mixture' as inherently good, and its principle of individual rights and a rhetoric of 'true romance' are values held dear to US citizens, while white supremacists advocate strict segregation, and the imposition of a social contract preserving white privilege and racialised integrity, by force if necessary. But there are many other discourses that occupy a more complex terrain existing between them, and encompassing aspects of their discourses. For example, among the many organisations of the media (including film, television, advertisements and music, and the press) significant images of 'race mixture' are represented through a discourse of consumerism. This discourse is expressed through linguistic and visual creativity, artistic innovation and poetic licence. The motivations are multiple – sell goods and advertising space, and support liberal democracy and individualism. The constituencies are the producers of films, videos, advertising and literature, and the corporations that sell goods. The underlying goal is to get the products sold, especially by promoting a way of life that looks cool (as in Hip Hop videos), and the designated methods are air space and air waves, huge billboards (as in the distinctive cartography of Los Angeles), and images and photos. The audience is the US consumer, especially the young, hip one. Films are paramount here. In *Jungle Fever* (1991), an African-American architect commits adultery with his Italian-American secretary. They attempt to develop a relationship but succumb to the pressures of racialised family and community. In *Lone Star* (1996), the legacy of the past – told through an aborted adolescent sexual adventure – reveals itself in a transgressive relationship of adulthood in southern Texas. It is made poignant, tragic and ridiculous through the accidental discovery of kinship and incest.

Topping all these films for its deep and pervasive reverberations of 'race mixture' is *Blade* (1998). Ostensibly about vampires, it constitutes an allegory for purity of blood, in which Blade, half-human, half-vampire, phenotypically black (Wesley Snipes), fights Deacon Frost, half-human, half-vampire, phenotypically white (Stephen Dorff), for the future of the human race. Frost is rejected by the pure vampires. 'Who are you to challenge our ways?' asks Quinn, the leader of the vampire council. 'You're not even a pure blood.' Frost seeks an alliance with Blade, but is rejected by him, as Blade aligns himself with the humans. Frost taunts, 'You think the humans will ever accept a half-breed like you? They can't. They're afraid of you. And they should be. You're an animal.' Neither man fits into a world of racialised purity, and they can only exist in its interstices.

One of American television's most popular shows – *ER* – featured a sexual relationship between a black man and white woman. The NBC programme – which relates the activities of an emergency room in a Chicago hospital and is currently (autumn 1999) in its sixth season – generated a controversial off-screen debate in spring 1999, as the actor who plays the lead character protested off screen that all his relationships with black women were 'dysfunctional' while his relationship with a white woman had 'a much better story line'. Television also runs special programmes on these issues, including 'An American Love Story', a ten-hour PBS series, in September 1999. Television advertisements deploy similar imagery – with portrayals of multicultural schools and colleges, workforces, sports teams and politicians, mixing and matching, embracing and kissing, and more.

To this can be added the numerous television celebrities whose photographs adorn the front pages of television magazines – David Bowie and Iman, Wesley Snipes and his Asian girlfriend, Donna Wong, Robert De Niro and black spouse, Grace Hightower, along with early practitioner, Sidney Poitier, his white wife, Joanna Poitier, and their daughter Sydney Tamiia. Hip Hop videos are replete with light-skinned, scantily clad women – could be black, could be mixed, could be white, could be Asian or Chicana – decorating the sets of Ghetto Gangsters. The Hip Hop prima donna, Foxy Brown, proclaims her mixed identity in her album *Chyna Doll*, resplendent with her diminutive self on the front cover, adorned with a tattoo (in Japanese characters, announcing 'peace, love and serenity') beckoning from above her left breast. From Janet Jackson and Michael Jackson, to Mariah Carey and Sean 'Puffy' Combs, video after video is suggestive of the increasing patterns of transgressive racialised relationships, especially among the nation's youth. Mariah Carey, herself the constant focus of attention about her mixed identity, did a show with Oprah Winfrey (November 1999) in which she described her background, her problems and issues, through the medium of personal trauma (she had to write poems to deal with her pain), personal accomplishment and success. On the show she is accompanied by a series of pretty, mixed children, all girls, who relate the plethora of problems they encounter just trying to be accepted as individuals, because both whites and blacks reject them. When one little girl recites a poem, Mariah Carey cries. In England the frequency with which blacks and whites date on television – in *EastEnders*, *Brookside*, in dramas and films (*East is East*, *Brothers in Trouble*), and the frequent portrayals of prominent couples in the British press – Lenny Henry and Dawn French, Frank Bruno and his wife – remind the British public that such practices are common.

Similar images are common in the UK, where US culture has always had an impact, particularly on blacks. In addition to films about transgressive relationships and people of mixed racial descent that are produced in Britain – *Sapphire* in the 1950s, *A Taste of Honey* in the 1960s, *Mona Lisa* in the 1980s, *Secrets and Lies* and *The Crying Game* in the 1990s – American films also have an impact – films like *Jungle Fever* and *Get on the Bus*, or *Sankofa*, played in the now defunct black film theatre in Portobello Road in the early 1990s. In *Get on the Bus* there's a scene in which two black men, one apparently mixed, one presumably unmixed, cross swords on the issue of slavery and preferential treatment for 'mixed-race' people. The unmixed one (nicknamed 'Hollywood' because he's an actor) tells the mixed one (Gary) that he must know what the white bus driver is thinking because the two of them, he says, 'share a white thing!'. A heartfelt renunciation of 'the white thing' follows, as he maintains he is black. After an intervention by another passenger who says 'the man's black', and if this were slavery 'old master' wouldn't care if he were 'half white', Hollywood explodes:

> He'd be 'a house slave pimpin' round the big house, and while the rest
> of us would be talking about grits . . . this fool'd be eatin' potatoes,
> he'd have the best of chicken, we'd have the neck bones, our women
> would be all blistered up and stinkin' from picking cotton, his would
> be all bathed, smelling good, and nine times out of ten, the honey
> he'd be hittin' skins with . . . she'd be a white girl.

Gary say's 'my lady's not white' and accuses Hollywood of wanting to sleep
with a white woman himself. The tension passes, for the moment. Similar
portrayals have appeared in other films about slavery in which men and
women of mixed origins received favourable treatment especially from
their white fathers. *Sankofa*, a progressive film that explores the complexities of slavery in the US, including rape, in empathetic and insightful
ways, still manages to reproduce all the derogatory stereotypes of blacks of
mixed origins. Joe, the 'mulatto', is the product of rape, idolises and
embraces white culture, in the form of an excessive devotion to Christianity,
deprecates all things African, and makes a libidinal fetish of the Virgin
Mary, while refusing to sleep with a dark-skinned woman. Poor Joe despises
his African mother, whom he eventually kills. These images continue to
have a key impact on attitudes towards transgressive racialised relationships
and towards people of mixed racialised descent. Similarly, the Oprah Winfrey show, the Jerry Springer show and others frequently air programmes
about people of mixed origins which frequently appear in Britain on cable
or regular television (Phoenix and Owen, op. cit.). And incidents like the
one in which Hugh Grant, the white British actor and epitome of the
upper middle class, was arrested for soliciting an African-American prostitute in Los Angeles in the early 1990s also provide images of 'race mixture'.
    Closely related are images of black beauty in black popular culture,
which speak to the desirable hair texture, skin shade and shape of lips for
black women. Describing several items that appeared in the black woman's
magazine *Pride*, and in her own research on images of beauty and mother-
ing among young black women, several of whom were mixed, Weekes
describes how such images frequently negate 'black textured hair and
darker shades of skin' in favour of straight hair and light skin (Weekes,
1997: 115). Several black women wrote in to *Pride* to complain that the
winner of a beauty competition looked white; these letters were followed
by several from 'mixed-race' women who asked why it was that only dark-
skinned women with flat noses were regarded as 'true black woman' (ibid.:
117). It is clear then that images of race and race mixture continue to play
an influential role in black attitudes and discussions. Relationships between
celebrities are another area in which images of 'race mixture' are common.
People like David Bowie and Iman, Naomi Campbell and her various
relationships with white men including Adam Clayton and Robert De
Niro, provide the impression that transgressing racialised boundaries is no
longer a problem.

Occupying a far more dubious celebrity status are the hundreds of 'brown-skinned blue-eyed boys' and girls that crowd the pages of the black press and the professional journals of social-work associations in Britain.[3] These children, with pretty smiles or sad faces, are the result of broken families that attempted to cross racialised boundaries, in the care of social-service departments. Disproportionatly over-represented among children in care, mixed-race children are like so many cats and dogs awaiting adoption. Their images suggest the inevitability of marital decline for people who cross racialised boundaries (didn't everyone warn their parents that such marriages wouldn't work?) and are a palpable reminder that it is the children who will suffer. Discussing transracial adoption, Phoenix and Owen (op. cit.: 126–7) examine the idea that white parents can't look after mixed-race children. They indicate that there is 'insufficient research' to draw such a conclusion, though blacks who support same-race placement do so largely because of fears that the children will face racism. Twine provides evidence to demonstrate that white mothers are very competent in handling racism, perhaps even more so than black mothers (1999).

Newspapers cover similar topics. An article in the *Guardian* in 1994 on black/white relations presents transgressive racialised relationships as the antidote to black nationalism and an apartheid mentality. It presents hostility to such relationships as antiquated and bigoted, as a Big Brother approach to issues that are best left to individuals. And it highlights black hostility to such relationships (Goodwin, 1994). And it does so without any comment at all on the pernicious stereotypes of black and Asian women as sexual objects which are pervasive in the British media, and which serve as the backdrop for many white men's interests in women of colour.

Constituting a section of the media in a number of respects, but veering off at a tangent to secure its own distinctive territory, is a discourse of carnal delight associated with the sex and romance industry in general, and with prostitution and sex tourism in particular. This articulation is dominated by innate heterosexual hyper-sexuality and natural licentious-ness; the motivation is personal sexual desire and an opportunity to taste the forbidden fruit. By purchasing the services of sex workers, pleasure is secured without guilt (women of colour do it because it's their nature to please, to serve, to deprave) and with privacy so that one's peers will never know about the trangression. The constituency is all men, especially white men; the forbidden fruit is privately consumed, and men seek to get maxi-mum value for money. The most common source is magazines and porn-ography; but also common are prostitution and sex workers. The primary audience of producers is after profits; the consumers are after value for money. At one end of this continuum are romance novels in which true love battles with hypocrisy and bigotry. Further along are factual and fictional accounts of sexual fantasies, as in the best-selling collection, *My Secret Garden*, in which one white woman relates, 'If I see a picture, for example, of a black man and a white woman, I'm ready for sex almost immediately.' Close by are advertisements in newspapers for sex partners from different racialised groups. At the other end of the continuum are requests by white men for sex workers of colour in San Francisco or New York. Or in Bangkok, and other exotic destinations, for those with a more heavily endowed exchequer. Somewhere in the midst of all this – unluckily for him – was the Hugh Grant manoeuvre in Los Angeles, which pandered to all the stereotypes – rich white desirable male, with beautiful, intelligent, white girlfriend, just had to get the forbidden fruit attributed to black carnality.

A final example can be found among agencies of the state where we can identify a discourse of economism and bureaucracy, with the Office of Management and Budget (the agency primarily responsible in the US for the Census) reluctantly acting as institutional fulcrum. The articulation is rationality and efficiency (cost effectiveness, bureaucratic containment and efficacy, reasonableness in the face of an infinitely expanding workload). The motivation is cost reduction and bureaucratic efficiency in a world of heterogeneous, uncontainable and infinitely multiplying categories. The constituencies are the bureaucrats of the federal government. The goal is for them to fulfil their responsibilities as public servants, while keeping racialised categories to a minimum, and themselves in jobs. The designated method is decisive rationalistic criteria – via meetings, forums, consultation with experts, memos, discussion and working papers, dissemination of options under consideration, decisions made and defended. The primary audience is academics, policy-makers, state and private agencies.

Taken all together, these institutional dynamics constitute an entrenched and trenchant range of discourses with diverse constituencies, drawing on the past, using innovative methods to reproduce images. They are characterised by people with very different motivations, and by vast differences in the resources under their control, and in the range and nature of their impact in British and American society. They constitute a fundamental challenge to any idea that race will disappear from contemporary society in the immediate future.

Concepts of 'race mixture' in the academy

How are we to approach this range of issues? Many insights can be provided, many suggestions made in contemporary academic books. Academia in the past contributed as much to the problems of 'race mixture' as it did to the solutions, with the most reputable and distinguished academics of Europe and the US both complicitous and duplicitous in reproducing stereotypes, false ideas and suspect evidence (Gossett, 1965). More recently academics have offered key insights, challenged faulty assumptions, introduced new concepts, provided new evidence, especially as we have seen more people of colour in the academy. They have helped articulate the many links between ideas of race and other variables such as ethnicity, gender and class, and dynamics of power and hegemony. And they have highlighted links between structural and institutional factors (employment, demography, education, political power, immigration) and discourses, images reflected in literature, film and television. Some significant problems remain, in particular, the deployment of faulty language, and the ultimate recourse to questionable theories, but substantial progress has been made.

The problem that confronts analysts, then, is how to engage with the range and diversity of discourses articulated around 'race mixture', and how to begin to challenge the assumptions and language deployed. The prevalent language reifies race and 'race mixture', and treats such relationships as anomalous. This is one of the fundamental challenges to those of us who try to swim in these murky waters – we find ourselves tossed about by the tremendous forces of a historical and linguistic legacy which we do not control, just as the tide sways the helpless weed. In this respect, the most important point of departure is to recognise that we don't have to use the language we have inherited, or the analytical framework which its usage implies or, in fact, requires. We have a decision to make. Some people want to embrace and resuscitate the language of race, and seek to build a new destigmatised discourse; others, like us, want to grab and strangle the language of race, choking the last breath from its moribund body, and finding an entirely new vocabulary, predicated on an entirely new framework. We believe that we can, and must, reject the existing framework, the existing language and most of its assumptions.

Ifekwunigwe offers a promising critical approach, one which challenges the entire conceptual apparatus, as she calls for an archaeological excavation, and makes concrete suggestions for alternative sources of conceptual clarity and rigor (op. cit.). Class analysis is central to her analytical enterprise, and she demonstrates that some concepts in vogue – like hybridity – are far more sullied than their proponents suggest. Ifekwunigwe herself is in favour of 'metissage', and she makes a strong case for it. It is not clear that the French concepts she embraces are entirely free from the kind of problems associated with their counterparts in English, especially given their incubus in the civilising world of colonisation and conquest. But if we pursue the path she has highlighted, we suspect that we might find more promising concepts and theories outside the civilising hemispheres that remain hegemonic. We believe that it is essential to explore theories of cultural and human mixing in Asia, the Middle East and Africa. By locating our analysis in this far wider geographical and cultural purview, we will make far greater strides in recognising that patterns of physical, sexual and cultural interaction are far more endemic than current analyses suggest – in fact, that every society in the world has been constituted through a comprehensive mixing of human populations and cultures. We put the cart before the horse when we work, even implicitly, from a model that implies original pure 'races' and societies that later became 'miscegenated'.

In 1991 one of us introduced the phrase 'blacks of mixed origins' in place of nasty little terms like half-caste, quarter-caste, mixed race (Small, 1991). The goal was to highlight what blacks of mixed origins and blacks (presumed to be unmixed) shared, while also recognising some of the distinctive problems which confront blacks of mixed origins. It was suggested that the power of whites to define racialised identities was important, and their tendency to impose what they see as an inferior identity on people who are not 'milky white' was often the most decisive factor. This appears to be still largely, but not exclusively true, and we propose to stick with that concept. But to that analysis we would add that white impositions and power are no longer the pre-eminent factor, nor should we allow them to be so. As with black identity formation there is more fluidity now for people to choose identity – less pressure to choose black, more options to choose an intermediate category (especially with so many more people of this status) – even if we continue to shape identity under the shadows of the continued villification of blacks, so pervasive in the media, from *EastEnders* to *Brookside*, from Little Black Sambo to the Robertson's Gollywog. The evidence from studies of young people of mixed origins in Britain shows a distinct trend towards choosing a mixed over a single identity. It is clear that white mothers have played a significant role here, in particular, when they have become estranged from the black father of their child. But there is also considerable evidence that many mixed people are comfortable with a black identity, in fact prefer it and embrace it ardently, and Liverpool is just one prime example. And, as is usual with academics, and the press, we have far more research on, and testimony of, the squeaking wheels that attract attention, with their own class bias towards the formally educated and professionals (press headlines that Daley Thompson says he's not black, for example), than we do on the majority that just live their daily lives. As Ifekwunigwe has pointed out, we still lack evidence on working-class identities, and, as Christian argues, we lack evidence on the ways in which families shape identities.

What we have suggested throughout this book is that the racialisation framework can facilitate a more informed and useful analysis of these issues. We also suggest that it can be more accurate, and inoffensive. Highlighting the racialisation problematic is helpful here, especially because it makes it indispensable to conceptualise ideas about 'race' and 'race mixture' as always and only one issue among many factors that shape racialised relations. It is clear that notions of race are often the most central factor, as discussions of race purity, stereotypes of black men (sexual studs), Asian men (bad), black women (sluts), Asian women (gentle and sub-servient) all shape sexual interactions. But there are many other pertinent issues that seem to have little apparent nexus to notions of race. These issues include class (for example, transgressive marriage rates reflect class standing); gender (conflict between men of different racialised identities over access to women, and the increasing exercise of their own decisions and expressions of their own sexuality by women of different colours); family (as parents try to control the sexual and marital choices of their children, especially daughters); demography (transgressive sexual relations show tremendous correlations with the distribution of racialised groups, by gender and age); nationality and citizenship (opposition to immigration predicated on alleged links between marriage and economics).

These connections are frequently apparent in films. For example, in *Jungle Fever*, as the micro-drama of the relationship unfolds it is juxtaposed against the destruction and decimation of the black community through poverty, inequality and drugs. Flipper's brother, Gator, a long-time drug addict, lounges in a drug-induced stupor in the 'Taj Majal', a massive drug den. In pursuing his brother, Flipper is introduced to the breadth and depth of these problems, and his own anxieties seem less salient. A pre-occupation with racialised identity and family, on their own, cannot resolve these larger problems, and until they are addressed the resolution of identity and family issues remains fleeting. When we consider the range of images in film and television it is clear that the key engine driving these images is the quest for profits, as the issue of race mixture becomes just one more peg for corporate business and media businesses to bang into the ground of profits. The issue will remain central as long as it lends itself to profit. The salience of demography is apparent in both England and the US when we consider the dramatically increasing rates of sexual relationships between black women and non-black men. These increases reflect the limited avail-ability of 'desirable' black men, and the increasing independence of women's sexual choices.

Other historical examples further exemplify this. When, under slavery, most blacks of mixed origins were defined in accord with the status of their mothers, rather than their fathers, it was not because they were of mixed origins but because white men in power sought to increase the number of enslaved persons. When the white fathers of some blacks of mixed origins freed them, it was not because they were mixed, but because of patriarchy, because they were their sons and daughters. In the film *Mona Lisa* the lead character was prominent not because she was mixed, but because she was a prostitute, with a lesbian orientation, and because she was a woman. The same might be said about sexuality in *The Crying Game*. When blacks of mixed origins identify with whites it is not because they are mixed, but because they have grown up in white communities, with little interaction with black communities, as Daley Thompson so frequently made clear.

When Bob Marley identified himself as a Jamaican his mixed ancestry was irrelevant, it was his upbringing by his mother, in the cultural context of Jamaica, that was important. When Nigerians and Kenyans, or Jamaicans and Barbadians disagree over politics, or music, or religion, it is in large part because of their national and cultural upbringing, rather than their black identities. When conflict occurs between Somalis and Liverpool-born blacks, or Nigerians and Liverpool-born blacks, it is often because of age, and issues around immigration and belonging, and perceptions of discipline and respect, rather than black identity per se. Blacks are attacked and abused, discriminated against, because they are black. But if they live in Hampstead, rather than Clapham Common, they are more likely to be able to do something about it, and to get more attention.

What this means is that with regard to 'race mixture' and people of mixed origins, ideas about 'race' might always be present, and might be the most decisive factors shaping a situation. But it is always and only one factor among many, and whether it is the most important factor or not cannot be presumed beforehand but must be proven by investigation, analysis and evidence. The theoretical and conceptual issues have been outlined in far more detail elsewhere. What we try to demonstrate in this book is that racialisation always involves a series of intricate factors – structural and institutional, ideological and cultural – among which ideas of 'race' and ethnicity are always prominent, but also always several among many other important issues, including economics and class, nationalism and gender, and age.

Working from within the racialisation framework adopted in this book, these findings come as no surprise because in this framework we assume that notions of race and experiences of racism are only one variable among many that shape social experience and identity generally, and they may not be the most important or the most consistent variable. This means that people of mixed racialised origin, whose experiences vary by class, gender, family, education, community and nationality, amongst other things, are bound to reveal a variety of identities at varying tangents of importance to an essentialised, single racialised identity. As Phoenix and Owen point out, this makes it far more 'important to document the range of ways in which young people of mixed-parentage think about themselves' (op. cit.: 127). And as Parker points out, 'The focus should be on specific processes of identify formation rather than subsuming them all into one state of hybridity' (cited in ibid.: 114). This enjoins us to identify the key variables that shape identity, of which notions of race will be one, and to explore the ways in which they have concrete impacts, on concrete social collectivities and individuals, in concrete socio-historic contexts. It is highly likely that many common elements will be present – demography, class, gender, family, collective imaginaries – but they will configure in different ways, and with different consequences. Any consideration of the experiences of people of mixed origins in contexts like South Africa, Brazil and the US make this clear. But the same set of conditions is also true of contexts that are less strikingly different – as Twine demonstrates in her work on white mothers of 'African descent children' in Leicester (1999). The globalised patterns emphasised throughout this book render all of these variables that much more complex. The movement of diverse populations, for temporary or permanent settlement, will continue to increase patterns of sexual interaction across racialised, national, religious and linguistic populations. The number of people of mixed origins, particularly those who insist on affirming such mixed origins, can only grow larger. The movement of goods and services across national boundaries will continue to break down the identification of products with particular identities. And the movement of images and icons – symbols, that is – across the globe will continue to transmute identities embraced at the local level.

Racialisation requires us to pay more attention to the social context and social processes rather than individual attitudes. Social and historical context helps us understand the laws against 'miscegenation' in the US, and attitudes towards 'race mixture' in England. The ideological context helps us understand why people of mixed origins were the subject of dehumanising discourses not because of anything they had done themselves. And, as Phoenix and Owen point out, it is the social context that leads opponents of such relationships to persuade potential partners in such relationships not to pursue them, by suggesting that the children might suffer (op. cit.: 117). While we must always consider individual attitudes, they cannot and should not be the first line of address. Instead, the focus should be on social-structural and attitudinal factors, and on the range of attitudes, and on the factors that shape these attitudes. And while we must consider local and national contexts, we should increasingly be cognisant of the increasing importance, sometimes decisive, of global processes.

Conclusion

In the US and the UK, and in so many other countries subject to the more dominant forces of globalisation, dramatic changes in patterns of racialised dating and marriage, and the growth of a population of diverse origins, offer us an opportunity to contemplate issues of race and racialised identity, and issues of class and gender. All factors suggest that patterns of sex and marriage across racialised groups will continue to grow, especially at middle-class level. The new international division of labour, the continued relocation of massive numbers of workers across the globe, tremendously high levels of tourism and student exchanges – all of these factors will sustain diverse patterns of dating and marriage across national, racialised and ethnic boundaries. The prevalence of images of 'race mixture' across all levels of media, and across nations, will keep highly varied and fluid identities at the forefront of the social imaginary and in popular discussion. These continuities provide the opportunity for rejecting the binary racialised classifications of the past, and finding a new, more humane, less coercive, nomenclature for identifying our various affiliations and affections across racialised and ethnic identities.

These patterns have been accompanied by, and are inextricably linked to, other institutional domains and discursive terrains that reproduce images of 'race mixture' and hybridity in the social formation of contemporary society. These discourses remain socially endemic, form a central constitutive component of the social imaginary and are reproduced throughout numerous institutional domains. These domains comprise agencies and agents who appropriate ideas and images of 'race mixture' to meet their own goals and priorities. These dynamics follow vectors intrinsic to these institutions, but are also shaped by, and refract, dynamics associated with broader patterns of racialisation and globalisation. While some of these developments offer the potential for a critical interrogation of racialisation and 'race mixture', of gender and class relations, and of nationality and identity, it is more likely they will contribute to the reaffirmation of an uncritical individualism, the denial of class advantage, the subordination of group identity and collective action to the pretext of individualism and romantic love, to increased demands for colour blindness and to an untenable heralding of the end of racism. In this respect, the roots of racialisation remain deeply embedded in contemporary life.

Images and discourses about race mixture, and blacks of mixed origins, are far more pervasive than ever before, and continue to both reflect and shape attitudes, expectations and patterns. Unlike in past decades when the dominant discourse was motivated by a largely hostile and similarly inclined racist response by white people, contemporary discourses reflect far more divergent political, economic and social groups. They take place across transnational lines of communication and media. And for the first time, people of mixed origins, and their parents and families, are central players in these discourses. Yet such images are far from free of the nasty stereotypes of the past, nor are they primarily motivated by a desire to erase such stereotypes. Many of the discourses described above are, by their very nature, predicated on ignoring contradictions, deploying selective evidence, judiciously highlighting examples and, ultimately, subordinating the discourse to the goals and priorities of those that prevail in that particular institutional domain. This is another pattern that contributes to the increasing array of options for blacks of mixed origins.

While dating and marriage across racialised identities will inexorably continue, it will do so far less slowly in the US than in Britain, and far less slowly than the advocates of such relationships would have us believe. Patterns of racialised segregation and inequality, and the continuing practices of discrimination and racist stereotyping, will continue to act as a drag on the expanding potential of sexual relations and marriage across racialised identities.

The factors that shape the identity of people of mixed origins today are complex. There is far more fluidity than ever before. In both the US and England the number of partners in sexual relationships across racialised identities has increased dramatically, as has the number of people of mixed origins. Whereas in the past the partners and children of such relationships tended to find less hostility in communities of colour (because of a virulent racism against them in white communities) this is no longer the case. More and more whites are less hostile. Also, more and more people of mixed origins are growing up in areas with few people of colour. This means that there will be far more diverse expressions of these mixed identities, and that they will be shaped far more directly by factors that appear to have little apparent correlation with race – economics, class, education, gender, nation and location. Globalisation will be central here – especially in the continued flow of people, goods and identities across local and national boundaries. As the patterns of globalisation continue to unfold, the factors that shape racialised identities will continue to be the focus of intense academic and personal interest. But, as we have shown in other chapters in this book, variations in expressed identities will not occur independently of transformations in economic and political power, or access to education, health and welfare. Nor will dramatic changes, and huge variations in such expressed identities, on their own, change these underlying factors. That is why we must continue to evaluate the relationship between expressed identities, institutional inequalities and variations in power, and do so in full awareness of the complexities which globalisation has created.

Notes

1 The term 'coffee-coloured children' comes from the hit record of the early 1970s in Britain, 'Melting Pot' by Blue Mink, in which miscegenation was advocated and promoted as multiracial harmony. The antidote to this was how the song was used for the video by Onwurah Ungozi, *Coffee Coloured Children*, to show that things were rather more sanguine.
2 As early as the 1970s Britain already had a rate of marriages across racialised identities that was three times the rate in the US (Bagley, 1983: 38). This reflects the particular histories of the two nations, and the distinctive cultural attitudes towards the practice. Attitudes towards such practices have overwhelmingly been hostile in Britain, as the surveys demonstrate, but they have never been as hostile as attitudes in the US, nor have they been supported by legal obstructions or levels of violence comparable to those in the US. For this history in the US, see J.W. Williamson, 1995, and Spickard, 1989.
3 The reference here is to the top-ten hit in the British charts of the early 1970s, 'Black Skinned, Blue Eyed Boys', sung by The Equals, whose leader vocalist was Eddie Grant.

Chapter 4

Sexualising racism

The previous chapter examined the impact of new and changing racialised identities. The discussion outlined the role of sexual mythologies in the workings of racism. This chapter will expand this discussion and argue that, even as the world changes, the heat of sex continues to lubricate the excesses of racism.

The chapter begins with a review of feminist debates and the attempt to encompass the experience of different women under a single banner. This fraught moment in feminist discussion anticipates later struggles across social theory and the question of whether universal categories are possible. It also introduces a global awareness and a sense that understanding requires dialogue between different locations.

It is this painful realisation that forces (some) feminists to develop an analytic language that could acknowledge and encounter difference, while still proposing some shared interests between women. This volume has borrowed heavily from this learned-from-feminism approach. We have attempted to retain an awareness of irreconcilable differences while outlining the continuities between the West and the rest and the deepening inequalities of rich and poor worlds.

It is the feminist critiques that come from the poor world and from black communities within the rich world that develop an analytic language of global relations. Although much of this debate preceded explicit discussions of globalisation, the building blocks of later discussions can be traced in the fraught battles that characterised divisions within feminism. In this chapter we wish to re-examine the framework of black feminist interventions and to suggest that a reappraisal of this earlier work can enhance our understanding of more recent global processes.

The critique of black feminism attempted to chart the construction of interrelated forms of agency as they were structured across an uneven and differentiated terrain. This critique always attempted to keep in mind the deep interdependence of women from different locations. Despite the anger at monolithic and exclusionary representations of womenhood, there remained an awareness that different kinds of women were connected in some way. Of course, the point was that this connection was not as white feminism imagined. Rather than a happy and conflict-free sisterhood of universal women, black and Third World feminism revealed that global femininity was constructed through the exploitative relations between women within the West and across the globe. The femininity of different locations remained connected, yet this was not a connection of similarity. Instead, women's experience was determined through the global connections of cheap labour and cheap products, through domestic service and career motherhood, through the devaluing of women from the poor world and hyper-protection of First World femininity. This realisation revealed that differential positioning made the issues themselves different.

The key insights of this realisation can be transferred to our current discussion of the racialised outcomes of globalisation. In chapter 2 we discussed the manner in which the forces of global change have created new forms of racial fear and new modes of racist practice. The analytic language of black feminism can allow us to articulate these two moments as part of the same process. By transferring the tools of black feminism to our account of more recent developments, we can begin to think of global processes as at once causing new and real pain to the relatively privileged inhabitants of the rich world, while also creating fresh sources of western privilege in relation to the global racialised poor.

The chapter takes this insight in order to understand in more detail the deep sense of interrelation which globalisation brings. In order to develop this argument, we examine the process by which the global imagination has extended into the space of intimacy. This confusion between matters of state and matters of the body and desire can be traced back through far longer histories of race-thinking. The chapter suggests that this longer history inflects contemporary understanding of global relations, not least in the extension to imagining the global as the space of intimacy.

Developing black feminism

This section looks at the role of sexual mythologies in various processes of racialisation and its attendant subordination. We argue here that this sexualisation of racism has a long history, but also continues in more recent and globalised forms of racial inequality. The chapter suggests that an analytic language for understanding the sexual heat in many different processes of racialisation can be learned from debates within feminism and other writing about sexuality. However, to understand the debates which shape our access to these processes, first we must reconsider some debates about gender, race and the ambivalent privileges of respectable gender roles. As always, the story of women starts with the West.

Universal woman

Orthodox accounts place second-wave feminism as a western creation – this is the feminism which transforms the consciousness of many women in western nations through the second half of the twentieth century, the feminism which takes imaginative and strategic resources from African-American struggles for civil rights (a struggle already borrowing from anti-colonial movements), anti-war protests and the various strange alliances of post-1968 liberatory politics (see Mercer, 1994: chapter 10). From this grows a feminism which demands equal rights and respect for women – because women everywhere have been denied. This liberatory call took the experience of womanhood as a universal experience – something that all women everywhere could understand and identify with. Much has been written already about the shortcomings of universalist feminism and the deep divisions within feminism. To quickly review, the crux of the discussion lies in the assumption that the experience of subjugation for women was a global, cross-cultural, cross-class experience. It was this shared positioning which linked all women to each other and the recognition of this link represented the possibility of change. In this account, all other social structures and divisions became insignificant beside the bigger experience of being a woman. This formative experience rendered all women the same at some level – and thus able to intuitively understand all other women and their concerns across the globe and across time.

Of course, even this much maligned imperial feminism brings us many new tools and insights. Although we understand that women are positioned differently, and live through many different identities, the broad conception of women's subjugation moves us all into a fresh terrain of social understanding. Now we can see that sexuality can mean both love and violence, that the powerful can desire and despise in one move and at one moment, that social relations extend beyond the formalities of a proper public sphere into the realm of the private and everyday. We learn to think in more detail about the effect a person's conception of self has on their ability to live their life and we begin to conceptualise agency in many more varied ways. These conceptual gains, however, have been tempered by the assumption that womanhood is a unitary and universal concept.

Difference

In response to this universalism, the critique of black feminism, and of working-class and lesbian feminists, has been that this version of what it is to be a woman does not include our experience. Instead, women who were not white, western, class-privileged, heterosexual (and later, able-bodied) argued that the troubles and joys of their lives were not encompassed by the name woman alone. The political and intellectual fall-out of this realisation has been well documented in other places (Anthias and Yuval-Davis, 1992; Barrett and Phillips, 1992).

Despite the considerable pain generated by these debates, notable gains were made in terms of the analysis of various identities and their inter-action. Although the comforts of simple naming were lost – so that people continue to tie themselves up in knots in the attempt to describe their position and not oppress others – the critique of white feminism took the lessons of feminist analyses and remade them for a diverse population. These debates within feminism allowed the shift into understanding multiple identities – not only or primarily woman, but also, say, migrant, middle-class, polysexual. The fighting about how and why these different identities matter and reorganise the experience of being also named woman, by the way, develops a way of talking and thinking about many identities at once.

This could be seen as the key analytic gain of discourses such as black feminism (its political gains are still being decided in many everyday settings). Feminism creates the space in which political critique can be couched in the language of personal experience. The idea is that political knowledge comes from living it – and raising your consciousness stems from the recognition that this is what you live. This starting premise, that people have the ability to know their own lives and build their politics from that knowledge, makes the space within feminism for debates about the political implications of women's diverse life experiences to happen. Sometimes the extreme bitterness of these altercations can obscure the role even white women's imperial feminism has played, albeit inadvertently, in making space for fresh ways of political thinking. If there are any doubts about this gift, we have only to review the impact of black perspectives on other forms of left thinking. The white labour movement across Europe has barely registered the political costs of failing to address the politics of whiteness – and black trade unionists and labour activists have struggled to make their own spaces largely on white terms. The idiosyncratic spread of white Marxism, from many schools of thought, nominally acknowledges the role of black community struggle – yet remains tied, overtly or covertly, to a dream of heroic white leadership. Despite black people's continuing involvement in the most significant aspects of labour organisation, the white left offers few spaces to articulate the specificity of black people's working experience, and their particular experience of racialised class identities. Whatever the considerable failings of white feminism, at least this debate had room to develop in relation to gendered identities (for more on the particular role of black women workers in British industrial disputes, see Wilson, 1978; Sivanandan, 1982; and the path-breaking and long-running disputes led by Asian women at Hillingdon hospital and by Skychef workers at Heathrow airport, both in west London).

Feminism not only created a space in which women from different communities could consider their particular construction by gender, it also provided a way of thinking about community histories as gendered events. Now the big stories of enslavement and occupation, war and upheaval, could be seen to have their own gender logics. Instead of subsuming the experience of women under a community history which was regarded as more central because male-centred, now a variety of women started to reassess the deepest tragedies of their people as gendered phenomena. This was of particular importance in relation to histories of racial attack – because women hold the future of the race.

> Because women bear the next generation of a collectivity, they are put uniquely at risk as members of a group targeted as 'racially inferior'. Taking into account the construction of women as ethnic and national subjects, the definition of genocide must be gendered, to include political projects involving slavery, sexual slavery, mass rape, mass sterilization, aimed, through women, at 'ethnic cleansing' and the elimination or alteration of a future ethnic group. Catastrophes, genocidal or otherwise, . . . target women in very specific ways due to their social, ethnic and national construction.
>
> (Lentin, 1997: 2)

This insight reveals the mythologies of gender at the heart of racist violence. When social boundaries are imagined as matters of blood or stock, then women's bodies assume their age-old role as conduits of male entitlement, power and identity. To attack and destroy an ethnic community, you attack and destroy their women in sexualised and dehumanising ways – cut away this root of a people, and nothing else will grow, says the logic of ethnic cleansing. The critiques of black feminism contribute to the development of a language to help us all understand the horrific gendering of these racist violences.

Global issues

Alongside these debates within the feminism of the (comparatively) rich world, another critique of western feminism wished to replace the battles of the rich world's women in a global frame. This critique argued that the obsession with the universal name woman veiled the privileges of the rich world – and the ambivalent social status of the western woman relied upon a much more straightforward exploitation of women (and men) from the poor world.

This critique paralleled that of black feminism in suggesting that the key tenets of white feminism were inappropriate for women from beyond the rich world. This critique targeted a number of issues, reflecting the central organising tenets of western feminisms.

First among these issues is the relation to paid work. The second-wave feminism of developed economies devoted much laudable activity to agitating for women's right to equal access and pay in the workplace – and through this to the public status, independence and political recognition accorded to waged workers. Against this, poor-world feminists argued that poor women had always worked outside the home and the struggle to leave the home was itself an imperial privilege. Domesticity for some women was bought by the hyper-exploitation of others. Instead of proclaiming women's right to work, they argued, an international feminism needed to develop a multifaceted approach to address the varied nature and conditions of work (Spivak, 1987).

A second point of contention focused on definitions of the politics of sexuality. White women of the rich world recognised that domestic confinement and exclusion from the public sphere formed key pillars of a culture of sexual control. Empowerment for women must, therefore, include sexual autonomy and a reclaiming of sexual pleasure. However, for many women facing more extreme conditions of violence and deprivation, the focus upon sexual fulfilment missed the more immediate economic hardships of their lives. Instead, they argued that physical survival must take priority over physical pleasure as an organising agenda for women. Equally, however, black women from many backgrounds asserted the value and sustenance of the sexual cultures of their communities (B. Smith, 1983). Linked to this debate came disagreements about what was understood by the right to reproductive freedom – while women in the richer nations focused on the need for contraception and abortion on demand, poor-world feminists argued that reproductive freedom must extend to the right to bear children in safety (Mies and Shiva, 1993).

The debates around both the politics of work and the politics of sexuality fed into the manner in which different groups of women conceptualised the threat of male violence – although racism and poverty made women more vulnerable to male violence, this violence was not only the private secretive violence of marriage and heterosexual coupledom. Instead, this violence against women was part of a global system of exploitation and terror – sometimes 'domestic', but often public, institutional and systematic (Carby, 1982).

Each of these critiques of the stated aims and priorities of the rich world's women's movement called into question this version of a politics built around women's experience of gender. Women from the poor world, alongside less privileged women from the rich world, argued that a focus on gender in isolation could never encompass the complexity of their lives.

Chandra Talpade Mohanty outlines the key characteristics of this 'third world feminism'.

[T]hird world women's writings on feminism have consistently focused on (1) the idea of the simultaneity of oppressions as fundamental to the experience of social and political marginality and the grounding of feminist politics in the histories of racism and imperialism; (2) the crucial role of a hegemonic state in circumscribing their/our daily lives and survival struggles; (3) the significance of memory and writing in the creation of oppositional agency; and (4) the differences, conflicts, and contradictions internal to third world women's organizations and communities. In addition, they have insisted on the complex inter-relationships between feminist, antiracist, and nationalist struggles.

(Mohanty *et al.*, 1991: 10)

The first point reiterates the discussion above – women who were not white, class-privileged, from the developed economies, all argued that gender was not experienced in isolation. Other structures of identity and entitlement always operated in conjunction with gender.

The second point has been less discussed in histories of feminist thinking, but is conspicuously present in a range of activist and academic material (see Grewal *et al.*, 1988; B. Smith, op. cit.; Southall Black Sisters, 1990; James and Busia, 1993). This point rests on the understanding that, in a world of gender oppression and racial privilege, white males embody power and run the whole show. White women, especially class-privileged white women, encounter this male power in their most intimate domestic spaces, in their family and kinship groups, and, in the case of heterosexual women who observe the stricture against mating outside the race, in their husbands and lovers. Therefore, white women encounter power and domination as a gendered phenomenon and imagine the powerful as (white) men. Women from racialised communities, and to some extent poor white women, do not experience significant male powers as being held in their communities. Instead, the power that counts, which is coded white and male, is embodied through the state rather than the home. Power, even in its most gendered forms, is encountered as an entity combining the forces of (at least) class, race and gender and operating through the various machineries of police, military, law and other social institutions.

The third point highlights the importance of voice in debates around feminism. Much of the critique of white feminism has focused on the exclusion of a variety of voices and perspectives, in favour of a notion of woman-hood as univocal because essentially the same everywhere. In response to this, black and Third World feminists have stressed the importance of recording many stories. Both writing and storytelling have been celebrated as central strategies in the construction of an alternative and diverse feminism which encompasses many histories while allowing space for com-munication between different women (P. Williams, 1997; Minh-Ha, 1991).

The fourth point acknowledges that even within the communities of race or nation, there are many other differences between women. If woman was not a unified category, then the same could be said of any identity. Many of the divisions identified within the white women's movement could be seen among the ranks of black and Third World feminists. Certainly, similar concerns about the issue of class and its various organising agendas arose. Sexuality also became a point of potential division. Most painfully, femin-ists were forced to acknowledge that the same divisions as men's politics scarred women's politics. For communities in exile in particular, the fraught struggles of back home impinged upon the work of the new space, even among women.

The new languages of feminism developed through black feminism and Third World or post-colonial feminisms placed women as far more variously made than through gender alone.

> It is the intersections of the various systemic networks of class, race, (hetero)sexuality, and nation, then, that position us as 'women'. Herein lies a fundamental challenge for feminist analysis once it takes seriously the location and struggles of third world women, and this challenge has implications for the rewriting of all hegemonic history, not just the history of people of color.
>
> (Mohanty *et al.*, op. cit.: 13)

Regendering through globalisation

Some commentators have suggested that developments in the global system – economic, political and cultural – have had a restructuring effect on gendering, for some communities at least (see Sassen, 1998). The suggestion makes sense. Once we have accepted gendering to be a socially based process rather than a finished product of nature, then it must follow that changes in social living have an effect on the process of gender-making.

This has been implied in other areas of debate. In various forums, the suggestion has been made that we are witnessing a shift in gender roles which dramatically alters the meanings of the names man and woman (see Walby, 1997). The following varied forces have all been cited as contributors to the reshaping of gender.

The cultural change brought by the impact of popular feminism and the resulting change in so many people's ideas of themselves and others has effected other wide-ranging changes. Despite the backlash, feminism (of a sort) has had an effect on the conduct and expectations of personal relationships, particularly for heterosexuals, on domestic arrangements for everyone and on all our ideas of personal fulfilment through work, love and life (Giddens, 1992). Alongside this culture shift, de-industrialisation in the rich world and the demise of the male breadwinner as an economic marker of true masculinity have destabilised previous markers of masculine status and security. This economic shift has had a knock-on effect on family structures and the life courses of very many working men and women (Walby, op. cit.). These economic changes have enabled the rise of service industries as the new mass employers of women, youth and minorities in the West and the related fall in influence of organised labour. This shift has remade conceptions of work and entitlement, and continues to painfully force changes in goals, practices and achievements of workplace politics (Aronowitz and Cutler, 1998).

As well as these varied pressures on social relations, the recent history of western nations has seen relatively rapid developments in sexual cultures. This has included the sexual revolution (for some), the contraceptive pill (for many), and changing attitudes towards sex before marriage, divorce and homosexuality (Haste, 1992; Segal, 1990). Public cultures of sexuality have been refracted through the spread of a commodified culture of the body which increasingly places the male body under levels of scrutiny and discipline previously suffered only by women (Nixon, 1996; Simpson, 1994). All this is taking place through a period in which the emergence of HIV forms part of a cultural shift through which the exercise of sexuality becomes as much a sign of mortality as life power (Singer, 1993).

There are some common themes in these diverse movements. On one side we see the factors which increase the choices, mobility and status of women – a language of political empowerment, technological advances which limit the pull of the body, greater access to the labour market (however ambiguous a choice this is). On the other, there are the much talked about symptoms of masculine crisis – the alleged threat and humiliation of women's comparative emancipation, the decline of traditional sectors of male employment, the new pressures of body culture. These two stories have been told as a zero-sum game – more choices for women mean fewer for men, for one to win the other must lose. However, these accounts also contain less obviously girls-against-boys stories. Changing attitudes to sexuality and a greater fluidity in domestic arrangements offer threats and opportunities to all. Radical shifts in the nature, meaning and quantity of paid work have brought hardship to many men and women, regardless of pockets of job growth (Martin and Schumann, 1997). New illnesses haunt all our experiences of body, albeit differentially. These more uncertain pressures remake our experience of gender as something other than the same old zero-sum game, because here it is not so clear that men's losses are women's gains. Instead, gender is remade for everyone because of other larger pressures from beyond the dynamic of gender struggles.

Of course, another less acknowledged factor in this reshaping of gender in the West has been the wider reshaping of the world order. The so-called crisis of (white) masculinity is as much a symptom of the end of empire and the loss of explicit and unassailable white power as it is a response to the unruly disobedience of white women and the global economy (Dyer, 1997; Gibson, 1994).

For the rest of us who feel the pressures of the global through (among other things) stories of western living, a shift in the heterosexual romance of whiteness has a knock-on effect on everyone's sense of self. It is significant that the demise of formal western power and the accompanying disappointment of white men in the far less flashy dominance of globalisation has been narrated as a form of sexual frustration. Just as western women's entry into the previously male spheres of employment, politics and the wider public is told, bitterly, as a constraint on male access to women's bodies, similarly, the collapse of western power is told as an unwelcome brake on sexual energy. In both cases, all that healthy testosterone goes to waste.

If the self-conception of white men is adapted, grudgingly and unavoidably, by changes in all of his significant others, then we significant others will feel the amplification of this responsive change. The identity of white men is not at the heart of global change, but when forces combine to remake white men and their orbit, there are implications for us all.

To revisit the themes of gender shift, we can see that the rise of popular feminism in the West makes a certain image of commodified liberation for women into the dream and danger of western influence – existing alongside the local struggles of women in the poor world, this fantasy of possibility informs aspiration and repression. De-industrialisation to the rich world is globalisation for the poor – economies dependent on the requirements of the industrialised suffer from the inevitable cutback in paternalism, economies struggling to industrialise find that this route may not be so prosperous after all and that the benefits and privileges of the nuclear family will never come to them.

The service economies of the West, on which so many hopes are pinned, parody the social structures of the poor world where cheap and plentiful human labour and wide disparities in wealth have made service rather than manufacture a central form of occupation. Again, the dream of industrialisation is spoilt almost before it begins.

Sexual cultures continue to shift throughout the world, in varying and uneven ways – but the fantasy of sexual liberation in the West still fuels libidos world-wide. Scrutiny of the male body can make the men of the poor world into sexual objects for exploitation – but also feed the consumer aspirations of nearly middle-class men globally. AIDS decimates a generation of gay men in the West, and scares others in the process – in the poor world HIV seeps through the whole community and becomes another event to make the poor more desperate and vulnerable.

Most of this hardens existing hardship. When times are hard in the West, things get even worse for the already suffering rest. However, some of these changes can be regarded as opportunities. Sassen identifies some relatively empowering aspects of globalised experience for women migrants, which include gaining access to new political arenas as actors in their own right and renegotiating authority and control in the home (op. cit.). Certainly, mimicking the gender proprieties of the West stops being such an attractive or straightforward proposition – and perhaps this allows more space for everyone to attend to struggles over gender identity which stem from their context and history. Crisis in the West is not necessarily a disaster for the rest – and perhaps could be seen as no more than a refinement of the horrors occasioned by the West's ascent?

However, other aspects of this western crisis are more threatening, a reminder that the securities of western gender patterns and privileges for men and women cannot be relinquished easily. It is important to remember that these shifts in gendering are an indicator of the demise of a whole way of life, a sign that western powers are slipping away and whiteness may change its meaning altogether. Unless we acknowledge the potential weight of these changes and their threat to some, how can we understand events such as the outbursts of white militias across North America and the corresponding racist and homophobic terrorism in Europe? In April 1999, bombs were set off in three well-known neighbourhoods of London – Brixton, famously home to a large Caribbean community, Brick Lane, equally famous for its association with the Bangladeshi community, and Soho, which has been remade and regenerated by the gay community. Without an analysis of the role of sexuality in racialised anxieties, there is no method to comprehend the particular heat and horror of racial privilege under threat. The next section returns to the idea that sexuality informs the violences of racism.

Racialisation operating through gender and sexuality

Another response to white feminism has been the suggestion that the process of racialisation transforms the experience of gendering. Rather than arguing that race plus gender equals a different category of operation, this work suggests that the assumption of racial identities happens through a differential process of gendering. This means that instead of conceiving of white and black women, for example, as sharing some common ground as women, but with this experience refracted through other factors such as race and class, now the name woman refers to different things for different communities.

In chapter 2 we reviewed the idea that social life is structured either through race *or* class or race *and* class. In both these conceptions, however, race and class each remain distinct entities with their own dynamics. The suggestion in relation to race and gender is that race parasitically inhabits and distorts the process of gendering in order to make racialised divisions. In this reckoning, 'proper' gendering – even with its attendant problems for women – is a privilege of those considered human. Racialisation is a process which splits humanity, rendering some lesser or not quite human. Less-than-humanness is proved, in part, through the improper gendering of some groups of people.

Like most racist mythologies, this is a tricky double bind for those concerned. The benchmark of normality is taken to be the lately developed model of gender relations of the industrialised West – another problematic story of modernity which has never been fully embraced even by westerners. The version of gender identities which we, the entire rest of the world, are judged against is a mythology of urbanised industrial living, in which brand new cults of domesticity, feminine propriety, privacy, monogamy and parenting as ownership are just slipping into view (McClintock, 1995). Despite the continuing ideological weight of these constructions, there are many reminders of how partial their take-up has been, even among the most privileged and unquestionably human elements of the world's population.

Industrialisation – perhaps most particularly the first-off-the-mark industrialisation of western Europe – requires a shift into more privatised living. Not only does this new regime of widespread wage labour demand a domestic system which will maintain individual workers at little cost to the employer (unlike the more intimate and substantial ties of feudalism), it also benefits from the creation of a whole host of new privatised households to consume the goods of these new production processes. The shift towards the nuclear family and the attendant rise of more privatised living arrangements helps to augment the culture of industrialised living, something which must always be more than work alone, but the shift is never quite absolute and complete (Stone, 1979, 1993). Even as the material pressures of employment and housing shove people into the nuclear norm, we see remnants of more extended family patterns surviving and re-emerging. Too many of the struggles of the century have entailed a clinging to some notion of 'community' for us to imagine that anyone retreated into private living easily (R. Williams, op. cit.). The parallel mythology of monogamy clearly never took hold at all.

Other aspects of the gender laws of industrialisation such as the idea of parenting as ownership have been transformed into horror stories of modern living. The western world is in the throws of a series of nightmare revelations about the dangerous status of children in a society shaped around private spaces of reproductive property. Children take the role of legitimisers – it is this repeopling of the world that is cited as the moral imperative behind heterosexual monogamy and nuclear living. Western propriety is built around this fiction of child rearing for the nation and the need to protect these vulnerable offspring from the assorted dangers of improper gender and sexual codes and the contamination of beyond the family. The recent realisation that it is precisely this hyper-sexualising of domestic spaces and the eroticisation of ownership that endangers children and makes abuse endemic to all industrialised nations reveals another crack in the relentless logic of modernity (Renvoize, 1993; Hester et al., 1996). On the one hand, even those supposedly living these relations dispute the proclaimed normality and desirability of particular gender roles, sexual behaviours and attitudes to family living. On the other, the outcomes of this propriety are revealed to be abusive and unacceptable.

The domestication of western women has been a highly contested process. The relation of the rest of the world to these western ideals is, therefore, uncertain, to say the least. Whether propriety as a route to civilisation is an imposition or an aspiration, the process is greatly complicated by the changeability of the norm (Bhabha, 1994). The deviant less-than-human status attributed to the rest of the world during and since European expansion is marked in relation to a standard of western behaviour which has never existed. The pristine and total humanity of white people is a fiction even on its own terms.

This fiction could be seen as similar to the fiction of heterosexual perfection described in the work of Judith Butler and others (Butler, 1990, 1993). This has been a key insight of queer theorising – that the much heralded norm which terrorises and demands mimicry exists nowhere. Just as we all perform sexual identities in approximation to a heterosexual standard which no-one achieves (however straight they believe themselves to be), whites and others have mimicked a white propriety which has no original. Unfortunately, if predictably, the outcome of this general make-believing has been that, rather than celebrate the pleasures of performance, the powerful have sought to hide their own fragile identities by casting others in the role of abhorrent caricatures of normality. The shouting about the moral laxity and sexual ambiguity of the rest of the world distracts from the strange and various behaviour of the West. The point is, of course, that too excessive an interest in the sexuality of others indicates some hidden and unresolved anxiety about your own.

Whiteness as virtue

> The problem is that whites may not be very good at it, and precisely because of the qualities of 'spirit' that make us white. Our minds control our bodies and therefore both our sexual impulses and our forward planning of children. The very thing that makes us white endangers the reproduction of our whiteness.
>
> (Dyer, 1997: 27)

The culture of white supremacy that marks the world as inevitably and thankfully under the sway of Europeans claims human progress as an insistently white affair. The unspoken message of supremacist discourse, from law-and-order anxiety to the white man's burden of global policing, is that it is better for everyone if we, superior beings, take charge. This is based on the belief that human development occurs through a progressive shift away from the animal bodily calls of physicality to the higher plains of reason and the mind. Life gets better when we stop being pulled this way and that by the arbitrary and unreasonable wants of the body and instead form complex social structures which defer physical calls in favour of the more lengthy projects of technology and social order. Through this process, humanity conquers nature and takes control of its own destiny. All of which is well and good, except for the hidden sting in the tail – the exercise of reason belongs, handily, to white people. Everyone else is tied hopelessly to the body, and with it backwardness and primitive culture. We need the interventions of white folks to make it in the world.

Across centuries, apologists for white privilege spin out a version of this story. The previous chapter spoke of slavery and empire, the big stories of white subject formation, and the legitimating mythologies of white control. However, the same structures can be seen in the more covert interventions of recent times – structural adjustment, global policing and market imperialism. The nasty ways of the powerful are legitimated still through an idea that the rest are distracted – if everyone else is too busy trying to keep up with the endless hungry demands of the body, then strategic thinking is left, necessarily, to the more far-sighted.

Previous chapters have outlined a number of the consequences of this phenomenon. In this chapter our focus is on the other side of this equation. If progress, science and human development belong to a white world of the mind, what happens to the constantly constrained and effaced white body? The inescapable implication of all this celebration of the cerebral is that white bodies are not up to much, and, as Dyer suggests, may not be very good at 'it'. It is the structure of white supremacy itself that spoils white people's relation to sexuality. By abandoning the body in favour of higher pursuits, whiteness relinquishes the everyday and inescapable business of the physical including, most troublingly, desire.

Desire, of course, confounds reason. Instead of order, desire makes disarray. Instead of boundaries, desire seeps liquids, leaks fragments, blurs edges. For a constructed whiteness built on (the fictions of) reason and order, strictly hierarchical social structure and strictly tight-lipped self-control, desire threatens to smash apart both self and society. The tightly bounded individual who knows their place in the social order is dissolved through desire – because now boundaries are there to be overcome and transgressed, others are incorporated into the pristine self, the lack at the heart of subjecthood is revealed. These are some of the reasons why desire must be excised from a modernity we have only recently learned to call white.

Of course such excisions are temporary and partial. Sexuality cannot be written out of human living altogether – and the attempt to tame its demands only alter its shape. The discussion that follows outlines some areas of this dangerous shape-changing and argues that the attempt to construct sexually pure cultures for some has led to racist violence against others. In particular, the chapter argues that white subjectivity – the mythic moment of racial privilege, for our time if not for all times – is made through a sexualising of racial boundaries and a containment of the dangers of sexual transgression. White culture is strewn with the fear of sexuality – the dirty secret waiting to be unleashed at any moment. To indulge the body is treason to the privilege of whiteness – so pleasure is suspect and sex is dangerous. White people must make sure that they are not very good at it, because to be good would make their whiteness suspect and inauthentic (Dyer, 1997; Brody, 1998). You give up the pleasure and weight of the body in favour of the privilege and control of the mind. Thus even in its own fictions, whiteness comes to signify both virginity and impotence – as if the sprint of civilisation at once made white people into higher beings and ensured that they could not propagate their race, ultra-good but not good at it.

Subjugation as seduction

The effacement of the body in white supremacist culture displaces sexual pleasure into other realms. Through a variety of documents we see domination of territory articulated as a sexual experience – from Columbus's famous conception of the earth as a huge breast, with the yearned-for riches of colonial expansion located at the nipple, to the countless penetrations into unknown territory, landscapes are owned as women's bodies (Pratt, 1992). It is because all that land is figured as feminine that it can be imagined as open, willing, needy of conquest. The land itself becomes a hungry female body, prostrate and waiting in pornographic expectation to get what is coming to her. The figure mobilises a familiar string of connotations, with femininity lined up with nature, passivity, emotion, childlikeness, against the masculine action-hero of conquering reason. The people of these feminised landscapes similarly become tainted by these connotations, or transformed into extensions of this sexy body. All of this sexualised and feminised matter, rolling hills, inviting valleys, close-to-nature natives and lush plant life, all of this makes the process of economic exploitation, military (overt or covert) occupation and theft into the most titillating of sexual encounters. Any resistance becomes mere love play, adding to the pleasures of seduction. Before you know it, expansion has become the ultimate sex substitute, reimagining a fantasy of heterosexual coercion for the purposes of occupation (Stannard, 1992).

This will to imagine domination as a sexual experience permeates the cultures of European expansion. The histories of slavery and colonialism are littered with examples of this nasty eroticisation of power and unseemly scrutiny of the bodies, practices and responses of the subjugated (McClintock, 1995; Gill, 1995). The traces of this fascination continue into the present day and can be observed in a whole range of everyday pornographies of racial domination, from adventure films to charity adverts. All the indications are that white supremacy is experienced as pleasure.

In one reading, the subjugation of other peoples stems from a need to compensate for a sense of sexual inadequacy (Fanon, 1967, 1968). This places sexuality at the heart of racial violence and oppression. Although there may be material factors driving the construction of racialised cultures, so that white people gain real and tangible benefits from a world that rewards whiteness at the expense of everyone else, Fanon suggests that the culture of colonialism is not purely instrumental. Instead, there is a helplessness and neurosis at its heart – and this neurosis is white people's sense of

sexual inadequacy. It is true that all over we see that white cultures prohibit sexual enjoyment or empowerment, and instead use violence to achieve
sexual gratification through other means. The terrorisation of the local
population that accompanied European occupation often used a rhetoric
and iconography of sexuality to mark its presence, as did the European
enslavement of Africans (Wiegman, 1995; Stannard, op. cit.; Gill, op. cit.).
When bodies of colour are violated and dismembered, our anatomies are
sexualised even when already dead. However absolute white power seems,
its exercise reveals a continuing fear of the sexual potency of the racialised.
The celebration of whiteness disrespects and banishes sexuality, marking it
as the terrain of us less-than-human peoples, yet is consumed with fear and
envy at the sexual lives of non-whites (Mercer, 1994; L. Young, 1996;
Kabbani, 1994).

White culture itself imagines the monsters who grow from the distortion
of sexuality into an exercise of power. This is one of the cautionary tales
of western culture, that sexual frustration will re-emerge somewhere, and
that re-emergence will be more frightening and uncontrollable than that
which was originally repressed. Rather than banishing sexuality successfully, the culture of whiteness imbues sex with a new status. Whether we
view this banishment as stemming from the culture of modernity, which
reorders human life to maintain the disciplines of waged working and
spreads its tentacles of limited leisure and pleasure across the globe, or
from a European culture steeped in a developing Christianity which
viewed the body as an entity to be transcended, the civilisation which is
built on the repression of sexuality has its birthplace in Europe (Stannard,
op. cit.; Sawday, 1995).

The question of the applicability of western psychoanalysis to the social
structures of the rest of the world is beyond the scope of this chapter. However, the discourse of psychoanalysis, with all its heat and myth, can offer
an insight into how the West imagines the formation of the perfect (yet
always imperfect) subject of modernity. And the insight is that the repressed
will always return, bigger and badder than ever – what you cast out of
yourself and project onto others will come back to haunt and consume
you – what civilisation tries to tame with cruelty becomes transformed into
wild violence and suffering. The attempt to crush the will to pleasure creates
the will to power in its most ugly manifestations.

Much has been said already about the figure of rape as a metaphor for
the conquest of a territory and people. There is something apt in this
which captures the violence and forced intimacy of conquest, and describes
the particular erotic tastes of the violator. As we have discussed above, it is
the exercise of force in itself which has held the erotic charge for conquer-
ors. However, what can be missed in this figure of rape is the particular
articulation of rape fantasy which has animated much European expansion.
These are double-edged fantasies which at once take pleasure from the

violation of force and imagine the conquered as lasciviously responsive to this aggression. This colonial fantasy dreams of both absolute power and perfect reciprocity (R.C. Young, 1995).

In the end, this is the central contradiction in the culture of white sexuality. Having banished sexuality to the realms of the unclean, Europeans embark on a global programme of expropriation and moralising. Sexual gratification is recoded through this process of getting goods and doing good. The fantasy of perfect reciprocity from the subjugated dreams of a time in which sexuality can be welcomed again as part of the healthy mission of whiteness, because it is both goods and good, not sex at all.

Otherness as a sexual characteristic

The developing use of the term 'other' to describe the process by which the powerful delimit their own boundaries itself comes from psychoanalysis. There is no great revelation, therefore, in remembering its sexualised provenance. The self is marked by casting out all that is other, and this includes the disorder of unsocialised sexual desire. In this process, the self is constituted as an orderly entity. The assorted confusions of the pre-linguistic, the irrational, bodily impulses, are all lumped into the supplement of otherness, and everything is made tidy.

The widespread use of this idea of otherness to describe particular social relations rests on the assumption that this story of individual subject formation can be used to explain the differential access to subjecthood of different people. If the subject is imagined as masculine, with the tricky extras of otherness projected onto femininity, it is a small step to see how this masculine subject centres a world of whiteness, western-ness and modernity. Everything and everyone else falls into the void of otherness – object to his subject, fragment to his whole, passive to his active. The unhappy historical accident of subjugation proves this retrospectively – the misfortune of enslavement, colonisation, defeat, capture can happen only to the other who is not yet equal to the western subject. It is this lack of reason, progress and consolidated will that leaves the rest of the world vulnerable to conquest. Lacking the subject's will to act, we others are all left swimming randomly in the flows of physical sensation, the calls of the body, the music of the pre-linguistic and the poetry before reason. The western subject envies the sensual freedom of our existence, but steals our labour and resources anyway.

The sexualisation of the category of race has its roots in the history of racialised relations. Once again, the big stories of slavery and empire haunt our contemporary existence. Just as the contemporary economic nightmares of the poor world have their roots in these previous forms of theft and exploitation, present-day mythologies of racism and its strange sexual obsessions can be traced back to the ugliness of slavery and empire. In relation to the contemporary effects of the Atlantic slave trade, a significant literature has developed which argues that the experience of enslavement has led African-America to come differently to gendering, family and sexuality (hooks, 1982; Spillers, 1987).

Slavery transforms human beings into chattels – to be traded and bred for profit. As many commentaries have noted, this disrupted affective relations – erasing black fatherhood, disempowering black motherhood and denying captives the humanity of affective bonds. We can only speculate about the quality of sexual pleasure which can be derived from a body which is not your own. Enslavement transforms heterosexual relations into a vehicle for (re)production – yet in this version the heterosexual male actor can claim the fruits of paternity only through legal ownership, paternity itself has no purchase (Spillers, op. cit.).

There has been extensive speculation about the contemporary consequences of this history. Both popular representation and policy and academic writing have suggested that this history of paternal disenfranchisement continues to shape communities of African descent in many locations (Reynolds, 1997). One mythology, a mythology which feeds others, is that African men in the forced diasporas of slavery have lost their sense of responsibility to the family – this is described as a cultural outcome of slavery. The parallel myth suggests that African women in the same diasporic communities develop greater self-sufficiency in order to compensate for this absence of responsible men. Although these mythologies grant a remarkable degree of determination to past histories and seem to imply that other more recent aspects of social determination have made no impression on communities of African descent, the idea that people still live their lives in response to the historical experience of slavery resonates deeply with many people of many ethnicities.

Rather than revisit debates about the formative or otherwise experience of slavery for the contemporary living styles of diasporic African peoples, this chapter has focused on the effects of historically informed narratives and mythologies of gender and sexuality. Previous chapters outlined the continuing weight of state resources which are devoted to restraining all of these mythically forceful and highly sexualised black men. This chapter has reviewed the manner in which racism operates through gender and remakes and distorts the gendering of certain communities through the processes of racialisation. Racism both demasculinises the men of racialised communities and raises these same men to a dubious pinnacle of hypermasculinity (see Mercer, op. cit.). The effects of racism in the public worlds of the labour market, the street, political representation and everyday respect result in men from racialised communities being denied many of the privileges of public manhood. Women from racialised communities, in a parallel experience, are not subject to the same respects or constraints of public femininity. While both black men and women suffer racism, their experience is both differentiated through gender and operates through expectations of 'proper' gendering.

Whether or not it is slavery which has caused African men to allegedly forget the socially useful aspects of masculinity, racism reminds us all again and again that some men are not up to the responsibilities of male power. Instead, their masculinity is represented as no more than undisciplined dick. Racialisation remakes gender in pantomime form, with none of the privileges, proprieties or compensations of racial respectability.

Empire – that assorted set of practices which improvises opportunistically to occupy other people's land – runs parallel to the monstrosities of the Atlantic slave trade. While these people are subjects, not slaves, their subjection promises none of the compensation of citizenship. The supposed quid quo pro of domestic subjecthood – you are my subject and subject to my authority, but in return you enjoy my protection and the indirect fruits of my power – cracks apart in the imperial setting. Even without the legal trappings of ownership, white supremacy still manages to wield absolute and brutal power in the colonies. The result is an unhappy echo of slavery – unhampered violence, stolen labour and people, brutality as an instrument of government. However, the central difference – that these people are not the property of their tormentors – reshapes the mythologies of inhuman and improper gendering.

As has been discussed elsewhere, the intimacies of empire are of a different order (Gill, op. cit.). There are the same relations of servitude and close proximity but, unlike the strange domesticities of slave societies, here it is the white man who is far from home. The relative absence and then late arrival of white women in the sexual arena of empire makes for an ambiguous dynamic. Although, of course, the natives are sexually threatening, white women are not always available to be protected. Instead there is an ambivalent movement between tacit acceptance of sexual contact with the local population (for white men with whomever they fancied) and a mythology of absolute white self-sufficiency and sexual abstinence as the core of white superiority. It is this ambivalence which characterises the discourse of exoticism, those stories which make some people at once most desirable and somehow lesser and less human.

Rather than charting similarities between slavery and empire, or suggesting that these processes disrupt family structures and remake gender in similar ways, the point here is to recognise that empire, like slavery, has a sexual articulation. This intrusion is sexualised not only by colonisers, but by colonised also. Just as slavery can be told as a proof that these men cannot protect their women and children as real men should, empire questions the ability of some men to wield hetero-phallic power with any effectivity. Just as foreign intrusion is narrated as sexual conquest by the victors, the occupied community tells it as sexual humiliation.

> The modern meaning of the word 'machismo', as well as the concept, is actually an Anglo invention. For men like my father, being 'macho' meant being strong enough to protect and support my mother and us,

yet being able to show love. Today's macho has doubts about his ability to feed and protect his family. His 'machismo' is an adaptation to oppression and poverty and low self-esteem. It is the result of hierarchical male dominance.

(Anzaldua, 1987: 83)

The charade of hyper-masculinity develops as a reactive and defensive strategy against the affronts of a world which disempowers some men through disrespecting their masculinity. Black feminists have long argued that this reactive performance distorts the gendering of communities of colour and, effectively, does the white man's work for him. The false machismo of Anglo invention valorises the most cruel aspects of traditional masculinity, while forgetting the burden of responsibility that even old-style patriarchy demanded. Instead of strength with tenderness, and protection with interdependence, false machismo mimics the white masculinity which wears male power as a metonym for so many other powers. In the process, masculinity becomes no more than abuse.

The loss of a sense of dignity and respect in the macho breeds a false machismo which leads him to put down women and even to brutalize them.

(ibid.)

In both these accounts of the continuing shadows of larger histories, the outcome is community damage. For communities under attack, the comparative luxury of gender war is not available. Even without the heteronormativity of popular accounts, which explain the antagonisms between men and women of colour as part of the destructive programme of white racism (because who will make black/brown/yellow/red babies for the revolution?), no struggle can give up on half its people. Regardless of sexuality, the need to find some space of ease and respect for each other haunts the women and men of all communities in struggle. Somehow we are still stretching to reach some model of gendering that does not parrot the fiction of white propriety.

Random terror and racial discipline

European intervention promises to enforce proper gender relations, and thus introduce propriety as a route to humanity. What results from these interventions is rarely recognisable as propriety on European terms. Instead, affective relationships within dominated communities reshape in response to this alien wedge.

In more recent times we could view this as a part of certain development agendas or, even, as tied to a human rights programme. The point here is not to question that good can come from such strategies, but rather to suggest that the wish to construct propriety plays a particular role in domination. Long after the civilising mission of the white man's burden, the residue of this wish to make others like yourself *for ethical reasons* survives in the expansionist aspirations of a range of would-be regional powers (Kaldor, 1999).

Alongside these (almost) benign interventions, the racialised exercise of power continues to require at least a threat of terror tactics in order to maintain its grip. In recent times, the invocation of this terror has taken a number of forms – from the renewed horrors of war rape to the resilience of lynching as a transferable method of everyday terrorism (Gutman and Rieff, 1999).

Discussion of the role of sexuality in racialised politics has identified the functional echo of myth in material strategy. The long histories which see large numbers of people subjugated through, in part, their devalued 'race' show that the practical business of violence and exploitation can be pragmatically supplemented by the mythologies of bestiality. The hyper-sexual man of colour who haunts the imagination of slavers and colonisers alike becomes the legitimation for endless violence against black men – in pre-emptive defence of white women. The hyper-sexual woman of colour who inhabits the fantasies of the same slavers and colonisers becomes the point of entry through which whole peoples can be entrapped – as if her putative openness marks a wider openness to all forms of conquest. The sexually lax natives who appear to people the waiting-for-whiteness rest of the world become another indication that these people need to be taken in hand – for them subjugation to the disciplines of European living is a blessing.

All these accounts seem convincing and common-sensical. Of course, some stories are dreamt up opportunistically to legitimise less than laudable actions. Some ideologies are built up from a base of material relations, and some social machineries engender their own narratives of interaction. However, now we enter a period in which less certain power structures are in play. Unlike the clear demarcations and legal covenants of empire and slavery, now white supremacy adopts more informal methods. Yet somehow, sexualisation still plays a role in the business of racism.

To return to the themes of racialised Armageddon, this chapter has sought to demonstrate that the mythologies of sex continue to inform the business of racialised class relations.

Death

The alleged threat to law and order (for which we can read unquestionable white entitlement) of dark-skinned peoples both on privileged doorsteps and across the globe is, still now, articulated through the language of sexuality. The threat to order is figured as the dangerous possibility of contamination – what is so overwhelming are the size, numbers and difference of these bodies. Now the myth of the black rapist is reworked to become a global scare-story – some populations fall prey to lynching by state and amateurs, across the world, because they threaten to claim their human entitlement to life, love and happiness. The extra heat in this process comes from the ideological construction that understands the possibility that the world's racialised poor may claim their basic human rights as a sexual assault upon the privileged.

War

Global policing and total war at home retain many of the sexual kicks of previous regimes of force. Of course, this is in part due to the theatre of domination – natty uniforms and bang-flash displays of technological prowess continue to substitute for more everyday sexual pleasures for the children of corporate technoscience.

However, in the (allegedly) more benign elements of the global policing agenda we can see the remnants of earlier agendas. The return of human rights as an organising principle/strategy/rhetoric of international relations makes space for a different model of western intervention in the lives of others. The point here is not to question the value of protesting against abuses wherever they occur. Rather, the point at issue is the role of human-rights discourse in a wider schema of global policing and militarisation. A sense of propriety still informs all sorts of neo-imperialist interventions.

Famine

Food crises have long been explained as an outcome of the unruly reproductive practices of the poor world – not so much too little food as too many people. We will discuss the new population scares in more detail in chapter 5. Here it is enough to recognise that global stories about scarcity of resources are retold as outcomes of sexual behaviour. People are too hungry only because there are too many people, natural disasters indicate the inability of some populations to manage nature – some people are expendable because they are too animal, too sexual, too bodily, hardly human at all.

Pestilence

Contagion has become once more, tragically, a key narrative of sexuality for rich and poor worlds. However, the particular horrors of global HIV and the differential experience of even this tragedy according to income, location, status, represent only one aspect of sexualised narratives of illness and ethnicity. The re-emergence of old killer diseases and the arrival of new incurable threats to the body give rise to new conceptions of the deadly danger of foreign bodies. The racialised boundary between rich and poor worlds is policed with increasing violence and vigour, for fear that physical proximity will lead to degeneration through the diseases of poverty. Even when these illnesses are not sexually transmitted, the mass panic they engender is a fear of sexualised contamination (Singer, op. cit.).

This chapter has taken the lessons of black feminism as a route to understanding the multiple positionings of global relations. Through reviewing these debates, we have argued that the construction of gender and sexuality also takes place through global structures and this impacts upon the lived experience of racialised class. The intertwined mythologies of race and sex continue to inform the construction of racialised boundaries and fears in the global era. Although an anxiety about sexual propriety can be traced from the early histories of European expansion, our argument is that this legacy adapts to the circumstances of the 'newly' global economy. The next chapter returns to discussions about racisms and resources, and suggests that the anxiety and fascination of unresolved sexuality are all too present in the racialised class relations of the rich world.

Chapter 5

Consumption and distribution

In chapter 2 we argued that the intensification of global networks creates new forms of racialised class relations, both locally and globally. In that chapter we examined this process through a number of locations of production and suggested that the exploitation and coercion of vulnerable workers continued to be facilitated by racialised mythologies. In this chapter, we want to focus on the other side of economic contracts – the consumption and distribution of goods, services and assets, as opposed to their production.

Discussions of the character of globalised living have privileged the realm of consumption as an arena of meaning creation and identity formation (for a critical account of these debates see Sarup, 1996; Lury, 1996). This celebration of consumer possibility has been subject to angry criticism from a number of commentators, who have argued that the fiction of consumer choice masks the material losses and political disempowerment suffered by ordinary people (for a critique of First World consumption fever, see Miller, 1995. For a discussion of the politics of consumption, see Clarke, 1991). Here we want to acknowledge that the processes of consumption construct people as different types of agent – and that an analysis of this moment of consumption can complement accounts of work and production. However, we also want to examine the constrained circumstances of consumption for the world's racialised poor. Our argument is that the globalised world severely limits some people's access to the most basic of resources. This inability to consume for survival, let alone for leisure-time distraction, becomes another characteristic of the racialised poor in the global economy.

Famine

Food represents the most archetypal of consumer products – its ingestion serves as the figure for the consumption of all other goods, pre-dating market relations and returning to the moment of intake. A good becomes ours when we consume it – making it part of ourselves by taking it into ourselves. Consumption recalls the satisfaction of this elemental need, even when the consumed object is frivolous, unnecessary and not nutritious at all. However, whatever the lifestyle choices of food shopping in the rich world, food (particularly when non-branded) remains among the most basic of consumer needs. For much of the world's population, the inability to engage in this life-sustaining consumer practice indicates their economic powerlessness more starkly than any account of their working practice. For this reason, our discussion of the uneven pattern of consumption and distribution in the global racialised economy begins with an examination of the consumption of food.

While celebrations of consumer agency stress the pleasures of choice, food distribution has been characterised by extreme inequalities in access. Later we will discuss the processes by which ethnic diversity is displayed and consumed through food and culture. For now, our interest is in the role of food economies in structuring global hierarchies of entitlement. In particular, we want to argue that continuing disparities in access to food operate through racialised myths – and, in turn, that food crises serve to confirm this mythology of differential entitlement across the globe. Since 1979 at least, popular debate about global food economies has been informed by the idea that world hunger is avoidable and continues because of the ugliness of western economic greed. Susan George had already written the following lines:

> The present world political and economic order might be compared to that which reigned over social-class relations in individual countries in nineteenth-century Europe – with the Third World now playing the role of the working class. All the varied horrors we look back upon with mingled disgust and incredulity have their equivalents and worse in the Asian, African and Latin American countries where well over 500 million people are living in what the World Bank has called 'absolute poverty'. And just as the 'propertied classes' of yesteryear opposed every reform and predicted imminent economic disaster if eight-year-olds could no longer work in the mills, so today those groups that profit from the poverty that keeps people hungry are attempting to maintain the status quo between rich and poor worlds.
>
> (1986: 23)

The key components of a more critical account of development are in place here in this quotation. The starting premise is that hunger is not a natural disaster caused by climate or over-population, but instead is the outcome of the structural inequalities of the global economy. Rather than offering a route out of this morass, trade, as it exists, only exacerbates this process and further ensures that the poor of the world stay hungry. As George states, what stands in the way of change are class interests on a global scale. This insight, coming from many quarters, informed critical development theory through the later twentieth century. While the rich world balked at the suggestion that world hunger was any responsibility of theirs, radical thinking across poor nations focused on the role of international trade and foreign intervention in their nation's economies (see Rodney, 1972). Imaginative solutions to world poverty and hunger become inseparable from critiques of the global economy shaped around the needs of the West.

The (long) gathering campaign to 'cancel the debt' is another child of this way of thinking. Although at the turn of the new century all these assorted movements against global poverty are reshaped through the development of media-orientated pressure politics (with associated celebrities) and the differently shaped street politics of a host of DIY tendencies, the germ of the analysis is contained in the earlier debate. The coalition of demonstrators who assembled around the World Trade Organisation meeting in Seattle in December 1999 – linking concerns about ecological sustainability, labour rights and the quality of life for poor nations to a critique of international trade – represented a new activism around these older ideas (see Klein, 2000). For our purposes, the point is to think about the circumstances in which class can be thought (and maybe even mobilised) globally. The key resource here is food, and we want to suggest that differential access to this most essential of resources is an issue of class. People's location and empowerment determine who eats what in a global system of distribution. This follows a version of Sen's concept of entitlement which has transformed discussions of hunger and food distribution. For our discussion, what is most relevant is the extent to which entitlement is determined by the historical traces of far more long-standing global inequalities. Endemic hunger remains the fate of the poor world long after the imperial high points of struggling for Africa or partitioning Bengal. Vulnerability to famine represents another well-documented instance of the disposability of some groups of people.

Agency here is marked around the ability to command food – the various overlapping structures of entitlement indicate the social status and power of the individual agent, and this in turn determines chances of survival and well-being. This has been the accepted insight of the groundbreaking work of Amartya Sen, among others – that hunger is determined by social status and power, not absolute levels of food in the world (see Dreze and Sen, 1990; Sen, 1984).

> The ability of some people to command (acquire) food may reflect their political, military, economic or inherited position within the international system and its national and subnational elements. The term 'command' is used because it suggests that an individual's or group's ability to acquire food is correlated with their access to power, however expressed and at whatever level.
>
> (E.M. Young, 1997: 6)

The debates around world hunger posit food as one of a number of essential resources and then chart access to this absolute can't-do-without-it entity as a way of modelling power. Of course, the rich nations of the West come out as the guzzlers, addicted to resource-heavy food habits and excessive calories, at the expense of the poor world which cannot eat enough to sustain healthy life. Not only do the rich eat more than their share, we also find that the poor are forced to devote energies to meeting the needs of the rich, before their own essential needs are met.

'In 1988 . . . the developed countries took three-quarters of all food imports (by value), the developing countries but a quarter; the pattern established in the late nineteenth century still survives' (Grigg, 1993). It is this disparity which prompts George's analogy between nineteenth-century class relations in industrialising economies and twentieth-century relations between industrialised and not-yet-and-never-to-be industrialised economies – the West is instrumental in creating and maintaining the bad times of the rest and we eat their resources just as the bourgeoisie eats the surplus value of labour. Whatever fictions of redistribution permeate the discussions of policy and media, from loans to aid to debt relief to radical development, somehow the equation of access and distribution remains the same.

In relation to world food supplies, there is a clear case of haves and have-nots and a range of commentators across the political spectrum have identified this (for an outline of debates, see Lappe and Collins, 1988; Goodman and Redclift, 1991; Grigg, op. cit.). However, class is not a concept which describes inequality – although this may also be an attribute of class relations. Rather, class as a category promises to explain the interdependence of the resource-rich and the resource-poor, and, from this mixture of injustice and supplementarity, pull out a theory of agency. The high-profile media-friendly begging of Jubilee 2000 and fellow travellers is an attempt to remind the world of this interdependence – and to suggest that global debt transforms the poor world into agents of change despite themselves. Whatever the various feel-good accounts of the West's change of heart, at root, hard economics again determines the response to the debt crisis. The rich world proposes to write off the debts of the poor world at just the time when the world begins to realise how vulnerably interdependent the global economy makes us. The agency of the poor is less an issue of their political organisation than it is a fear of their destabilising numbers here. Now whether or not the children of the poor world can eat has become an issue of global stability – because that dangerous mix of financial and political instability threatens to topple the West itself. In the catch-phrases of the new centre-left consensus of the rich world, (slightly) more equitable distribution is good for capital – and extremes are dangerous and unsustainable.

Gordon Brown, British Chancellor of the Exchequer and architect of New Labour economic policy, proposes a writing off of the debt of the world's poorest nations, a declaration that puts pressure on other rich nations –

a millennium gesture out of keeping with his public persona of absolute caution and tight budgetary control.[1] However, the desire to halt the debt cycle of the poor world echoes the desire to end Britain's own debt dependency – Brown has used his skills in financial management to pay back quantities of Britain's public debt, resisting the calls to pump available cash back into disintegrating public services.

This gesture around debt repayment coincides with an internal struggle in IMF to elect a new managing director and to refocus the aims of the organisation. In this context, campaigns for debt relief add to the wider pressures on the IMF to reconsider its role.

According to one report,

> Mr Summers [head of the US Treasury] said the IMF should concentrate on providing short-term financing for countries threatened by balance of payments problems, financial contagion or market panics. He proposed the IMF should do more to collect and share financial information, and to disseminate that information to global markets and investors. It should promote better assessments as to whether countries are likely to run into trouble, for example by running unsustainable exchange rate regimes. But he said the goal should be for emerging market economies to 'reach the point where calling on the IMF for financial support is unthinkable'.[2]

For a range of reasons, including US doubts about its continuing efficacy, the IMF has been attempting to constrain the extent of new debt crises and to shed development responsibilities in favour of the power-house influence of the World Bank.[3] For now, the global impact of currency crises has made the debt cycle too risky an option – whatever the short-term profits to be made. Whether this will correct the skewed distribution of food is yet to be seen.

Of course, another old argument has it that this distorted distribution is another effect of the pursuit of profit – an outcome of the actions of the international bourgeoisie (whoever they may be). Whatever the needs of the world's poor, need does not enfranchise you in the marketplace. Instead, and as usual, the rush for money skews production towards the whims of the resource-heavy of the world. What people need has no influence at all. The debate around national self-sufficiency in food acknowledges the impact of these pulls.

> National self-sufficiency in food production, whatever its merits, does not in itself guarantee all citizens the right to food. In reality, preventing hunger depends on the following minimum arrangements. First, all citizens must have the means to produce or purchase food for an adequate diet. Second, national policy should cause food to be available for purchase in the quantities required for good nutrition. And,

third, there should be national and local capacity to handle disasters effectively where and when they occur, and the country must be able to prevent excessive fluctuations in national food availability resulting from external events.

(Omawale, 1984)

Food production in itself cannot guarantee food distribution. In order for the world's poor to have a chance of eating food that they produce, many other factors have to change. Citizens must become entitled to food and this entitlement must be strong enough to compete with the international market. Planning must prioritise the citizens' entitlement to food before any other call for supply or repayment. These provisions have proved almost impossible for poor nations to achieve.

A key factor has been that the hunger of the poor world profits the rich – the question is the name we give this mechanism, unequal development, neo-colonialism, old-style global capitalism, bad planning, government corruption. Whatever explanatory model is chosen, it has become commonplace to point out that there is sufficient food in the world to feed everyone – but that the problem is distributing this food to those in need (Lappe and Collins, 1988). This distribution problem mirrors older relations of coloniser and colonised, discoverer and discovery, merchant and unfree labour – and is, of course, inescapably racialised. How did we ever get into this mess except through the global politics of racialised profit extraction? For these reasons, we want to suggest that the manoeuvres to address global hunger are a key site of class negotiation and race politics in our time. The framing of entitlement to food – and by implication to life itself – takes place through a racialised mythology that depicts some groups as active and striving and others as passive and receiving. Within this framework, hunger once again becomes the self-appointed destiny of the racialised poor.

Genetic modification

In recent times, these global relations of racialised class which fight over access to natural resources have become extended through technological development. Global food economies have always been a battle for access to these most essential resources – now we find that the battle is also a matter of profit-making and ownership. The will to own the very formative structures of the organic is the basis of fresh and hard-fought battles across the globe. The growth of biotechnology, and the impact of its commercial applications, has extended the struggle to own and control the organic world.

Popular debate has depicted this leap in knowledge as another threatening move towards colonising nature. The influence of ecological concerns and the fall-out from a variety of industrial and technological mistakes have combined to create a populist distrust of scientific expertise. As a result, a significant amount of everyday discussion has centred on the ethical inappropriateness of tampering with nature. Although this can be explained as an outcome of insufficient levels of scientific understanding among the general population, there is also an unease about the power and control such knowledge will bring. As always, the deciding factor will be the ownership and application of this technical development.

> This realisation has been reached by the movers and shakers of the so-called new economy – the mishmash of communications and bio-technology which has been identified as the next agent of economic growth and change. Biotech shares have overtaken dot.com companies as favourite buys for the new portfolio – and the resulting speculation has drawn concern about the impact of the market on scientific development and, in turn, human well-being.[4]

On the one hand, knowledge about the make-up of human gene patterns opens new possibilities for medical research. Better and more accurate understanding of the genetic blips that 'cause' disease allows accelerated and targeted research. Morgan continues,

> But for the real benefits of the genome to be realised, the promise of science has to meet commercial demands. At one level, the picture seems bright. Big drugs companies which have invested in genomic technology have seen their research efforts accelerate. With the completion of the genome they can effectively go supersonic. SmithKline Beecham (S.B.) says before it began genomic research in 1993 it would explore six to eight drug targets a year. With genomic research it examines 200.
>
> (Ibid.)

However, this acceleration is in answer to potential market calls – unless there are profits to be made, research may be diverted. Paradoxically, the hype around biotechnology may prove to be its worst enemy – the explosion of market interest may damage long-term research in the area.

> Analysts are comparing this year's biotech boom to dot.coms last year. The sector has been driven by the US and the position of biotech in the new economy, as investors have moved out of dot.coms looking for other high-growth sectors. Internet stock performance in 1999 woke the world up to the fact that traditional valuation models were not applicable to the new economy.
>
> (Ibid.)

Most immediately, commentators fear that the impending crash in bio-tech shares will push some companies and some research out of the market. This jeopardises future investment in an area that has yet to demonstrate its profit potential. Most worrying of all, research which is not judged to be sufficiently profit-generating – too small a target group, too rare a condition – may fall out of future funding altogether.[5]

Defenders of the biotechnological revolution point to the vast potential benefits of this knowledge area. Understanding the make-up of the human body opens new arenas of medical understanding and progress. Developing more nutritious, higher-yielding and more resilient crops through genetic modification promises to alleviate the pressure of world hunger. The wide-spread fears of a burgeoning world population can be tempered by the promises of biotechnically engineered plenty. Chapter 6 will examine the racialised aspect of these anxieties about a scarcity of global resources. Here we focus on the critique that biotechnology represents an intensifica-tion of existing structures of dependency. According to Cathy Atkinson, 'Farmers from both rich and poor worlds have complained that the intro-duction of genetically modified seeds and their partner pesticides reduces agricultural labour to a new form of "bio-serfdom"'.[6] Elsewhere, Catherine Ainger writes,

> Masipag Farmer–Scientist Alliance takes the charge further, saying that the expensive chemical required by the IRRI's [International Rice Research Institute] rice varieties have forced farmers into a cycle of debt, and over the years depleted the soil, poisoned workers and caused massive loss of on-farm diversity. They argue that the costs of these inputs actually outweigh the outputs of increased yields.[7]

Although there is an acknowledgement of the need for more and better-distributed basic foodstuffs, farmer and development groups argue that hunger stems from other structures, not a lack of resources. Instead the push to modify and control the basic dietary components of large sections of the world's population is regarded with suspicion – a new attempt at world domination.

> The IRRI has some of the world's leading rice scientists, and was the organisation that developed high-yielding crops for the green revolu-tion of the 1960s and 1970s. But it is deeply unpopular these days at the grassroots. Rafael Mariano, leader of the powerful K.M.P. peasant movement, charges the IRRI with locking rice farmers into dependency on the market. 'Rice is a political crop,' he says. 'He who controls the production and distribution of rice has an invaluable weapon to con-trol the whole of Asia.'

> (Ibid.)

Recent years have seen a backlash against the supposed victories of the green revolution. This revolution proposed an end to world hunger through the use of chemically enhanced farming methods across the poor world – and in the short term, many areas saw an increase in crop yield, if not in the equity of food distribution. However, over time it has become apparent that these methods of intensive farming are unsustainable on a number of counts. Firstly, this approach depletes the soil over time – a process that is difficult to reverse. Secondly, crop yields become increasingly dependent on escalating pesticide use – this not only has adverse environmental costs, but more immediately it increases the economic dependency of small-holding farmers. Most dangerously of all, the combination of pesticide dependency and the need for ever larger units of production effectively pushed many poor farmers off their land and out of business. With no alternative source of employment and income, the increased crop yields of the green revolution served to increase the hunger of former farmers. In the light of this history, the rural poor of Asia, Africa and Latin America have good reason to be sceptical about the claims of technological development in food production. Vandana Shiva writes,

> Five hundred years after Columbus, a more secular version of the same project of colonization continues through patents and intellectual property rights (IPRs). The Papal Bull has been replaced by the General Agreement on Tariffs and Trade (GATT) treaty. The principle of effective occupation by Christian princes has been replaced by effective occupation by the transnational corporations supported by modern-day rulers. The vacancy of targeted lands has been replaced by the vacancy of targeted life forms and species manipulated by the new biotechnologies. The duty to incorporate savages into Christianity has been replaced by the duty to incorporate local and national economies into the global marketplace, and to non-Western systems of knowledge into the reductionism of commercialized Western science and technology.
>
> (1998: 8)

The battles around genetic modification and food cultivation are gaining pace in rich and poor worlds alike. In the rich world, the covert introduction of genetically modified foodstuffs to our diets has reawakened wider fears about the safety of our food chain. Concerns about farming methods have already raised alarm about much meat and animal produce. Genetic modification joins pesticides in the developing fear that even vegetables are not safe to eat.

However, legitimate and real as these concerns are, the concerns of the poor world are more basic still. The process which Shiva entitles bio-piracy is the new imperialism which seeks to own the very organic material of people's lives. Shiva argues that previously the rich West wished to expropriate only the labour and wealth of the rest of the world. This was done through the heady mixture of violence and legal contracts – so that theft could be rendered legitimate ownership through a staging of witnessing (Greenblatt, 1991). Thus piracy becomes transformed into international trade, moral responsibility and the resolutely legal contracts of the white man's burden. The complaints of those who lost property, liberty and lives to these bargains could not be voiced within this framework of legitimacy. Instead, the language of rights and law is framed to reward aggressors, rendering initial crimes into legitimate interests which then, paradoxically, can be defended through law.

Shiva describes the transformation of this process for the purposes of biopiracy. The new era of biopiracy updates this system of retrospective legitimation, so that now the development of biotechnology renders the organic world not only knowable, but, through the trickery of patents, ownable. We are witnessing a corrosion of scholarship which blurs the boundaries between understanding and owning, between describing and inventing. Now corporate science forgets all humility before creation, and instead imagines itself as ultimate creator. From this comes the strange spectacle of the assertion of intellectual property rights over long-used plant remedies, the genetic makeup of coveted basic foodstuffs such as basmati rice, or even the DNA of communities under threat (Shiva, op. cit.: 9).

The harnessing of biotechnology by international corporations who see a prosperous future only through an imperialistic deepening of capitalist integration leads to yet more suffering for the world's poor (Biggs, 1998). Now the small-scale sustainability of traditional farming methods is under attack from the irresistible pressure of international capital – backed up by both economic and military threats. Once the local environment is contaminated by these crops that are created for profit not well-being, local farmers cannot resist their fall into a new version of debt bondage. Biotechnology coupled with the imperialist protection racket of intellectual property rights skewed in favour of corporate interests contributes to the demise of small-holder farming across the world. Unable to weather the uncertainties of a market shaped by much larger economic players, farmers in the rich and poor worlds, in the US and in India, fall into debt, despair and suicide (J. Dyer, 1998; Vidal, 1999).

Despite the continuing crisis around the production and distribution of food for much of the world's population, the application of technologies which concentrate even more power in the hands of global corporations, at the expense of small- and medium-holding farming across the world, is unlikely to feed the hungry. The much vaunted green revolution is a recent indication that an increase in production alone cannot reshape skewed patterns of power and distribution. Without the safeguards of democratic ownership and control, even an increase in food production can serve to further immiserate the poor.

The move into biopiracy represents the most total attempt to colonise and commodify the life world. Once the world's disposable people are caught in this trap of dependency on slow poisons, the chance of escape into any form of autonomy again is slight.

Pestilence

Disease

The final nightmare section in this descent into Armageddon returns to versions of materiality which precede class, or, at least, operate alongside class as another order of materiality. This volume has tried to argue that the troubled intersection between race and class is best understood in terms of the lived effects on differentiated bodies. Here we consider supposedly organic scourges of the body – and remember again that the fate of the body is always remade through the social.

We have written in other places about the role of disease in the rise to ascendancy of the white race – and this account is well documented in a number of well-known texts (Bhattacharyya, 1998; Crosby, 1986; Diamond, 1998). This recent flurry of interest in the role of regional immunities in the material development of various societies and the possibility of conquest and expansion which stems from a luck-of-the-draw ability to withstand certain disease forms is only one aspect of a wider wish to think again about the role of so-called nature in human culture and development. Of course, a common-sense recognition of the role of disease in the rise of white supremacy has been with us for some time. In this account, some groups of people, the unfortunate objects of colonisation and conquest, are decimated through the bad luck of their unprepared immune systems. In its worst incarnations, this account uses the immunity argument to veil the extent of western violence – as if the misfortune of influenza was the only blight upon the admirable curiosity and will to knowledge of European man, and as if this loss of life was an unforeseen by-product of innocent exploration. However, in its more interesting and recently popularised forms, this account of the role of disease in human history rethinks the place of the organic in our ideas of ethnic conflict and conquest (Diamond, op. cit.).

Writing on issues of race can be divided (still now, after all these years) into the two camps of nature and culture. The debate on what race is, how it is formed and how it has effects as a category in the world remains a discussion about what is determined by biology and what is determined by society. Sadly, this debate has solidified into a polar opposition between those (largely on the right, largely against attempts to foster racial justice) who argue that the destiny of different ethnic groups is made through their blood, or some other equally non-negotiable characteristic which is based in the body, and those (largely more liberal and concerned to right the wrongs of history) who argue that ethnic identity is made through culture, with no recourse to the biological. In this two-way fight, attempts to uncover the role of biological factors in the comparative advantage of certain communities in certain historical moments have been all too often assigned to the first camp of blood and destiny. No talk of nature without a dishonourable slide into fascism, apparently.

The shift that allows a reconsideration of nature as a historical factor is the shift that sees nature as a complex system, rather than a singular and one-way determination through blood, stock or gene pool. According to Diamond,

> Throughout the Americas, diseases introduced with Europeans spread from tribe to tribe far in advance of the Europeans themselves, killing an estimated 95 percent of the pre-Columbian Native American population. The most populous and highly organized native societies of North America, the Mississippian chiefdoms, disappeared in that way between 1492 and the late 1600s, even before Europeans themselves made clear their first settlement on the Mississippi river. A smallpox epidemic in 1713 was the biggest single step in the destruction of South Africa's native San people by European settlers. Soon after the British settlement of Sydney in 1788, the first of the epidemics that decimated Aboriginal Australians began. A well-documented example from Pacific islands is the epidemic that swept over Fiji in 1806, brought by a few European sailors who struggled ashore from the wreck of the ship *Argo*. Similar epidemics marked the histories of Tonga, Hawaii, and other Pacific islands.
>
> (Ibid.: 78)

The world we all inherit, the world which is already scored deeply with the marks of a western ascendancy which becomes indistinguishable from white supremacy, is already necessarily shaped by these materialities which are not strictly economic. The particular configuration of economic development which gives rise to a European ascendancy also gets some extra help from the chance benefits of cultivatable basic crops and the ability (given by climate) to domesticate animals. The domestication of animals also gives rise to new immunities in European populations – people who live close to livestock learn (through generations) how to withstand the disease strains of other species, as well as to wear animal skin and wool and to drink animal milk. These material extras improve the physical comfort of European populations enough to allow population growth and societal development – now there are resources to support technical innovation and invention – and the added extra of steel makes the armies of early European expansion unstoppable. When other people first encounter these Europeans raised by animals and armed with hard metal, their weapons and their immune systems provide no defence. European technology and biology triumphs (Crosby, 1986).

However, in recent years it has become apparent that the technological adaptation of the natural environment – precisely the innovation which has fostered white supremacy and global capitalism – always has hidden consequences. Now the factors which were once enablers become burdens instead. Some aspects of technological advance return to haunt us. Antibiotics – the wonder drugs which have eradicated so much disease and also fattened so much livestock – now herald the possibility of new plagues. Over-use of antibiotics to treat inappropriate ailments or to make farming livestock more profitable has led to the development of resistant strains of bacteria.[8] This is happening in a period when many of the world's population have lost their immunity to diseases believed to have been eradicated. New strains of old diseases such as tuberculosis raise the possibility of epidemics of illness for which there is no effective medicine and for which human bodies are ill-prepared.

> Medical science has given doctors the means to control TB. For 40 years, there have been effective therapies. But because the treatment – and money to pay for it – has not been taken to the areas affected, the world is not planning its extermination but preparing for an epidemic. Drug-resistant strains are spreading.[9]

In the time of inescapable interdependence, the return of old styles of pestilence to the rich world via the conduit of globalised impoverishment offers a version of capitalist self-destruct for the era of biotechnology. It is true that this is more Nemesis than dialectics – rather than forging anew from irresolvable contradictions, here diseased chickens come home to roost – but it is some kind of forced reunion between rich and poor. We end on this note in order to remember that even when the lot of the poor seems endless and unchanging, class is a concept that reminds us that we are all more interdependent than we think. Somehow or other, the suffering of the poor creeps back to undermine the rich.

Contamination

The new and intensified networks of globalisation reawaken long-standing fears about the boundaries between different categories of being. The fictions of 'race' differentiate between groups on an assumption of biological difference – a boundary that is always in danger of being transgressed and collapsed through human contact.

Colonisation enables this threat of contamination – population movements in all directions collapse the spatial boundaries between groups, the creeping colonisation of the organic creates new ruptures in western safety. Proximity brings the horror of lost differentiation and permeated boundaries on many levels.

Excessive access to global resources brings some satisfaction and fleeting security to westerners, but the accompanying intensification of global inter-dependence reignites fears of being entered and made dirty by alien others. Contemporary manifestations of pestilence threaten to materialise these deep-running racist fears. The re-emergence of 'Third World' diseases in rich nations confirms the fear that the horrors of racialised status can be caught through contact. Migration itself becomes refigured as a threat to the immune system – because these people, as always, bring dirt, poverty, disease. In response, rich nations engage in a reinvigorated building of many borders, both within and between nations.

Although it becomes increasingly difficult for the poor to enter the rich world, the issue of immigration becomes more hyper-politicised than ever. While globalisation renders all spaces permeable and interconnected, rich nations devote resources to fortifying their national boundaries against the incursion of unwanted foreign bodies of all varieties. At the same time, the desire to keep clean by keeping separate is manifested locally through the active segmentation of residential and business spaces within white nations. As the next section discusses, these processes represent attempts to manage white national space and to cleanse and make it safe by other means.

Cities

A recurrent theme of this volume has been the relationship between globali-sation (interconnectedness, permeability, etc.) and new forms of racialisa-tion. Yet ideas of interconnectedness and the collapse of spatial boundaries do not sit easily alongside talk of contamination, disease and threats to the immune system. The consequences of such contradictions are lived out in what have been characterised as 'global cities'.

Cities like London, New York, Los Angeles and Tokyo constitute highly compressed spaces for the forced reunion of the rich and poor. On the one hand they have to accommodate the headquarters of multinationals and an advanced financial and business services sector (insurance, banking), and act as centres for the inward and outward flows of capital and finance. A key aspect of the emergence of global cities has been the transformation of capital into an interconnected system. This development has depended on a number of factors including the deregulation of financial markets and their freedom from national control, the revolution in information and communications technologies and the creation of organisations for the pro-cessing of capital flows (Castells, 1989: 339). Such affluence has spawned and valorised a class of specialised and highly paid professional workers, e.g. property-rights lawyers, fund managers, insurance and estate agents, bankers. On the other hand, and equally importantly, it has devalorised many traditional employment sectors whilst at the same time creating a new class of low-paid service workers, of necessity on hand to meet the daily and diverse needs of the new commercial elites (Sassen, op. cit.: 142).

The service sector has thus been polarised into high- and low-income workers, the latter made up of fast-food workers, porters, cleaners, nannies, sex workers and 'ethnic' restaurateurs. Castells is quick to point out the ironies of such spaces. While global in its spread, capital requires spatial proximity of its command centres and, despite the virtual nature of its information flows, it relies on face-to-face interaction amongst its anonymous masters. Castells goes further to suggest that whilst appearing to control the destinies of economies from the far-flung corners of the earth, such global centres of capital live in constant fear of implosion from within (Castells, op. cit.: 344).

There has been a pronounced racial dimension to these urban changes. For example, in Los Angeles, the collapse of the automobile and steel and tyre industries and the corresponding decimation of traditional trade unions disproportionately impacted on minority workers. The location of the sunrise industries coincided with processes of white suburbanisation which we come back to below. What was left were the low-paid unregulated and non-unionised service sector and sweatshop jobs in the secondary labour market. In Los Angeles, these were labour markets open to new influxes of Asian and Latino immigrants. The uprisings in Watts in 1965 and in the aftermath of the Rodney King verdict in 1992 were expressions of political disaffection and social and economic polarisation in the city. White flight, which resulted from such uprisings, fuelled the creation of white enclaves like Simi Valley where Rodney King's assailants were tried and found not guilty. Hence the pattern of de- and re-industrialisation is a function of industrial location, political ideologies, demography and spatial characteristics of the city (ibid.: 431).

A consequence of these processes, which can only be understood as simultaneously economic, political and spatial, has been the peripheralisation of the centre. Thus the straightforward geographical distinction between the First and the Third Worlds has been complicated in the case of global cities. Here, both First and Third Worlds co-exist. Differences still exist in terms of macro-economic wealth and power; witness the significance of western-owned TNCs, banks, governments, etc. However, continuing disparities of wealth and ownership, which remain a feature of the global economy, should not conceal the fact that marginalised groups in the West are excluded from the benefits/profits/decisions distributed or taken in their own countries.

As we have suggested, the above global processes did not take place in a political vacuum. The role of central and local governments, alliances and grassroots campaigns have all played a role in mediating and shaping such processes. Neo-liberalism, which dominated economic debate from the mid-1970s, gained ground in the 1980s as it became synonymous not only with the political ideologies of Ronald Reagan and George Bush in the US and Margaret Thatcher in the UK but also in the thinking of organisations like the World Bank and International Monetary Fund and amongst a then growing number of think-tank bodies and academic advisers. Such was its sway that the displacement of right-wing by centrist governments across Europe and the US during the 1990s made little impact on the key principles of deregulation, privatisation and a minimal welfare state/social budget, all of which had underpinned the expansion of the finance sectors in New York and London in the 1980s.

The emergence of global cities has also inevitably challenged traditional ideas of 'place' and identity, based as these were on relatively fixed and ordered notions of belonging, boundary and hierarchy. According to Harvey, globalisation has led to the 'disarticulation of place-based societies' (cited in Massey, 1995: 54). Space, another concept forming part of this new urban vocabulary, is no longer defined by place but, as we suggested above, by flows. Spatial movement is so fast, thanks to global communications networks and supersonic transport, that social relations have been transformed. Places now are what Massey and Jess refer to as 'meeting places, intersections of particular bundles of activity spaces, of connections and interrelations, of influences and movements set within a wider space' (1995a: 218). Such forces call into question the traditionally held view that where we live is a key source of ordering and making sense of our lives, that is, of cultural identity. Such has been the sense of loss and crisis that attempts have been made to maintain and mobilise old identities and values. These efforts, whether by politicians, corporate planners or community or religious leaders, have invariably built on romanticised and nostalgic versions of local and/or ethnic histories as well as a reinvention of 'place' as we suggest below.

The racialisation of city spaces and the phenomenon of 'gated' cities

The partial and inevitable failure of rich nations to fortify national boundaries against the incursion of unwanted foriegn bodies has displaced the problem of fortification to the locality. The forced and quasi-forced concentration and ghettoisation of different ethnic groups has a long history as do the popular myths surrounding the lifestyles of different ethnic groups. For example, Engels wrote about the concentration of the Irish in Manchester, whilst the popular press wrote lurid tales of opium and prostitution amongst the Chinese communities in the Limehouse area of London's Docklands at the turn of the century. In the 1930s, Robert Park and his associates at the Chicago School pioneered their ecological thesis of the development of urban spatial locations in the city, and more recently western sociologists have sought to examine patterns of settlement in terms of discrimination in the public and private housing markets. John Rex and Robert Moore, for instance, explained patterns of settlement of what were in the 1960s immigrant communities in Birmingham, England, in terms of direct and indirect racial discrimination (1967). In the case of the former this operated in the private rented sector quite openly and blatantly through advertisements for tenants suggesting that 'coloureds' and the 'Irish' need not apply. Indirect discrimination applied in the public sector, via Birmingham housing department's 'five-year rule' which meant that only those who had been resident in the borough for five years (i.e. not recently arrived immigrants) were eligible for council housing.

Mike Davis (1990) cites two important developments which helped to shape patterns of racial segregation in Los Angeles. The first was the emergence of homeowners' associations during the First World War. The uses of restrictions and covenants enabled community builders to make possible the exclusion of all non-Caucasians (and sometimes non-Christians as well) from occupancy, except as domestic servants' (cited in Davis, 1990: 161). The effect of this was to prevent blacks from buying homes outside the ghetto (ibid.). Throughout the 1920s and 1930s, homeowners' associations such as the Anti-African Association and the White Homeowners Association, whose memberships overlapped with that of the Ku Klux Klan (ibid.: 162), conspired to confine African-Americans and Mexicans to particular districts and to exclude them from others. In fact, until whites began moving to the San Fernando valley and to the south-east of Los Angeles County, they had sought to keep blacks out of the Watts and Compton areas of Los Angeles. Crosses were burnt, riots broke out and one home was blown up in efforts to keep those areas white (ibid.: 164).

The idea of 'gated' cities in Los Angeles emerged in the aftermath of the Korean War when the town of Lakewood was allowed both to contract its own services like fire, police and library and exercise control over zoning. This meant that towns like Lakewood (and, between 1954 and 1960, twenty-six more cities followed suit) were able to restrict government use of land, keep taxes low and keep 'undesirables' out. The result was that, by providing such an attractive escape hatch from ordinary municipal citizenship, the Lakewood Plan fuelled white flight from Los Angeles, while at the same time reducing the city's capacity to deal with the needs of increasing low-income and renter populations (ibid.: 166).

Luxury enclaves like San Marino, arguably the richest and most Republican city in the US, closes its parks on weekends to exclude Latino and Asian families from adjacent neighbourhoods (ibid.: 245). Others, like Rolling Hills, built walls, literally, to provide physical, spatial insulation for middle-income earners in what used to be 'wide-open tractlands of the San Fernando Valley' (ibid.). Brian Weinstock, a leading Valley contractor, boasted of more than one hundred newly gated neighbourhoods, with an insatiable demand for more security. According to Weinstock, 'The first question out of their [the buyers'] mouths is whether there is a gated community' (cited in ibid.: 246).

The rise of gated cities for the rich emerged alongside initiatives to 'fence off' low-income areas inhabited by the poor. In Sepulveda, for example, barrio residents supported police in their efforts to seal off an area as a deterrent to drug buyers and other 'undesirables', despite the protests of younger residents who complained about the Berlin-wall quality of neighbourhood quarantines (ibid.: 248). According to Davis, 'carceral structures have become the new frontier of public architecture' (ibid.: 256).

On a smaller scale, Frank Gehry's walled compounds, enclosing the School of Dance and Gemini GEI, the Loyola Law School and the Goldwyn Library with its fifteen-foot security walls of stucco-covered concrete block, anti-graffiti barricades covered in ceramic tile, sunken entrance protected by ten-foot steel stacks and its stylised sentry boxes, 'offer powerful metaphors for the retreat from the street' (ibid.: 238). Likewise, the Watt's Centre has realized a panopticon vision with its eight-foot security fence, video cameras and lights which illuminate the centre at the flick of a switch, infra red to detect intruders who try to cling to the walls, security observatories which contain a sub-station of the Los Angeles Police Department and round-the-clock security guards (ibid.: 243).

Such surveillance and security measures have enabled the 'truly rich' to insulate themselves at home, at work and in their leisure activities against unsavoury groups. Even so-called public spaces 'are full of signs warning off the underclass' (ibid.: 226). According to Davis, 'In Los Angeles the city government has collaborated in the massive privatization of public space and subsidization of new, racist enclaves (benignly described as "urban villages")' (ibid.: 227).

The development of downtown Los Angeles is proof, Davis argues, of a conscious policy to erase all signs of its multicultural past and to make secure the financial district. This entailed cutting off all pedestrian links and not developing public transport links where they were likely to be heavily used by 'Black and Mexican poor' (ibid.: 230). Redevelopment thus reproduced spatial apartheid. Design deterrents included no public toilets, 'bumproof' benches which were designed to be so uncomfortable as to discourage the vagrants who were most likely to use them (ibid.: 233), enclosures for rubbish bins, including 'the ultimate bag-lady-proof trash cage: made of three-quarter inch steel rod with alloy locks and vicious outturned spikes to safeguard priceless moldering fish-heads and stale french fries' (ibid.).

London, too, has its fortified counterparts to the Loyola Law School in Los Angeles. Walled office complexes, private clubs, restaurants, shopping malls, roads, blocks of flats with their own underground parking and security arrangements are interspersed with the poorer districts of the city. One example is Cutler's Gardens in East London which has gone through a number of incarnations since the land on which it stands was granted to an order of knights by the king in the twelfth century and later, in colonial times, used as an industrial warehouse. It now stands at the end of a narrow lane opposite Liverpool Street Station. True to its past its gated compound encloses cobbled courtyards and, as if to remind onlookers of the ancesters of the modern security guard, there stands a larger-than-life-sized bronze statue of an armoured knight. The insurance workers who inhabit its buildings are made 'safe' by the presence of security guards and surveillance cameras at all the entrances. And, since there are cafés, dry cleaners, newsagents, gift shops and a gym within its walls there is little need to venture out except to walk the hundred or so yards to and from Liverpool Street where train links take one to the heart of rural England within an hour. At the other end of the compound the gate leads out onto Petticoat Lane, the old boundary of the City of London and the East End, an area which has thrived on myths of contamination and crime, of unwanted bodies of all varieties.[10]

Selling cities

Social polarisation and the juxtaposition of affluent and poor locales have created urban tensions which the state has sought to defuse. Multi-culturalism has been one such strategy aimed at bridging the periphery and the centre (Sassen, 1994: 121). This has taken different forms according to local political conditions and the ethnic make-up of the city. In Singapore, like many western cities, superficial symbolic differences are supported through multicultural festivals whilst efforts are made to de-racialise the political arena through a largely rhetorical commitment to formal equality. The promotion of an Asian, communitarian, capitalist work ethic has also served to undermine ideas of difference and inequalities between Malay, Chinese and Korean immigrants. Elsewhere the creation of ethnic enclaves resulted from a combination of factors, including zoning policies, employers' recruitment practices and the preferences of different immigrant groups to live in particualar areas. These older patterns of settlement have more recently been harnessed to new forms of ethnic tourism. The market-ing of 'Little Italies', 'Chinatowns', 'Irish quarters', etc., have sought to lure the international business tourist class to global cities with offers of authentic cuisine (what Grace *et al.*, 1997, refer to as culinary cosmo-multiculturalism) museums, craft shops, pubs, with the odd festival or monument as backdrop (pagodas, mosques, etc.).

In Birmingham, England, such manipulations have gone hand in hand with efforts to celebrate a white colonial history marketed around the entre-preneurial activities of the pioneers of the industrial revolution such as James Watt, the political enterprise of Joseph Chamberlain and the toil of the industrial (white) working classes, and expressed in the city's architec-ture, monuments and museums. The prosperity of Victorian Birmingham, like other British cities, was closely tied to British colonial history, a fact which sits uneasily with attempts to portray contemporary Birmingham as a culturally diverse and vibrant cosmopolitan city.

Cities are thus imagined as a result of an increasingly sophisticated marketing apparatus. How they are 'sold' depends on the prospective business and/or young, professional consumer. Ethnic quarters of the kind described above are incorporated into this wider cultural strategy. They offer a taste of diversity to an increasingly affluent and mobile class, a class Featherstone refers to as 'third cultures', by which he means 'sets of practices, bodies of knowledge, conventions and lifestyles that have developed independent of nation-states' (1995: 114). Such local offerings provide this cosmopolitan transcultural class with a taste of home, or a taste of the 'other'. Likewise, the growing reliance on heritage industries has proved an effective strategy for offsetting the impact of globalisation and the displacement of the locality by the satellite television, transnational giants and, in political terms, decision-making structures in Brussels or New York.

Predictably such places have experienced industrial decline, like Birmingham and Docklands in England and Cleveland in the US. In the case of Cleveland, this has involved transforming 'the mistake on the lake' into a commercial centre, attractive to banks, law firms and insurance companies, tempting such businesses with new lakeside leisure activities including the Rock and Roll Hall of Fame. In London the development of Docklands emerged out of an alliance between commercial and political interests which effectively excluded local residents of the area and once again sought to promote the area as attractive to private-sector investment and middle-class housing. Regeneration meant that the area (has) 'effectively been emptied of its past meaning by the LDDC [London Docklands Development Corporation], and then recomposed as an aid to financial and property speculation' (Goodwin in Kearns and Philo, 1993: 160). Such processes were made easier by the creation of enterprise zones and/or other agreements which gave significant powers to unelected bodies as well as tax concessions and regulatory exemptions (e.g. planning) for would-be private investors.

Localities are in part created by image-makers of the kind described by Davis (op. cit.: 21 ff.) working to a marketing plan, but they are also the product of strategies pursued by local people themselves. The extent to which people assimilate or adapt or resist through the reassertion of ethnic boundaries is an open question. Little Englandism expressed in the Malvinas/Falklands is one kind of cultural fundamentalism (Featherstone, op. cit.: 119). The desire to hold onto a sense of genealogy, kinship and residence is what Hall refers to as ethnicity. The reasons for maintaining such boundaries are complex. Ethnic mobilisation may be linked to business opportunities and/or the importance attached to religion and family ties. Such strategies inevitably clash in what Hall calls 'the culture wars' (1995: 199). The battle lines are thus drawn between those whose preferred option might be to accelerate processes of hybridisation and globalisation and those seeking to resist it who use ethnic or national identities as strategies for mobilising and defending interests as well as expressing self- and collective identities.

This last point reminds us that behind the gloss of the tourist brochures, festival guides, websites, Hollywood blockbusters, etc., there invariably exists a highly segmented (both racialised and feminised) city. Los Angeles is not atypical in this respect. In the nineteenth century, Chinese immigrants came with the gold rush and ended up working on the railroads and in the mines and on the fields (Ong and Blumenberg, 1996: 323). More recently African-American, Latino and other Asian immigrants have been drawn to low-wage jobs in agriculture, domestic work, manufacturing and the service sector (ibid.: 325). Of these groups only African-Americans have made some occupational progress, moving into higher-paid manufacturing and government service (ibid.). For some African-Americans this has provided opportunities to move to the affluent Ladera Heights neighbourhood (Soja, 1996: 148). But, for many, such processes have been reflected in poverty rates which are disproportionately high for Latinos and African-Americans (ibid.: 327). According to Soja, 'well over half a million (live) precariously in housing conditions little better than those of the worst Third World squatter settlements and shanty towns' (ibid.: 445–6). Elsewhere, 40 per cent of the population of Cleveland live below the poverty line and 65 per cent of the population of three black neighbourhoods on the east side is in poverty (cited in Holcomb, 1993: 141).

We have argued that the spatial proximity of rich and poor is needed because insurance companies, law firms, banks, etc., need cleaners, porters and gardeners; they also need entertainment both for their own workforce and for their international clients, Featherstone's third cultures. The rise of the ethnic quarter emerged in the 1980s as part of a marketing strategy by city governments and corporations intent on promoting themselves as commercial (instead of manufacturing) centres with amenities for a new international business tourist class.

This strategy of selling places is both selective and manipulative (Kearns and Philo, op. cit.). As we have argued, the representation of 'diversity' hides real patterns of segregation and exclusion of which gated communities are one example. It is historically selective too, since the wealth of cities like Bristol and Birmingham in England which now boast of difference were built on the profits of exclusionary practices of slavery and colonialism. Managing diversity as Ghassan Hage (1998) argues is not the same as diverse management, as local black businesses which have been subject to processes managed by local government planners, corporate finance and multinationals will testify. Hage recounts the tale of 'The Stew that Grew', a recipe which was enriched by the arrival of new immigrants to Australia but in reality was only added to at the behest of the white chef. In other words the strategy of multiculturalism is bound up with terms like tolerance, acceptance and enrichment which are all defined from a white perspective. Hage goes on to argue persuasively that diversity is always extrinsic to the 'white we' for if the 'we' were genuinely diverse then there would be no room for valuing anything other than the all-inclusive 'ourselves' – hence the limit of white multicultural discourse.

Clearly, the kinds of conditions described by Soja and Holcomb above are not the kind of multicultural realities corporate marketers are seeking to highlight. Global processes have been absorbed into the local political landscape. The local representations of diverse global interests have sometimes been harnessed to more local commercial and political interests whilst clashing with others. Oppositional strategies range from passive quiescence to direct action of varying kinds. A recurrent theme of this book has been to explore whiteness in its new global incarnations (both neo-liberal and liberal) as well as its more overtly racist manifestations. An example of the ways in which cities reflect and refract global forces through the prism of the locality can be seen in the history and recent conflicts in Spitalfields in east London, just a few hundred yards to the east of Cutler's Gardens.

According to Whimster and McGuire (forthcoming), Spitalfields is a classic example of what Robert Park *et al.* have referred to as a Zone of Transition. In their words, 'it was ever the area outside the City's walls, both Roman and Medieval . . . being without walls it was to an extent without the law' (unpublished paper, p. 11). In the nineteenth and early twentieth centuries the area became 'the conduit of the imperial economy', that is, where raw materials were brought into London's docks and turned into products for export. Successive waves of immigrants, migrants and refugees have settled in the area and worked in local manufacturing industries. In the eighteenth century, Huguenot Protestants, fleeing persecution in France, settled in the area, followed by Irish immigrants in the mid-nineteenth century, and Polish and Russian Jewish refugees in the late nineteenth century, Bangladeshis from the 1960s and most recently in the 1990s refugees from the civil war in Somalia and from eastern Europe. The markets of the area grew up around the weaving and clothing industries, as well as Spitalfields market itself which sold fruit and vegetables. More recently the area has attracted a gentrified class of artists, designers and those working in the new media industries. Like other such zones of transition it 'provides economic services to the adjacent financial services district such as printing, computing, restauranting and sex tourism' (Whimster and McGuire, op. cit.: 11).

The density of the area in terms of both people and markets in part reflects the area's proximity to, yet crucial separateness from, the City of London. It is this separateness which has recently been called into question with the gradual and in one view the seemingly inexorable eastward push of the City. The key players in the resultant conflict have included financial-services firms seeking to build purpose-built offices to the east of Bishopsgate, the City of London Corporation (and their allies), property developers seeking to exploit relatively cheap and/or abandoned sites, a local heritage lobby including gentrified homeowners who are also well connected to the property developers (at times one and the same – see Taylor, 2000) and the local Bengali community. Much of the debate in this process of urban transformation turned on what Spitalfields meant to people and whose claims on it were paramount. It thus raised important questions of identity and community.

Historically the area has proved a popular base for fascist organisations and parties. In the 1930s, for example, the confrontation between the police, Oswald Mosley's blackshirts and Jewish demonstrators, known as the battle of Cable Street, happened just a few hundred yards from Spitalfields. Less extreme but more widespread has been a strong nostalgic commitment to return to a white ('ethnic-free') community. Enoch Powell's 'rivers of blood' speech in Birmingham in the 1960s, feeding as it did fears of loss of nation and indigenous white identities, provoked a spontaneous support march of dockers from London's East End (ibid.: 75). In the 1970s the Brick Lane area (to the east of Spitalfields market) became the focus of an increasing number of violent attacks on members of the Bangladeshi community and their businesses and homes. The history of the area is also thus the history of mobilisation of alliances of anti-fascists and immigrant groups who have been forced to mobilise in defence of their communities.

More recently and at the other end of the class spectrum, communities of gentrifiers and heritage lobbyists combined to mount a campaign to defend 'the indigenous history' of the area. According to Jane Jacobs, poverty and popular perceptions of the area ensured that the local eighteenth-century Georgian architecture, which housed the studios used by Huguenots for their silk weaving, remained largely intact and, by the mid-1970s, most such buildings had been listed for conservation (1996: 76). Between 1977 and 1987 Spitalfields Historic Buildings Trust purchased forty such properties (ibid.: 79). Taking a cynical view of events, Jacobs writes, 'in the nineteenth century imperialist heroics were rewarded by territorial possession. So too in 1970s Spitalfields' (ibid.). This became the basis not only for the revalorisation of architectural Spitalfields but also for the foundations of a new 'community' of gentrifiers (ibid.: 80). One such property doubled as a museum and dwelling where 'the paying customer is taken back to the civilised everyday life of a family of Huguenot weavers' (ibid.: 81). The result of such schemes was reflected in rising property prices (houses fetching an average of £15,000 in the late 1970s were sold from anything between £140,000 and £500,000 in the late 1980s).The upward pressure on land, property and rents contributed to the closure of local manufacturing businesses and the outward movement of 'local' people. In an effort to stem this tide, the Trust restored an industrial building as a garment-manufacturing workshop to be used by those displaced as a result of the gentrification of the area (ibid.: 83). The impact of these local, seemingly benign forces (i.e. the liberal heritage lobby) has been to all but destroy the local clothes-manufacturing industry (Rhodes in Budd and Whimster, 1992).

The 1980s witnessed bigger development plans including the decision to relocate the fruit and vegetable market. In this instance the Trust saw redevelopment as an opportunity to 'rid the area of elements which contradicted its vision to transform Spitalfields into a restored monument to early Georgian London' (ibid.: 85). Opposition to the development was organised around the Campaign to Save Spitalfields from the Developers, an alliance of Labour and left activists and the community service sector. In the course of the campaign, the protesters pointed out the employment and housing implications for the local, predominantly Bengali, community (ibid.: 261). According to Jacobs, in doing so, the campaign presented a version of Bengali culture as pre-capitalist and village-based. The result was that 'Bengali residents were absorbed into an all-embracing "indigenous" narrative . . . thus incorporated in and displaced by this paternalism' (ibid.: 96).

The racialisation of the area has worked in different ways. Fascists sought to drive immigrant communities out of the area and to return it to the white working class (this latter view has been echoed by people not formally associated with fascist groups – see Taylor, 2000 and McGuire, 2000). City firms have been more successful in their efforts to drive out local Bangladeshi buisnesses and thus to redraw the eastward boundary of the City. So, too, have the heritage gentrifiers who, whatever their intentions, have also successfully forced up property values and effectively driven local businesses and families out of the area. The dilemma facing the local Bangladeshi community, like communities elsewhere, has been to weigh up the possible advantages to be gained from temporary alliances with groups like the heritage lobby or the benefits from the adoption of corporate labels ('Banglatown', 'Chinatown', etc.) versus the drawbacks, e.g. being 'spoken for', manipulated and ultimately marginalised with the consequence of ending up in a similar or weaker position than at the outset.

Interdependency and eco-disaster

This chapter has reviewed the diverse outcomes of global interdependence at global and local levels. We have argued that continuing inequalities of access to global resources and local entitlement reveal the racial divisions of an otherwise interconnected world. On the one hand, intensified global networks threaten to collapse boundaries of all kinds – racial, economic, bodily. On the other, those attempting to cling to the privilege of their racialised class position find new and innovative ways of reconstructing protective boundaries. Once again, race and class are remade through the battle for resources.

However, the global is more than the simply economic, and the complex interdependence of our world has been more poignantly recognised through other aspects of materiality altogether. The major lesson of our globalised

existence is that the deepening of capitalist integration has many unantici-
pated effects which rework the experience of the body for many different
people. Globalisation has reminded us again of our shared materiality and
of the strange vulnerabilities of the organic body. It is only recently, as we
come to appreciate the environmental consequences of the profit motive on
a global scale, that we can once again imagine the ravages of class relations
as an attack on the body. The varied processes of globalisation reveal class
as the most embodied of processes – not only marked by the incarceration
and disposability of some bodies, but also by the hunger and disease of
others. This chapter has outlined some areas in which racialised class
relations are remade through diffuse means. The argument has been that
the diffusion of economic relations does not detract from their bite, or
from the simultaneous deepening of racism and class exploitation.

The most interesting writing on class does not only berate others for
having forgotten the concept. The most interesting writing tries to think
afresh about the manner in which economic arrangements place people as
actors and agents, and suggests that different economic structures may
throw up not only new and even more unpleasant forms of exploitation
and inequality, but also different kinds of subject and agency (Aronowitz
and Cutler, 1998). The experience of physical deprivation pushes people
into particular forms of agency – if not into the history-making role of
irresolvable contradiction, at least into situations which are unsustainable
because the body has some limits. If the processes of globalisation extract
profit through the machineries of racialisation so ruthlessly that people are
left with nothing – then many die or something changes. A new politics of
class must address the possibility of this change.

None of the above has been an advocation of the real new site of struggle.
Rather the suggestion is that the diffuse economic effects of globalisation
can restructure a number of everyday areas of life, and that the trouble
that comes from that must breed its own resistance. Unlike a previous
generation of commentaries, there is no suggestion here that the outcome
is decided already. Class does not swing in as the answer to all our prayers,
because now the formative agents of history are in town. In fact, this
account of racialised class formation is far more pessimistic, identifying the
workings of a global economy without a clear idea of how people organise
against its ravages. However, ultimately, without an account of this
racialised class system the racist nature of economic hardship remains
incomprehensible – and this volume argues for this as the bottom line, at
least an openness to understanding what is going on in our world.

Notes

1 'Brown Challenges West to Write-off Poor Nation Loans', *Independent*,
 22 December 1999: 987; Bob Geldof, 'I Didn't Believe it Would Ever
 Happen. I was Wrong', *Independent on Sunday*, 19 December 1999: 1281.

2 'Summers Urges IMF to Focus on Preventing Crises', *Financial Times*, 15 December 1999: 538.

3 'A New Mandate for the IMF', *Financial Times*, 15 December 1999: 1118.

4 Oliver Morgan, 'Biotech's Gene Blueprint', *Observer*, 16 April 2000: 4.

5 Oliver Morgan, 'Appliance of Gene Science', *Observer*, 28 May 2000: 2.

6 'Seeds of Doubt', *Guardian*, 2 February 2000: 4.

7 'GM Crops: Grain Damage', *Guardian*, 12 April 2000: 4.

8 Paul Brown and Sarah Boseley, 'Medicine's Over-performed Miracle', *Guardian*, 23 April 1998: 5.

9 Sarah Boseley, 'TB on the Rampage Again', *Guardian*, 19 March 1998: 2.

10 The idea of the gated, walled compound has its parallel in package holidays in the tropics. West European tourists visit countries in the Caribbean, Africa and Asia only to experience these regions from behind the gated enclosure of a multinational chain hotel with its private beach, shopping facilities and organised tours, all of which aim to protect the tourist (and their money) from the local economy as well as limit interaction with local people. The odd trip to the local market for gifts or to restaurants, bars and night clubs for entertainment of different varieties may be the limit of the tourist's contact with life outside the compound.

Chapter 6

Diasporas, population scares and new aesthetics

In this volume we have collected together a range of recent debate, from accounts of global economies to analyses of identity formation. This chapter pulls together a number of these earlier themes in order to examine contemporary frameworks of racialised anxiety. Our contention is that new fears around the form of ethnic allegiance, the extent and location of population movements and the ecological consequences of population growth can all be regarded as symptoms of a globalising culture of racism. Alongside these scare stories, global forces also create fresh pleasures for the consumer with ethnically marked products. The chapter suggests that the unspoken connections between the fears and pleasures of global racialisation indicate new trends in racist culture.

Forming allegiance around faith, tribe, religion

The chapter reviews some competing ways of thinking about identity and its relation to diaspora. In the course of this discussion we link debates about diaspora and its cultural productions to issues of migration and population control. While the term 'diaspora' has been used to describe the experience of movement and to analyse the social formations that occur from this movement, the terms 'immigration' and, to a lesser extent, 'migration' have been addressed primarily as problems (Gabriel, 1998). This chapter seeks to make links between these two areas of debate and to suggest that there are connections between the development of new fears about population levels and new opportunities through new cultural forms. As part of this, we look again at the impact of ecological thinking on debates about population movement and control. This anxiety about how many people the world holds, and where in the world they are held, easily becomes a fear that these hordes of people are coming here, to live in the affluent world. Diaspora may describe the contradictory and productive experience of movement, but population scares indicate the continuing defensive response of western nations when it seems that people may be moving towards them. This chapter tries to register these two moments – population movement as cultural enrichment and population movement as a threat to resources. Ultimately, we argue, both moments rely on the fiction of race as an absolute divider of people and represent yet another example of global integration remaking ethnic divisions.

However, before this we begin with a discussion about the changing role of faith in wider social formations. Although writing about population movement and diasporic cultures has not usually focused explicitly on issues of belief and religion, we want to argue that shifts in global faith cultures are deeply connected to the development of global and diasporic consciousness. On the one hand, faith can offer an alternative globality, both a network of connection across the world and a competing account of how globalisation works. On the other, new variants of faith cultures emerge from the processes of population shift, people amalgamate different influences and adapt to new circumstances. The initial focus on issues of allegiance leads to a discussion of the concept of diaspora, because it is in diaspora that these questions arise. This chapter attempts to register both positive and negative accounts of population movement through an analysis of debates about population and ecology and a revisiting of debates about global culture. In order to place this discussion in the context of how people imagine their identities and allegiances, we begin with the contention that we live in a secular world and examine the limits of this conception.

The view that industrialisation brought about a decline in religious values was widespread amongst sociology's early thinkers. Secularisation was thus seen as an important expression of modernity (see e.g. Cox, 1971). Only recently has this view been challenged and academics forced to acknowledge the continuing significance and revival of older religions as well as the proliferation of new religious cults and movements. This new religiosity has been explained in terms of migration (Barker, 1995), the role of media and new information technologies in promoting religious values worldwide (e.g. tele-evangelism) and the revival of various core fundamentalist belief systems. These processes take place against a background of growing scepticism with regard to science and technology to answer the world's problems, a moral vacuum left by the end of the Cold War and the failure of different political systems to eradicate poverty, and, in the West, a crisis of national identity (see e.g. Bruce, 1996; Kurtz, 1995; Heelas, 1998). Faith cultures emerge as the popular response to seemingly incomprehensible global processes. As we have argued in previous chapters, globalisation impacts on the everyday lives of many people in catastrophic ways. The renewal of religion is one manner in which ordinary people attempt to make sense of these changes and construct an alternative world-view. Perhaps, inevitably, this populist take-up of faith mirrors the racial divisions and hierarchies of the globalisation it seeks to resist.

The racialisation of religion has taken many forms. Most notable amongst these has been the revival of the religious right in the US and the close affinity between Christian fundamentalist groups and groups on the far right whose political agenda is white supremacist (see e.g. Aho, 1990).

Its revival has been attributed to a number of factors including: a crisis of national identity (Barnet and Cavanagh, 1994) fuelled by the loss of the war in Vietnam in the 1970s (Gibson, 1994); the questionable moral role played by US governments in Latin America in the 1970s and 1980s; the fall of the Berlin wall and the thawing of the Cold War leaving the US bereft of an obvious demon on which to build its collective self-image; the rise of the internet in the mid-1990s as a means of transnational communication between Christian groups with affiliations to the far right; and finally to the third millennium itself which took apocalyptic forecasting (based on obscure readings of biblical texts) to new heights. Overall the forces of white Christianity form part of a backlash seeking a return to allegedly traditional American values, notably a society in which white, heterosexual norms prevailed, where federal government left frontiersmen to make their own laws, and minorities, i.e. indigenous native Americans, were eliminated by means of genocide. Inevitably, then, fundamentalist Christianity has remained at odds with both federal government and the liberal media establishment which it saw as representing 'special' interests, whether these be defined by ethnicity or sexuality or political outlook or all three. Such developments led to a small but culturally significant tendency within US Christianity which has articulated faith as the basis of a new politics of whiteness (Dyer, 1998). This is one manifestation of the new 'fundamentalist' approaches to faith that emerge in an era of global flux.

Despite the many accounts which suggest that religion is no longer a significant force in social relations, alongside the decline of certain forms of worship, other faiths have rediscovered the ability to inform people's wider social understandings. For minority communities facing persecution in a variety of locations, faith has re-emerged as the vehicle to articulate political claims and community allegiance. This is happening not only through the much publicised growth of populist Islam in many places and in many forms, but also in the return of younger people to more traditional faith forms in other communities (Bhatt, 1997; Castells, 1997; Kiely and Marfleet, 1998). Alongside this, we see a renewed will to place issues of faith at the centre of the national politics of many regions of the poor world.

This is taking place at a time when many are heralding the crumbling of national identities – and perceiving a re-alliance around region (Ohmae, 1995). In part, the re-emergence of faith runs parallel to these supranational alliances, representing a language of allegiance that straddles national boundaries. The comparative vibrancy of faith cultures in a time of loosening ties and uncertain boundaries means that religion has become a key aspect of diasporic cultures. Rediscovering and sharing practices of worship emerges as an unexpectedly popular and accessible tie to homeland and community. The conscious adoption of traditional cultural rituals operates as a resistance to western cultures which offer secular modernity as the only route to freedom. As we have discussed, many diasporic peoples have encountered this secular modernity as violence and degradation – the

rebirth of tradition refuses the West's claims of moral superiority and re-
forges the imaginative link with fellow believers all over the world.
Although it is beyond the scope of this work to construct a more sustained
account of the role of faith in diasporic communities, we wish to acknowledge this key insight – that populations in movement may refuse commodified progress on western terms, and instead negotiate their own route
between tradition and modernity.

Debates about diaspora

The unpredictable impact of faith on political identity and allegiance cuts to
the heart of debates around diaspora. These questions have suffused the
discussions of this book – what does it mean when populations move and
are remade in this movement? What identities, cultures and politics are
made in these dynamic encounters? Much recent debate has focused on the
conscious experience of being in movement – naming this cultural moment
'diaspora'. Although we will go on to suggest that this term misses some
key characteristics of population shift, first we must review the emergence
of the term.

The concept of diaspora was both revived and expanded in the new
discourses of ethnicity in the 1990s for reasons which, in part, date back
to the anti-colonial independence struggles in the 1950s and 1960s. Post-
coloniality brought about a shift in global power as well as a shift in
consciousness, a process (still ongoing) in which Britain's stature began to
shrink in accordance with its real geographical size and declining economic
significance. During this period, i.e. post Second World War, what had
been assumed to be characteristics traditionally associated with white
English culture were increasingly called into question by the settlement of
immigrants, often UK citizens, from the Caribbean, Indian sub-continent
and Africa. Added to both these political and demographic questions, the
rapid expansion of telecommunications technologies on a mass scale from
the 1950s and the arrival of the internet in the 1990s created yet more
opportunities for developing new transnational relationships and communities. Diaspora became the term to capture those conditions and experiences as well as those communities caught up in these changes. In other
words, the traditional meaning of diaspora, that is, the scattering of peoples
of a particular faith or background, has been expanded to refer to a mix or
fusion of cultures which express new ethnic identities and which cut across
as well as articulate with such social factors as class, region, age, gender
and sexuality.

A number of leading 'diasporan' intellectuals have helped to rework the
concept, each offering a somewhat different emphasis. For example, in his
book *The Black Atlantic*, Paul Gilroy (1993a) uses the term diaspora to
reject what he refers to as ethnic absolutism, that is the idea that ethnic

groups (majority or minority) can be defined according to a set of fixed and mutually exclusive characteristics. In his study of late-nineteenth-century and early-twentieth-century intellectuals he demonstrates the ways in which 'African-American' thought drew on as well as contributed to so-called 'western' culture. Each tradition was implicated in the other, thus any talk of a unitary ethnic culture is inaccurate. For Gilroy, the concept of diaspora captures the means by which such ideas and knowledges are fused. Likewise, Clifford (1994) and Stuart Hall (1990) use diaspora to highlight the idea of identity formation and the processes, experiences, practices and aesthetics associated with such cultural shifts. Migration is one important factor in explaining changing ethnic boundaries in so far as it creates opportunities for new social hybrids and syncretic cultural forms to emerge which cut across old ethnic divisions. Avtar Brah (1996) and Rey Chow (1993) are also interested in exploring diaspora both as a condition and/or an experience and in Brah's case, in particular, the ways in which diasporan identities enmesh with other sources of identity.

Besides migration itself, new patterns of mass consumption as well as cultural products have become associated with new sources of ethnic difference. In an interesting piece on hyphenised identities, Ayse Calgar examines the importance of consumption as a source of identity and the ways in which it forges new links across old ethnic boundaries. Ethnographic accounts of young people by David Parker (1995), Roger Hewitt (1986) and Les Back (1996) illustrate the ways in which new identities are built around such things as music, fashion, language, television and the internet. The strength of such studies lies in their emphasis on the cultural experiences and practices of young people as elicited through participant observation, rather than just relying on secondary sources and/or quantitative data.

Robin Cohen (1997), on the other hand, is less concerned with the diasporic condition or experience and more with particular migratory movements and the different reasons for migration in the first place. For example, some diasporas result from persecution, others from economic hardship, whilst others from opportunities to be reunited with family and friends.

These ambiguities have fuelled a number of critical responses to the concept of diaspora, one of the most cogent of which has been offered by Floya Anthias (1998). One difficulty with the term, she argues, is that however much its aim is to capture difference and change, at some point it inevitably relies on some notion of origin and that such origins are somehow the foundation of identities. Notions of Asian, African, Jewish or Islamic diasporas all, by definition, attach importance to the source of the diaspora, whether this is defined in ethnic, national or religious terms. The concept thus entails a primary attachment to origin, however much experiences change or fuse as a result of migration.

Secondly, although the concept is said to offer greater opportunity for analysing complex processes of identity formation, in practice this has not happened. In practice, according to Anthias, despite its avowed commitment to complexity and formal commitment to other sources of identity, in substantive terms diaspora has invariably eschewed an analysis of gender and class differences. Simply rejecting the view that ethnic groups can be understood in terms of a set of fixed characteristics, associated with such factors as language, religion, diet and custom, does not in itself guarantee an analysis more attuned to gender and class differences.

Thirdly, according to Anthias, the term serves to gloss over very real political differences between and amongst diasporic groups. For example, diaspora might be used to mobilise around a global allegiance to conservative, religious forces and/or to backward, reactionary political movements as well as to progressive cultural/intellectual aesthetic ones.

Overall, Anthias offers a powerful critique of the concept of diaspora which reminds us how new terminologies can often reproduce old problems. Nevertheless, the term has captured experiences and influences otherwise lost in the overly determined discourses of nation, race and old-style ethnic difference. And although the term itself does not guarantee complexity or particular political outcomes, it can offer ammunition in what Trin Minh-Ha calls a verbal struggle (1991). Its success, like other concepts, depends as much on its effects as on its intellectual coherence. Anthias is right in our view to use a political benchmark to unpack the concept but by this token the term would merit support in some instances and not in others, depending on when and how it is taken up. In what follows we shall explore the ways in which this new discourse of ethnicity underpinned by the concept of diaspora and tied to a new discourse of globalisation has begun to inform our understanding of ethnicity and social divisions. In particular, we are concerned to place these ideas about the empowerment of diasporic experience in the context of population scares as a threat to western privilege.

Migration and (over-)population

The debates around the idea of diaspora take place against a backdrop of long-standing discussion about the implications of population movement and growth. Although the softer edge of social science has developed (recently) a language which understands the movement of people as a lived experience, encompassing hard material imperatives and contradictory cultural stories, the longer debate about population movements has viewed moving masses as a problem to be contained (Miles, 1993). The concerns about who will produce and who will consume, and the excessive anxiety that racial privilege will be eroded through sexual temptation, can be understood as variations of population scare. Each racist mythology centres on an anxiety about the numbers and location of the racialised other. The discussion that follows revisits the terms of this earlier debate and suggests that old fears of population movement live on in new guises.

Debates around race and ethnicity have long taken population movement to be a formative event in concepts of difference and boundary between communities. While it is not quite the case that 'race' is taken to be born through the movement of populations, the history of 'race' as a concept has been closely linked to wider histories of population movement (Goldberg, 1993). In the most orthodox account, it is the movement of people in itself which gives rise to the various fictions of 'race'. In this account, it is contact with unfamiliar populations – through travel, trade and plunder – which fuels the language of race in European cultures. Historical accounts of the concept of race have taken as their framework the era of European expansion – with travel revealing a varied world population, the development of trade requiring a hierarchical classificatory system and a European culture steeped in Christian in-fighting looking for more others to mark the boundaries of salvation (Said, 1978; Kabbani, 1994). More recent writing has concentrated heavily on the development of multi-ethnic societies through population movements of various kinds – from the forced migration of enslaved peoples to the economic migrancy of many formerly colonised peoples to the desperate and barely planned movements of those fleeing war, violence, natural disaster. At bottom, reading the literature leads us to believe that race only becomes an issue, perhaps only comes into being, when somebody leaves home.

In the light of this, the era of globalisation is characterised as a new era of population movements – and this is the reason why the proliferation of literature on interethnic relations develops. In fact, much of this literature is an attempt to understand and manage the crises of the new and deeply interconnected world. Once again, the sociology of race and ethnicity portrays newcomers as the problem demanding a solution, and we see fresh versions of all too familiar narratives about the relations between host and migrants, majorities and minorities, citizens and refugees or guests or illegals. Rather than revisit these debates here, this section seeks to review the role of population movement in contemporary ideas of race and ethnicity, and to suggest that the figure of migration, if not the reality, still shapes the spectre of race in our world.

In parallel with these debates about racialised cultures and the experience of population movement, another more extensive and more scary debate has been going on. Population has become an object of study and anxiety in itself – with much debate focused on the imminent dangers of having too many people in the world (McMichael, 1993). Although an abundance of people could be viewed as a positive asset – with more people to do more work, produce more things and make more value – the expansion of the world's population has long been a cause of policy concern. Of course, these debates need not necessarily become racialised. It is self-evidently the case that the world is limited (in ways we have only recently come to understand) and that population growth without end cannot be sustained. For this reason, the move back to older versions of racialised fear stories seems worrying – both an indication that we have not moved on from this phobia of proliferating people and a sign that the more substantial issues around population growth cannot be addressed.

Although debates about the over-population of the planet use a rhetoric of whole-planet concerns, the danger of over-population is seen to stem from poor and dark-skinned regions of the world. Population scares are articulated on the assumption that the lifestyle and survival of western peoples are under attack from less deserving and burgeoning populations of the poor world. However much concern is expressed about the limited resources of the globe, the real concern is too often the threat of a limit to western living (Athanasiou, 1996). Rather than the problem being too many people in the world, the problem is that some parts of the world are producing people at such a rate as to endanger the living standards of those who live in other more privileged parts of the world.

Any doubt about this can be allayed by looking at the various solutions which have been proposed (by the West) to the world's population crisis. Population control is a problem only for the poor world – and the solution has always been focused on remaking the fertility of the poor world in the image of the rich (Mies and Shiva, 1993). Famously, and suspiciously, these solutions have advocated more contraception, better advice about birth control and incentives to have fewer children, and have led, on occasion, to forced sterilisation, punishment for having too many children and a terrorisation of ordinary people through state policing of fertility. More recently, and benignly, the solutions have stretched to include a concern for the general living standards in poor nations, access to education, the social status of women and the promotion of consumer lifestyles through choosing smaller families (McMichael, op. cit.: 120–2). The common thread between old and new styles of population-scare talk is the over-arching will to limit certain (dark-skinned) populations, as opposed to population per se.

Alongside the barely hidden fear that it is some sorts of people who produce too many children in the world, western fears about over-population reveal another familiar anxiety of the privileged – that the less privileged will appear to demand their share. Although little explicit connection is made between the various anxious discussions about numbers of people and the equally anxious debates about where people are and where they should be allowed to go, both sets of anxieties chart similar stories of the rich world under attack.

A great deal has been written already about the metaphors of xenophobia and the psychic drama of anti-immigrant hysteria (Mercer, 1994; Sibley, 1995; Gabriel, op. cit.). It is enough to say that those tropes of engulfment and swamping, faceless hordes and loss of individuation, are all articulated around a sense of excessive numbers of alien and unwelcome people. While one logic of racism regards the slightest contact as a source of contamination, another sees each incursion by the unwanted other as the first of an endless stream. Fears about migrants almost always are articulated as fears about the numbers of people involved – if not yet, soon, unless we stem the flow now. It does not take a huge leap of imagination to see western concerns about the growing populations of the poor world as yet another fear of immigration. The more poor people there are, the more likely it is that some will make the move towards the rich world – as the poor world becomes more desperate, the poor will find more ingenious and reckless methods of migration, moving towards survival however they can.

Once again, the crux of the issue is the maintenance of privilege, a privilege which we want to argue is highly racialised, although racialised in the different register of global relations. When the extensive discussions about population growth and impending global disaster occur, it is never said openly that the disaster is conceived as the end of western lifestyles. However, even a cursory examination of the terms of the debate reveals that the point at issue is western privilege. The poor of the poor world have remained painfully impoverished and numerous for many years already – yet this long-standing state of almost living, almost surviving, with so many of the world's population living short and brutal lives, is not what the phrase population crisis describes. Despite the half-truths of common-sense development talk – hunger is caused by too many people, not issues of access and distribution; health suffers from over-crowding, not a long-term lack of an array of basic living standards; national infra-structures crumble under the weight of too many people, not the accumu-lated mismanagement of larger histories – the population problems of the poor world are not a crisis in themselves. Crisis only threatens when popu-lation growth is seen to have an impact upon the living standards of the rich world. There is no question, after all, that global resources, however limited, are the rightful property and entitlement of the inhabitants of the rich world – for which we can read, the rightful inhabitants of the rich world, the light-skinned descendants of north Europeans. Crisis hits only when the proliferation of people in the poor world begins to impact upon the chosen lifestyles of the rich. The next section considers the role of a rhetoric of ecology in the articulation of this crisis.

Sustainability and new populations

In recent years a concern for the state of the ecosystem – expressed variously as a local or a global issue, an interest in local wildlife, the ozone layer, recycling or sustainable agriculture, as well as a whole host of other targets, only occasionally articulated against each other – has entered mainstream parlance in many places (Castells, op. cit.; Shiva, 1989; Mies and Shiva, op. cit.). Although these popular concerns have been evaded by most of the globe's wealth-owners, ecology has taken on the aura of holiness for a secular society, an unarguable good on which all right-thinking people agree (Athanasiou, op. cit.). In this, the ascendance of ecological politics resembles the resurgence of faith cultures. Ecology also proposes an alternative global consciousness, based on inescapable interdependence and shared vulnerability. In some incarnations, ecological politics can form alliances with local groups in order to organise against the excesses of a global free market (as in the demonstrations against the World Trade Organisation in Seattle). However, when transplanted to older debates about population, the rhetoric of ecology can augment the politics of new global racisms. This section examines ecological debates around population and suggests that even the absolute feel-good of ecology can veil a covert return of familiar old-style racisms, particularly when coupled with the rhetoric of the West's fears of global population growth.

In more recent times, anxieties about too many people in the world have been subsumed into more general worries about the future of a limited world which is being consumed too quickly. In popular discourse this ecological account has overtaken the fear of burgeoning population as western horror story number one. Now we understand that the promises of endless economic expansion as a route to prosperity for all can never be fulfilled. This most central tenet of optimistic modernity is, of course, no longer sustainable. However painfully and partially, recent decades of lobbying, research and all-too-tangible climate change impress on all but the most hardened green-resister that there is a limit to the current habits and plans of humanity. Given that most of the world is still waiting to reach prosperity through the western route of industrialisation and reckless over-use of natural resources, this realisation of global overload has been somewhat disheartening. After all, what other way of reaching decent and enjoyable living standards for the many has anyone imagined? Even the various attempts at planned economy have assumed that industrial growth will underpin the pleasures of more equitable distribution (Kiely and Marfleet, op. cit.). If consumer culture through industrialisation is not available to all, then there clearly is a limit to progress. And if there is a limit to progress, if we are not going to learn how to make enough of everything for everyone to have plenty, then redistribution is the only promise of a better life left to most of the world. Of course, there is nothing the rich world fears more than the threat of redistribution. Fortunately, the unarguable good of ecological concern enters to veil this selfish self-interest.

In its most populist incarnations, the rhetoric of the ecology movement can appear misanthropic. Among the serious arguments about the future of the planet, and the proposals for slowing this hurtle into self-destruction, there is a deep-seated assumption that it is people that are the problem. Others have commented on the modern-day Malthusianism of too much green rhetoric – as if the excess of inconvenient people will right itself through their early deaths, allowing the earth to reach equilibrium again (L.Young, 1996). For our purposes, the significant elision is between the dangers of more people living unsustainable lifestyles and more people per se.

Of course, these assumptions cannot escape the implication that some people are more of a problem than others. As with other versions of Malthusian thinking, the notion that some people are dispensable, because that is the way the world works, is not so far from the idea that some people are worth less than others and are therefore dispensable, because that is the way the world works. Although this is rarely spoken explicitly, the macabre glee in the face of impending doom can be enabled by the racial otherness of those about to die. However quickly Armageddon may be coming, we all know that it is coming more quickly to some than to others.

Ghassan Hage suggests that this springs from a fantasy of white nationhood which regards nature as the property of white nationals alone.

> [I]t is mainly nationalist ecology that often operates the fusion between the national and the natural fantasy, seeing the nation as both a social and a natural domesticated space. In such a space, otherness exists as a social and/or a natural value for the domesticator. Nature is perceived as a national value that needs to be exploited and/or saved, depending on how it is classified by the domesticators.
>
> (Hage, op. cit.: 168)

Hage suggests that ecology-talk for white nations assumes white ownership of the natural, in all its many splendoured forms. There may be a crisis, but it is a crisis about the use of white people's inalienable rights and effects. Everyone else is just another part of this landscape – a potential spoiler of the environment or another aspect of valuable biodiversity, but always an object in a field surveyed and controlled by whiteness. However phantasmic this may be, the belief in white ownership explains the skewed agendas of much popular ecology-talk.

This is the case even though racist versions of ecological thinking acknowledge that it is the rich (coded white) world which consumed the vast majority of the earth's resources. On every scale of consumption, it is the already rich world that wastes, over-uses and squanders, with seemingly little thought of the consequences. We see this in the international agreements to cut carbon emissions and to develop global strategies towards sustainability – at every point it is acknowledged that it is the developed nations which have led the world to this pass. Yet despite this recognition, the crisis talk only becomes truly hot in relation to the potential threat of the becoming-more-affluent world. The real monsters in this horror story are the newly industrialising nations and the big emerging markets – those places that threaten to remake themselves in the economic image of the old industrialised world and replicate all their bad habits many times over. Once again, this is articulated as a fear of population – the poor world is a problem because it produces too many people, but when this world becomes a little less poor, these people become another kind of problem because of their numbers. In the end, sustainability is imagined as the ability of the West to sustain privileged lifestyles by denying these wasteful habits to others.

We do not wish to suggest that this has been the only impact of ecological thinking on popular political consciousness. Much of the most dynamic activism in pursuit of social justice of recent years has come through eco-logical understandings of economic relations. However, without the con-textual attention to global economy, ecology can become another terrain on which people compete for entitlement – and the realisation of scarcity can reignite white fright again.

Local cultures and ecological arguments

This relearning of white fright on a global scale returns in struggles over the meaning of the local. The scarcity of global resources easily slips into an anxiety about loss of privilege on your own doorstep – the over-arching fear that there is not enough to go around reanimates the culture of racial terror. This section explores the ways in which localism is celebrated as a resistance to global eco-fear. Previous parts of this book discuss the impact of globalisation on local economies and mobilisation of ethnicity within local responses to global forces. Here we wish to focus on the notion of local cultures being lost to global processes. This idea that the authenticity of local cultures is being lost to the forces of globalisation can appear in a number of guises. On the one hand, critiques of tourism and cultural imperialism argue that resource-hungry parts of the world lose themselves and their traditional ways to the call of the market (Mies and Shiva, op. cit.). On the other, exclusionary racists use the language of roots and authenticity to argue that their locality must be defended as theirs alone (Daniels, 1997). In both instances, the local is figured as an almost lost space of nostalgia – a place without social division or contradiction, unified through organic connections not social relations. The global smashes in to ruin all this and to mark the fall into the ways of the market.

Of course, there is a sense in which local cultures of many kinds are disrupted and spoiled by the processes of globalisation. In many cases, this spoiling takes the form of a deepening of social divisions, of hyper-exploitation and increasing poverty – as we have discussed in previous chapters. Here we want to look at the different forms of racialised work performed by the idea of locality in the era of globalisation. In particular, we discuss the idea of a local ecology to be protected against the encroach-ment of global forces. Our interest is in the manner that the injunction to 'think global, act local' is mobilised for racialised ends.

The local has long held the status of absolute feel-good in accounts of spatial relations – local is the place of community and transparent social relations, a place where people are bonded through proximity, or even through nature. Despite the romanticism of this view, a whole range of responses to the threats of globalisation have taken the local as their focus and rallying point. Resistance to the homogenising forces of the global has been articulated as a wish to retain the values and identities of local communities – because in the local, people have an identity with their place and a right to remain the same (R. Williams, 1983). As suggested above, this argument can be used by both left and right, with occasionally scary and violent outcomes.

These debates about the various resistances of the local to global forces often forget the longer history of global encroachment into the lives of some communities. Long before the new technologies of media imperialism and communications networks, European expansion reworked other people's localities for its own globalising ends. Among the longest-standing attacks on local cultures by global forces has been the dispossession and genocide of the native peoples of the Americas and Australasia. It is now widely acknowledged that European incursion into the Americas, Australia and New Zealand led to the displacement and genocide of the indigenous populations of these areas, not by accident but in order to create the optimum conditions for white domination.

> In the Caribbean, Newfoundland, and Tasmania all but a remnant of the resident aboriginal peoples had been murdered. In practice, the choice between killing and 'a temperate line of conduct' was often beyond the control of colonial administrators. As settlement expanded, aboriginal peoples were deprived of their lands and conflict was inevitable. However, once a sufficient number of aboriginal peoples had been killed (i.e., enough to ensure British dominance), a set of policies based on a 'temperate line of conduct' frequently became possible. These policies relied upon a dominant military or civil police force for their ultimate enforcement and were aimed at managing aboriginal peoples by controlling their land use, settlements, government, and daily life. They also called for the introducing of aboriginal peoples to missionaries.
>
> (Armitage, 1995: 5)

In the later part of the twentieth century, we have seen First Nation people beginning to use the machinery of colonial administration itself as a route towards community reparation. There have been attempts to revisit the original 'treaties' between European settlers and indigenous populations as a method of reasserting entitlement through the language of European-framed law (Hazlehurst, 1995; Pritchard, 1998). Alongside these struggles, we see a resurgence of support for the rights and claims of indigenous peoples through an interest in conservation. Although this may appear to be another echo of the new exoticism that pervades globalised culture and another example of a fantasy of white subjecthood that views the world as its terrain and other peoples as movable pawns in the landscape, ecology does open fresh possibilities for the struggles of indigenous peoples. Although there is a history of using ideas of conservation as yet another method of dispossessing indigenous populations and their claims to sovereignty and self-determination, or of attempting to freeze indigenous lifestyles as part of the timeless display of national parks and protected areas, the ongoing debate about what it means to sustain biodiversity opens the possibility of recognising the rights of indigenous populations (Stevens, 1997).

Stevens argues that changing awareness of the role of indigenous populations in maintaining both the inhabitability and biodiversity of their homelands enhances the chances of indigenous rights gaining recognition on what are, still now, European terms.

> Protected areas in which indigenous peoples achieve recognition of settlement and subsistence rights and have at least some voice through consultation in resource management and protected area management may continue to be the most common form of indigenously inhabited protected areas and the approach most popular with central governments. Co-management and indigenous management, however, are likely to be increasingly important in coming years in the global protected area system, and represent the most effective means of truly building conservation on indigenous knowledge and indigenous rights.
>
> (Stevens, op. cit.: 62)

For the much abused indigenous peoples of conservation zones, ecology-talk can translate community interests into the more appealing global interests of sustainability. At issue is the extent to which we view some fantasies of the environment as matters of national or community heritage, and others as more global resources, whether they are to be saved or squandered. Other writers have commented on the conservative politics of heritage and the construction of new 'traditions' which privilege dominant populations at the expense of racialised groups (Wright, 1985). At issue in the concept of heritage is: who has the right to decide? Although First Nation peoples are using the machinery of colonial occupation to challenge their long dispossession, as always it is the resource-heavy who can define and defend their heritage most effectively. As a result, the beauty and leisure spots of the rich world can be (partially) protected through an appeal to ecological heritage, while the biodiversity of the poor world is more likely to cave in under the pressures of economic imperatives. As Ghassan Hage suggests, once this white right to determine the proper business and use of national terrain is established, the desire to safeguard heritage by keeping local ecologies clean of outside contaminations, such as landscape-altering processes and people, becomes indistinguishable from the other good and sustainable approaches to nature.

Ultimately, we must imagine a way of including the inevitable movement of people in our ideas of healthy localities. Whatever the various exclusionary nostalgias at work in fictions of local ownership and belonging, there can be no return to the pristine locality untainted by newcomers. If such places ever existed, they do not exist now. Instead, we all live journeying lives and come to inhabit localities through a nexus of economic need and diasporic shift. Rather than celebrate the authenticity of shorter journeys – so that village to city in one country makes you a native, while village to city across countries makes you a migrant – the local is better celebrated as the space in which social relationships may defy the logic of the global, not because these local relationships are organic and outside history, but precisely because they are created through the different histories of the local.

The next section examines some instances of these local articulations and argues that globalisation has caused us all to become marked by the cultures of population movement. As Gilroy has argued, the culture of the West is permeated with the traces of the colonised and enslaved and dispersed others who supplement western identity.

Diaspora aesthetics and minority cultural production

A range of debates in recent social theory has suggested that cultural production serves as a key site of identity formation and performance – and this suggestion has held particular resonance in relation to diasporic peoples.

Previous orthodoxies have held that culture and representation are domains of the dominant – particularly high cultural forms. Access to these routes to self-articulation have been regarded as a manifestation of cultural capital, and often as access to hard cash. A host of cultural and literary critics have questioned the structure of cultural values which mirror capital values. A possible outcome of these discussions is a disparagement of all cultural production – because all this culture can do no more than document barbarism. Against this, diaspora communities have adapted these forms for their own ends and made culture their space of articulation.

New ethnicities

In 1988 Stuart Hall published a paper called 'New Ethnicities' in which he registered important cultural changes particularly amongst young people of different ethnic backgrounds who had been born and were growing up in Britain. The use of the term ethnicity was something of a surprise at the time to academics and activists who had come to associate the term with academics and policy-makers who (1) wanted to avoid talking about racism and (2) attributed fixed often stereotypical 'ethnic characteristics' to different groups on the basis of religion, diet, family norms, etc. New ethnicities were not defined in terms of religion, diet, etc., but on the contrary were based on the idea that cultures were changing and that new hybrid or syncretic forms were emerging amongst younger people whose family backgrounds were different but whose cultural terrain was defined by class, gender, age and locality as much as by 'ethnic background'. 'New' ethnicities described dynamic, mixed cultural formations which, moreover, could accommodate racism within the range of possible experiences. In other words the revived concept of ethnicity was not an alternative to a discourse on racism but merely acknowledged that peoples' experiences and identities were varied and complex and could not be reduced to racism or its effects.

The diversity of new syncretic cultural forms was testimony to these changes. Hanif Kureishi's screenplay for *My Beautiful Laundrette* (Dir. Stephen Frears, 1985) and his novel, *The Buddha of Suburbia* (1997), Gurinda Chadha's *Bhaji on the Beach* (1994), Isaac Julien's *Young Soul Rebel* (1976) and BBC TV's *Goodness Gracious Me* were about being young/old, gay/straight, male/female in the 1970s (*Young Soul Rebel*), 1980s (*My Beautiful Laundrette*) or 1990s (*Goodness Gracious Me, Bhaji on the Beach*) and being of African, Caribbean or south Asian origin. Different social identities thus combined to produce new syncretic forms, which reflected fragments of different languages, styles, dress codes (see Back, 1996; Hewitt, 1986). Studies of the school playground for example have demonstrated the development of new languages incorporating Punjabi, Caribbean creole, New York street colloquialisms with English. In fact as Ben Rampton (1989) found, the use of the term *gora* (white) by a group of young people of different backgrounds including white English to refer to middle-class white pupils from another school illustrates the way in which such cross-cultural language codes have an important class dimension to them. Studies of young people of mixed origin could be accommodated within this new problematic although they added further levels of complexity to the understanding of identity and allegiance (see also Parker, op. cit.; Rampton, op. cit.)

One effect of acknowledging changing ethnic boundaries in this way is to question the idea of old ethnic cultures and more particularly specific cultural forms which are defined in terms of an old ethnic label. For example, can we talk about such things as 'black' music, 'Jewish' humour, 'Hong Kong' cinema, 'Asian' dance, 'Latin American' literature? In accepting these ethnic traditions are we not simply buying into the idea of absolute and fixed ethnic differences, of one ethnic essence or another expressed in musical, literary terms, etc.?

The argument for recognising such ethnic traditions is a strategic more than an intellectual one. Historically such labels have been important in maintaining collective identities in the face of exclusion and oppression.

The effect of treating dominant culture as the norm marginalises everything which does not conform to the white western benchmark. The idea that white western musicians have imitated, borrowed lyrics and instrumental styles from a black tradition to make successful careers for themselves is part of this process of marginalisation, yet even to be able to acknowledge this rests on the assumption that there is such a thing as a 'black' musical tradition to be plundered. On the one hand most people would acknowledge the debt that white super-groups in the 1960s and 1970s like Led Zeppelin, The Rolling Stones and Cream owed to African-American artists like Robert Johnson who died relatively unknown and poor. On the other hand, to acknowledge the perversity of this process is not the same as saying that what was appropriated was something which can be described as pristine or pure in ethnic terms.

The main difficulty with the idea of 'black music' or 'Jewish humour' or ethnic anything for that matter is that it assumes a principle of pure or authentic culture and one which remains this way indefinitely (see Hall, 1992b). The counter-argument to this is that all cultural traditions are inevitably mixed and that to try to suggest that anything has been somehow untouched by other cultural influences flies in the face of common-sense notions of cultural change and development. There are no such things as pure cultures or pure untainted cultural forms. According to advocates of this thesis we would be better off exploring the inherent syncretism and hybrid forms of white western culture than to search for the authentic musical or literary essence of another culture. Martin Bernal's epic study *Black Athena* (1987) traces the origins of western civilisation not to the Greeks as is commonly assumed but to Africa and to Egypt in particular. His evidence which draws on an enviable scholarship shows how etymologically indebted the Greek language was to Egyptian, how mathematicians and scientists studied in Egypt before making their mark in Greece, how many of the literary myths were borrowed from Egyptian tales and how classical political philosophy synonymous in many people's minds with Plato and Aristotle also took many of its ideas from Egyptian scholarship. Likewise, Paul Gilroy's analysis of the cross-fertilisation of scholars of African and European origin are examples of cross-over influences and exchanges which are reproduced across the cultural sphere as a whole (op. cit.).

Understandably, the polarisation of the debate regarding authentic cultural forms has made it harder to strike a middle ground. Such a compromise is possible if, instead of seeing the 'black culture' as fixed, we see it as a strategic designation forming part of a political agenda which seeks to redress forms of social exclusion and to mobilise and empower marginalised groups through an appeal to shared cultural allegiances. To acknowledge the significance of such forms of ethnic mobilisation should not preclude the idea of cultural exchanges and influences and the emergence of new self-consciously hybrid, cultural forms. In Britain the novelists, filmmakers and other cultural practitioners mentioned above would fall into this category. The varying forms of 'ethnic' cultural expression are in part a question of strategy and in part an unconscious effect of traditions, both old and new. Either way it is through ethnographic grassroots political research that such questions can be addressed rather than through abstract, formalistic debate.

Cultural imperialism and glocalisation

One powerful argument used against ideas of cultural mixing, hybridity and syncretism is that these terms imply a balance or equivalence between the different ingredients of the cultural mix. The concept of cultural imperialism has, in different guises, sought to establish the dominance of western and US culture in particular and to explore its destructive impact on local cultures, of how it serves to promote capitalistic consumerist values and how it induces a convergence of global culture around the dominant US norm rather than promoting a genuine respect for difference. A popular example of this has been the proliferation of McDonald's fast-food restaurants which not only testify to the growing appeal of American hamburgers (which are actually Russian in origin) but to what Ritzer refers to as the process of 'McDonaldization' (1993). The impact of what has been referred to as 'Americanisation' on local cultures and identities and whether or not it is a good or a bad thing have been the subject of hotly contested debates. At the heart of such discussions is the idea of cultural imperialism, that is the imposition of dominant (US/western) cultural values and products on the rest of the world. Arguments therefore often focus on the role of the media, the swamping of consumer products, and the associated values and the corresponding destruction of local cultures.

The revolution in media and communications technologies has transformed the way people understand the world and their own sense of themselves in it. Many authors have recognised the importance of the media and information technologies in contemporary culture (Bauman, 1992). One of the most often cited consequences of this revolution has been its effect on popular understandings of time and space. This was first noted by Marshall McLuhan in the 1960s and later by postmodernist writers.

Nevertheless, as we suggested above, the 'internationalisation of image markets' as Nick Stevenson refers to them (1995: 203) is nevertheless dominated by US television and Hollywood film. According to Morley and Robins (1995), communications empires have become increasingly responsible not for one but for several media products including film, television, press and publishing, music and video (ibid.: 32). What is more, alliances between IT giants like Microsoft and media conglomerates have strengthened this monopolistic grip.

Media imperialism refers to the way multinational media conglomerates spread their tentacles around the world. Western news dominates through international news agencies like Reuters, Rupert Murdoch's Sky TV and CNN, all of which are beamed across the world by satellite and digital technologies. Noam Chomsky's analysis of the Gulf War illustrates the way in which giant media conglomerates monopolise coverage of such events and, although there remains some room for dissent, how the dominant propaganda model helped to set the terms in which the war was explained, understood and accepted as necessary in the West (1989).

In effect, the model encouraged viewpoints sympathetic to the West and in opposition to the Iraqis and the anti-war lobby, through the use of different discursive techniques. The success of the media in winning popular support for the war relied more heavily on the mobilisation of popular, including racist common-sense notions of difference, evil, war and national identity (Kellner, 1995; Gabriel, 1994). The media thus drew on a well-established repertoire of stereotypical images to interpret the Gulf crisis, couched in a language of violence and male and female sexuality, as well as playing on national symbols associated with patriotism and heroism. Since the war was waged over the Christmas period, the media was able to strengthen western/Christian loyalties through heart-rending tales of separation during a period traditionally associated with family reunion.

Like the Rushdie affair which preceded it, the Gulf War provoked a reworking of orientalist themes and an escalation of racist violence in Britain, particularly amongst young people who used the term 'Saddam' as a term of racial abuse aimed not only at Muslims but anyone of south Asian background. However, the coverage was not fool-proof and there remained a vocal anti-war movement throughout the conflict. According to Stevenson we need to look at the quality press to find evidence of this dissent rather than just at television coverage (op. cit.).

War is not the only opportunity to tell stories of action heroes, individuals struggling against adversity, as well as those of romantic love; the happy and the not so happy endings. Hollywood films are saturated with such narratives, images and icons. Even in the seemingly more innocent genre of cartoon such cultural icons as Donald Duck are used to disseminate the values of western capitalism and justify global domination. *How to Read Donald Duck* by Ariel Dorfman and Armand Mattelart was published in 1971, two years before the CIA-supported coup which brought General Pinochet to power in Chile and which overthrew the democratically elected socialist government of Salvador Allende. According to the authors' reading of the cartoon strip, the seemingly innocent adventures of the creature helped to sanction imperialistic exploits in general including the US-backed coup in Chile.

This last point raises the question of audiences and of diverse contradictory interpretations of such allegedly global systems of meaning. For example, Katz and Leibes's study of *Dallas* discovered that ethnic groups in Israel were less attached to consumer values than to the melodramatic narratives (cited in Stevenson, op. cit.: 110). Important writing on ways in which women interpret popular cultural forms like TV soaps (Gray, 1992), romantic fiction (Radway, 1984) and videos have implications for thinking about different class and/or ethnic readings of cultural products.

The transnationalisation of media forms has had implications for questions of citizenship. The emergence of new transnational blocs has resulted in new transnational identity formations which result not just from political and electoral changes but the changing framework within which communications are produced and distributed. Public-service broadcasting linked to democracy and national community is giving way to global broadcasting, consumer identities and depoliticisation (Stevenson, op. cit.: 204). One reaction of public broadcasters to this threat has been to promote, and appeal to, more regional identities reflected in TV drama, film and specialised programming (for different ethnic groups, women, etc.). According to Stevenson, this can lead to fragmentation and parochialism which averts attention away from the significance of the global structures within which such regionalisation or localisation is taking place. The growth of pay per view, internet shopping, and a plethora of locally run websites and TV programmes is both suggestive of new forms of citizenship but also alerts us to the danger of the ever growing monopoly of ownership and influence of the likes of Rupert Murdoch and Bill Gates.

Another way of thinking about cultural imperialism is in terms of its impact on national identities. One argument here is that the values and traditions of countries are swamped by the imposition of western products. The latter range from Marlboro cigarettes to Tommy and Nike designer leisurewear to hamburgers and Coke. The question here is to what extent local values, choices and products are overturned by such consumer goods. An alternative view suggests that, far from thinking of consumers as both passive and easily manipulated, we should give people credit for making conscious, reasoned choices between products and that this human capacity applies as much to poor as it does to rich countries.

However, the idea that ethnic national differences are being erased in such processes appears at odds with the view that neither the sources of such information nor its effects on its global audiences are as straightforward as this model suggests. According to Douglas Kellner, media products encode relations of power but also provide the means for contradictory readings in which different audiences make a significant difference (op. cit.). Likewise John Thompson (1995) calls for an analysis of both structured patterns of global communication and the local conditions under which such products are appropriated (113 ff.).

The idea that cultures world-wide are becoming increasingly the same rests on the idea of the growing domination of the West and its ability to shape the rest of the world in its own image. The dumping of the banned contraceptive depo provera on poorer countries suggests not just a growing similarity but the continuing subordination of Third World peoples to the West and that the Third World is seen as a giant laboratory for testing and dumping products considered unsafe in the West. However, the idea that consumers from poorer countries are more susceptible to cigarette advertising or are more easily duped into the wrong choices by manufacturers of Nestlé powder milk, for example, smacks of a paternalism and sense of superiority associated more with an older, colonial mentality.

Moreover, the assumption that western products from hamburgers to US television soap operas mean the same the world over has been challenged by research which highlights the complex processes, patterns and meanings attached to consumption. A big Mac, for example, might mean a cheap meal in the US, whereas in Russia its price is beyond the reach of most Muscovites. The meanings attached to going to McDonald's thus differs depending on 'local' economic and cultural circumstances.

Not only do local cultures 'absorb' global products differently but they also help to shape those products. Where did the concept of designer leisure-wear embraced by the hugely successful Tommy Hilfiger label originate if not on New York streets housing people whose employment opportunities and mortality rates in the 1980s and 1990s were on a par with poorer parts of the Third World? Of course the cultural exchanges and influences are by no means equal. The role of 'ethnic' tourism is testimony to those inequalities and incorporates a range of practices from sex industries and safari excursions to multinational hotels employing local labour in the service sector to restaurants, museums, craft shops and pubs all of which reproduce, in their different ways, old-style colonial relations.

Finally, the idea of cultural imperialism encourages us to generalise in terms of a rich manipulative West and a poor, supplicant and compliant Third World. In chapter 5, we examined the idea of global cities where people living in extreme poverty live cheek by jowl with the upwardly mobile, affluent class occupying the gentrified quarters of the inner city. Moreover, even amongst the dominant cultural group there are differences of outlook and perceived interest, debates between commercial and public-service lobbies within broadcasting or between political and economic interests articulated by domestic manufacturing and international finance, etc. The idea that dominant culture is both uniform and consensual misses some important internal differences and contradictions. Equally, the reduction of Third World peoples to the rural poor glosses over important class, ethnic and gender differences both within and between urban and rural populations. Moreover, 'local' political and business elites in poorer countries have both challenged and colluded with western governments, multinationals and agencies like the World Bank or International Monetary Fund, in ways which require a more complex discussion and analysis than that offered by the concept of cultural imperialism. An important counter to the cultural imperialism arguments is that they underestimate the extent to which minority cultures have, in turn, influenced dominant western traditions and tastes. In the next section we look at the significance of consumption as a catalyst for other kinds of social change.

Consumption as acceptable interaction

This section re-examines the processes around consumption and ethnicity and suggests that consumption appears as the least threatening encounter with difference. The question remains, can these non-threatening encounters shift social relations?

Although a variety of types of ethnic display have been commodified for a long time, and this process is not tied to this new era of migration, a heightened sense of the meanings of diaspora has been accompanied by a greater range of commodification of ethnicity (on previous commodifications of racialised difference, see McClintock, 1995; Pieterse, 1992). In part, this can be linked to a wider cultural shift which regards the assumption of identity as a process of consumption (Lash and Urry, 1994). However, this process of commodified ethnic experience also continues a longer history of the West consuming the rest. If whiteness is constructed as an absence of demarcation and ethnicity, then the desire and ability to experience the flavour of difference through consumption and ownership is also part of this construction (R. Dyer, 1997).

The era of globalisation sees this phenomenon re-emerge with a vengeance. Transnational companies market global products through fantasies of white ownership, white subjectivity or deracialised Americanism (think Calvin Klein). Previous mythologies of consumption reappear – tropical idylls, dusky maidens, eager-to-please natives (think Bacardi) – and transmute into more contemporary models – the anti-glamour of a fantasy US underclass (think Nike) or the high-cultural pretensions of world cultures as conspicuous consumption (think 'ethnic' furnishings in stripped-back, minimalist urban homes). In both incarnations, we see that 'race' continues to make good product, despite the uncertainties of global identities.

The advent of a variety of cultural production which stages and explores ethnicity from the perspective of racialised communities has not gone unnoticed by the sellers and shakers of the world, as explained above. However, it would be wrong to suggest that this process of commodification is solely the business of the dominant culture. A key development in the articulation and sustenance of migrant and minority communities has been their ability to stage their own ethnicities for economic survival. Although established communities may resist this performance, commodification can itself offer a form of legitimation to communities under attack. Therefore we see music which seems to replicate racist stereotypes, film which takes the sight of the white eye as its starting point, community cultural forms which seek to cross over on the terms of the masters. In all these instances, diasporic communities remake their disparaged home cultures into a form of cultural capital and saleable good. This performance for western markets remakes cultures into distinctively diasporic entities – these are not the performances of 'home', they appear with transplantation. A sizeable literature has arisen which describes this ethnic entrepeneurship as a strategy for community survival (Waldinger *et al.*, 1990). As always, migrants sell what they can.

A paradox of global markets has been that while the white cultures of the West have seeped across the globe and continued to dispossess all other peoples through a variety of forces, cultural, economic and military, a certain version of racialised otherness has become saleable to the West. We can understand this as corporate multiculture – the process by which multinational capital embraces the gestures and images of a mixed culture of different-looking people who can be imagined to be located anywhere and nowhere at all. This trope appeals, presumably, to a fantasy of American prosperity as global melting point – a consumer fantasy which provides a point of identification for everyone. Unlike imperial cultures which sell the exotic to the white folk back home as a supplement to their always embryonic white identities, corporate multiculture addresses a global and multiethnic audience. The global market imagines everyone to be a potential consumer – however unlikely their access to resources – and the fantasy of ethnic performance through commodities must address this varied constituency. Therefore, we see the advent of multinational products which sell a saccharin version of US multiculture – complete with beautiful youth with a rainbow of skin tones. This fantasy can sell white people an old-style supplement of racial otherness, and everyone else a point of identification in the wholesome world of branded products.

Sadly, the glaringly obvious lesson of corporate multiculture and the commodification of ethnicity is that shopping does not change social relations or attitudes. In Britain we see that curry has been adopted as the new national dish – more popular than chips, which also can be eaten with curry sauce now – yet Asian restaurants and takeaways continue to be sites of racist violence and attack. Despite various attempts by informal bodies and local government, the undoubted desirability of ethnicised consumption does not take the violent sting out of other forms of social interaction. In chapter 5, we reviewed the difficult local interactions which occur from these initiatives.

Of course, this only confirms what we all must know. Consumption is a process which may not touch political consciousness at all. The very pleasures of difference packaged by local ethnic entrepeneurs and corporate multiculture play on the dangerous boundaries of race – if you don't believe in the difference, there is little pleasure in the product.

Ultimately, the global marketplace recreates structures of difference as a smart marketing ploy. Whereas in previous eras the prohibitions against contact across racial divides served the purposes of colonial structures, now the residual titillation of these taboos is repackaged as the exhilarating taste of global multiculture. Somehow in the process we experience a method of marketing which retains the boundary-marking required for exoticist fantasy, while peddling products which appeal to an ideal global consumer beyond racialised difference.

For the economic survival and well-being of the racialised, this contemporary exoticism represents a tricky bargain. In a way, the hunger for difference is an opportunity to enter the market, to make a living, to capitalise on attributes which have not been valued. However, in an echo of older exoticist structures, this disparaging commodification confirms the structures of racialisation. However innovative the performance, selling ethnicity lets the buyer see what they want to see.

In the end, this may be a reminder that the business of economic survival is rarely the same as the business of social change. Rather than berate participants in these fictions of the new exotic, perhaps we should applaud their ability to survive and thrive – because then there is a possibility of something else.

Concluding thoughts

In this volume we have sought to analyse a variety of new and shifting forms of racism that appear in the era of global intensification. In the main we have examined the manner in which these new racisms harden existing racial boundaries, while also seeking out new objects of racialised pain. However, alongside this gloomy picture, we have stressed the dynamic nature of racialisation processes. The end meanings and outcomes of the new world we describe are not yet decided.

This volume has reviewed debates in the areas of racialisation and globalisation. These debates have only recently begun to inform each other. We have attempted to chart key areas in which the processes of globalisation are inseparable from those of racialisation. Although we do not suggest that the intensification of global networks can be reduced to no more than a remaking of racist cultures, we do argue that global processes also restructure racism.

Our argument begins by reviewing ideas of racial naming and the role of class relations. We choose this starting point in order to acknowledge the importance of ideas of identity and the experience of economy. These are the two central themes of the book. Firstly the suggestion that culture, performance and sense of self are central attributes of contemporary living, most particularly in its racialised incarnation. And secondly, a reminder that race is still the mode in which class is lived, that racialisation is most starkly seen in its material outcomes.

The opening chapter reviews the construction of whiteness in various locations. This is a central debate in recent discussions of the process of racialisation. This work starts from the assumption that the privileged identities of race politics are themselves constructed, strategic and changeable. The discussion of whiteness as itself a constructed category opens far wider questions about the strategic nature of all racialised alliances. We wish to suggest that people inhabit identities strategically, yet that this is not a process in their overall control. Instead, racialised identities of all kinds are formed in the intersection between community alliances and self-articulations and wider structures of power. The focus on whiteness offers an opportunity to unpack the workings of these constrained negotiations.

Each chapter addresses these two ideas. We begin with a discussion of productive relations in a changing world order as a means of revisiting the relation between race and class. While our account is informed by the knowledge that all social spaces engage more complex interplays between multiple identities, with important differences coming from the articulation of gender, sexuality, faith and age, we wish to regain a focus on the economic outcomes of racism. For this reason, the old battle between race and class permeates our account of globalised racism. Here we argue that racialisation continues to be an intensely economic process – not the same as class formation, but operating through the same structures. In the globalised economy, we see once again that class and race reinforce each other, albeit in unforeseen ways. The chapter on production argues that the globalised economy renders large numbers of people 'disposable' – available to be worked to death, or exterminated, or, as argued in a later chapter, dispossessed through man-made famine and pestilence. The shift in social organisation to a view that regards human labour as endlessly replaceable and therefore dispensable inhabits the handy fictions of race which show us that some people are born only to die. Old-style racism makes the excesses of exploitation more palatable – and business, of all sorts, goes on as usual.

The discussions of whiteness and of evolving mixed identities examine both the uncertainties of racial naming and the strategic performances of new identities. Both chapters insist that we remember and acknowledge the continuing violence of everyday racism. However, equally, both sections reveal the malleability of the category of race. We learn that each moment and location develops its own racialised language – and that each has its particular racialised outcomes. The challenge remains to reveal this categorisation as arbitrary – no more inevitable than other forms of inequality.

Alongside this, we have discussed the growth of mixed-origin identities as a significant segment of many societies. We have argued that while, on the one hand, there are many more trajectories of ethnicised identity and far greater contact and intermarriage between so-called ethnic and racialised groups, on the other, old-style racism persists with a frightening virulence. While identities may be developing and transforming, social relations are not, sadly, completely transformed by these new articulations.

This chapter argues that racialisation is a process which touches all identities, but which adapts and transforms to new situations. The self-organisation and representation of mixed-origin peoples and the rearticulation of resistant white identities, both through backlash and through refusal of race privilege, reveal the manner in which racial naming itself can become a terrain for renegotiating social relations.

The chapter discussing the close relation between sexualisation and racialisation reveals the centrality of race-thinking to western concepts of self and intimacy. Although the structures of race pervade the public arenas of political and economic life, here we see that more private articulations of self and desire can also be suffused with the distortions of racism. More than this, the maintenance of public structures of racialised order require precisely this internalisation of racist myth. The section goes on to argue that this dehumanisation has its roots in the convoluted sexual mythologies of racism. The pathological inattention to the bodies of some, in all their frailty and possibility, masks a guilty but obsessive interest in that same flesh. This chapter argues that even in the contemporary world, old fascinations structure the mythologies of race. Even if the racialised object changes, the terms of this relation seem to endure. In particular, the economic ordering of contemporary racialisation mobilises the attractions and anxieties of this sexual neurosis – and disciplines us all in the process.

This sexualised conception of the racialised body informs debates about entitlement and safety. The discussion of consumption and distribution argues that access to resources is determined, in part, through these assumptions of entitlement and non-entitlement. The notion that renders an individual worthy is refracted through a racialised lens. The fear that the disprivileged will break through the protective boundaries of the privileged is amplified through mythologies of race and sexuality. The last two chapters pull together the themes of the volume in order to look at the impact of the global on the lived relations of race, class and locality. We describe this as an ongoing struggle – the terrain on which competing interests are articulated and, occasionally, realised.

Ultimately, the uncertainties of the emerging global order increase existing racist anxieties of being swamped, overwhelmed, sexually possessed, economically dispossessed – in fact, unable to wield racialised privilege effectively. The last chapter replaces these anxieties in a global frame and argues that global forces are pushing us all into new forms of racial articulation, despite ourselves. Although our analysis reveals little reason for optimism, we conclude by arguing that racial identity is changing and contextual. We can characterise this as the struggle between those whose preferred option might be to accelerate processes of hybridisation and globalisation and those seeking to resist it who use ethnic or national identities as strategies for mobilising and defending interests as well as expressing self- and collective identities. Our argument is that neither position can be easily located in the political spectrum. Hybridity can be the call of both corporate multiculture at its most imperialistic and of liberatory alliances seeking justice; localism can be a positive resource for forming an inclusive community or an aggressive warning that some people will never belong here. We hope we have offered some ways of understanding these contradictory processes. However bad times may be, nothing is yet decided.

The project of this book has been to revisit debates about race and ethnicity in the era of globalised economy. We have attempted to rework the languages of race to analyse both new social formations and the transformation and development of older, more familiar, social relations. Our argument is not that globalisation (or the new world order or post-modernity or life as we know it) is all about race, but rather that without attention to the role of racialising processes, the remaking of contemporary global inequalities becomes incomprehensible. Race may not be all there is, or even the main motor of social change, but its pernicious mythologies continue to inform and shape the life chances of all too many of the world's poor and disenfranchised.

Our main contention has been that racialisation is an adaptable and opportunistic process – and that its workings have shifted to fit new contexts, using older myths to construct new racialised meanings. Although this is anything but a polemical treatise – if anything we have sought to acknowledge the complexity of the contemporary social world and to argue that over-arching theoretical claims rarely fit all circumstances – the book does stress three key points.

The first is the insistence that race still matters. Despite the many claims that globalisation creates homogenisation – claims that we affirm in relation to some forms of social organisation, commodified culture and physical vulnerability to eco-disaster – we also want to reassert the counter-claim that globalisation thrives on the business of difference. Globalisation is a deeply differentiating process, reconstructing the world into a free-for-all fight between regions and localities while marketing particularity as the tastiest of commodities. Along the way, it also remakes ethnic divisions. These divisions may be remade for a new era, the boundaries and stigma between groups may shift and fresh stories of racialisation may appear, but in all these circumstances the languages of race and ethnicity retain their social force.

Our second key point is that issues of ethnicity are deeply implicated in questions of economy. Whereas we have avoided a headlong sprint back into the debates around race and class and their never-quite-decided relation, we have revisited this dilemma via another route. At the levels of both global and local economies, we argue that advantage and exploitation still occur through the mobilisation of ethnic division.

Our third key point is that although identities change, structures of inequality remain in place. Much of the book is an examination of shifting ethnicities and we argue that racialisation and its seemingly benign sibling ethnicisation are ongoing, never finally completed, but always in a process of becoming. Although this argument is heralded as an optimistic realisa-tion, with the implication being that some of the benighted racialised may escape into the normality of racial invisibility, our discussion has suggested the opposite. Rather than melting away, ethnic divisions harden and harm more people. Rather than a new celebration of fluidity and changing identi-ties, we see old models of racist demonisation include more and different people – not only blacks, but Albanians; not only 'pakis', but all Muslims, everywhere.

Our response to this alarming prospect is to propose the most eclectic of academic approaches. If global capital can inhabit various cultural forms without prejudice, borrowing from everywhere while acknowledging no debts, our attempts at understanding must be similarly innovative and unorthodox. Rather than suggest new theoretical models to fit all occasions, we want to suggest that the answers lie everywhere and that the only viable approach is to keep on looking, as attentively and as diligently as we are able.

Bibliography

Abelove, Henry *et al.* (1993) *The Lesbian and Gay Studies Reader*, London: Routledge.

Abu-Jamal, M. (1996) *Live from Death Row*, New York: Avon Books.

Abu-Jamal, M. (1997) *Death Blossoms: Reflections from a Prisoner of Conscience*, Farmington, Penn.: Plough Publishing House.

Ahmad, A. (1994) *In Theory: Nations, Classes, Literatures*, London: Verso.

Aho, J. (1990) *The Politics of Righteousness: Idaho Christian Patriotism*, London: University of Washington Press.

Alba, R. (1990) *Ethnic Identity: The Transformation of White America*, London: Yale University Press.

Alibhai-Brown, Y. and Montague, A. (1992) *The Color of Love*, London: Virago.

Allen, T. (1994) *The Invention of the White Race: volume 1: Racial Oppression and Social Control*, London: Verso.

Altman, D. (1999) 'Globalization, Political Economy, and HIV/AIDS', *Theory and Society*, 28: 559–84.

Amin, S. (1980) *Delinking: Towards a Polycentric World*, London: Zed Books.

Amin, S. (1988) *Eurocentrism*, London: Zed Books.

Amnesty International (1999) *Killing with Prejudice: Race and the Death Penalty in the USA*, London.

Ang, I. (1991) *Desperately Seeking the Audience*, London: Routledge.

Anthias, F. (1998) 'Evaluating Diaspora: Beyond Ethnicity?', *Sociology*, 32, 3: 557–81.

Anthias, F. and Yuval-Davis, N. (1992) *Racialized Boundaries: Race, Gender, Colour and the Anti-Racist Struggle*, London: Routledge.

Anzaldua, G. (1987) *Borderlands/La Frontera, the New Mestiza*, San Francisco: Aunt Lute Books.

Appadurai, A. (1997) *Modernity at Large: Cultural Dimensions of Globalization*, Minneapolis: University of Minnesota Press.

Armitage, A. (1995) *Comparing the Policy of Aboriginal Assimilation: Australia, Canada and New Zealand*, Vancouver: UBC Press.

Aronowitz, S. and Cutler, J. (1998) *Post-work*, New York and London: Routledge.

Athanasiou, T. (1996) *Slow Reckoning: The Ecology of a Divided Planet*, London: Secker & Warburg.

Australian Government Publishing Service (1991) Royal Commission into Aboriginal Deaths in Custody, Canberra.

Axford, B. (1995) *The Global System: Economics, Politics and Culture*, Cambridge: Polity.

Back, L. (1996) *New Ethnicities and Urban Culture*, London: UCL Press.

Bagley, C. (1983) *Multicultural Childhood: Education, Ethnicity and Cognitive Styles*, Aldershot: Gower.

Bales, K. (1999) *Disposable People: New Slavery in the Global Economy*, Berkeley: University of California Press.

Barker, E. (1995) *New Religious Movements: A Practical Introduction*, London: HMSO.

Barkun, M. (1994) *Religion and the Racist Right: The Origins of the Christian Identity Movement*, Chapel Hill: University of North Carolina Press.

Barnet, R. and Cavanagh, J. (1994) *Global Dreams: Imperial Corporations and the New World Order*, London: Touchstone.

Barraclough, S.L. (1991) *An End to Hunger? The Social Origins of Food Strategies*, London: Zed Books.

Barrett, M. and Phillips, A. (1992) *Destabilising Theory: Contemporary Feminist Debates*, Cambridge: Polity.

Bauman, Z. (1992) *Intimations of Postmodernity*, London: Routledge.

Baumann, G. (1999) *The Multicultural Riddle: Rethinking National, Ethnic, and Religious Identities*, New York and London: Routledge.

Benhabib, S. (1999) 'Sexual Difference and Collective Identities: The New Global Constellation', *Signs*, 24, 2 (winter): 335–62.

Bennett, J. and George, S. (1987) *The Hunger Machine*, Cambridge: Polity.

Bernal, M. (1987) *Black Athena: The Afroasiatic Roots of Classical Civilization*, London: Free Association Books.

Bhabha, H. (1994) *The Location of Culture*, New York and London: Routledge.

Bhachu, P. and Westwood, S. (1988) *Enterprising Women: Ethnicity, Economy and Gender Relations*, London: Routledge.

Bhatt, C. (1997) *Liberation and Purity: Race, New Religious Movements and the Ethics of Postmodernity*, London: UCL Press.

Bhattacharyya, G. (1998) *Tales of Dark-Skinned Women: Race, Gender and Global Culture*, London: UCL Press.

Bhattacharyya, G. and Gabriel, J. (1994) 'Gurinder Chadha and the Apna Generation: Black British Film in the 1990s', *Third Text*, 27 (summer): 55–63.

Biggs, S. (1998) 'The Biodiversity Convention and Global Sustainable Development', in R. Kiely and P. Marfleet (eds) *Globalisation and the Third World*, London: Routledge.

Birch, E. (1994) *Black American Women's Writing: A Quilt of Many Colours*, Brighton: Harvester.

Boldt, M. and Long, J.A. (1985) *The Quest for Justice: Aboriginal Peoples and Aboriginal Rights*, Toronto: University of Toronto Press.

Bonanno, A., Busch, L., Friedland, W., Gouveia, L. and Mingione, E. (1994) *From Columbus to ConAgra: The Globalization of Agriculture and Food*, Lawrence: University of Kansas Press.

Brah, A. (1996) *Cartographies of Diaspora*, London: Routledge.

Brah, A., Hickman, M.J. and Mac an Ghaill, M. (1999) *Global Futures: Migration, Environment and Globalization*, Basingstoke and London: Macmillan.

Brodkin, K. (1998) *How the Jews became White Folks: And What that says about Race in America*, New Jersey: Rutgers University Press.

Brody, J.D. (1998) *Impossible Purities: Blackness, Femininity, and Victorian Culture*, Durham, NC and London: Duke University Press.

Brody, J.D. (1999) 'The Returns of Cleopatra Jones', *Signs*, 25, 1 (autumn): 91–122.

Bruce, S. (1996) *Religions in the Modern World: From Cathedrals to Cults*, Oxford: Oxford University Press.

Budd, L. and Whimster, S. (eds) (1992) *Global Finance and Urban Living: A Study of Metropolitan Change*, London: Routledge.

Butler, J. (1990) *Gender Trouble: Feminism and the Subversion of Identity*, London: Routledge.

Butler, J. (1993) 'Imitation and Gender Insubordination', in H. Abelove *et al.*, *The Lesbian and Gay Studies Reader*, London: Routledge, pp. 307–20.

Cable, L. (1986) *Conflict of Myths: The Development of American Counter-insurgency Doctrine and the Vietnam War*, New York: New York University Press.

Campaign against Racism and Fascism (CARF) (1998) *Racism Goes Global*, 40 (June/July): 3.

Carby, H. (1982) 'White Woman Listen! Black Feminism and the Boundaries of Sisterhood', in Centre for Contemporary Cultural Studies, *The Empire Strikes Back: Race and Racism in 70s Britain*, London: Hutchinson, pp. 212–35.

Carnoy, M., Castells, M., Cohen, S.S. and Cardoso, F.H. (1993) *The New Global Economy in the Information Age: Reflections on our Changing World*, University Park: Pennsylvania State University Press.

Carter, A.B. (1999) 'Adapting US Defence to Future Needs', *Survival, International Institute for Strategic Studies*, 41–3 (winter): 101–23.

Castells, M. (1989) *The Informational City: Information Technology, Economic Restructuring and the Urban-Regional Process*, Oxford: Blackwell.

Castells, M. (1996) *The Rise of the Network Society*, Oxford: Blackwell.

Castells, M. (1997) *The Power of Identity*, Oxford: Blackwell.

Castells, M. (1998) *End of the Millennium*, Oxford: Blackwell.

Centre for Contemporary Cultural Studies (1982) *The Empire Strikes Back: Race and Racism in 70s Britain*, London: Hutchinson.

Chanley, V.A. (1999) 'US Public Views on International Involvement from 1964 to 1993: Time–Series Analyses of General and Militant Internationalism', *Journal of Conflict Resolution*, 43, 1 (February): 23–44.

Cheyette, B. (1989) 'Jewish Stereotyping and English Literature, 1875–1920: Towards a Political Analysis', in T. Kushner and K. Lunn (eds) *Traditions of Intolerance: Historical Perspectives on Fascism and Race Discourse in Britain*, Manchester: Manchester University Press, pp. 12–32.

Chomsky, N. (1989) *Necessary Illusions: Thought Control in Democratic Societies*, London: Pluto.

Chomsky, N. (1993) *Year 501: The Conquest Continues*, London: Verso.

Chomsky, N. and Barsamian, D. (1996) *Class Warfare*, London: Pluto.

Chow, R. (1993) *Writing Diaspora: Tactics of Intervention in Contemporary Cultural Studies*, Bloomington: Indiana University Press.

Christian, M. (1997) 'Black Identity in Liverpool: An Appraisal', in W. Ackah and M. Christian, *Black Organisation and Identity in Liverpool: A Local, National and Global Perspective*, Liverpool: Charles Wootton College Press, pp. 62–79.

Clarke, J. (1991) *New Times and Old Enemies: Essays on Cultural Studies and America*, London: HarperCollins Academic.

Clegg, J. (1994) *Fu Manchu and the 'Yellow Peril': The Making of a Racist Myth*, Stoke: Trentham.

Clifford, J. (1994) 'Diasporas', *Cultural Anthropology*, Summer.

Cobham, R. and Collins, M. (1990) *Watchers and Seekers: Creative Writing by Black Women in Britain*, Cambridge: Cambridge University Press.

Cohen, D.W. and Greene, J. (1972) *Neither Slave Nor Free: The Freedmen of African Descent in the Slave Societies of the New World*, Baltimore: Johns Hopkins University Press.

Cohen, P. (1988) 'The Perversions of Inheritance: Studies in the Making of Multi-racist Britain', in P. Cohen and H. Bains (eds) *Multi-Racist Britain*, Basingstoke: Macmillan, pp. 9–118.

Cohen R. (1997) *Global Diasporas: An Introduction*, London: UCL Press.

Cooper, N. (1997) *The Business of Death: Britain's Arms Trade at Home and Abroad*, London: Tauris.

Cornish, P. (1995) *Controlling the Arms Trade: The West versus the Rest*, London: Bowerdean.

Cox, H. (1971) *The Secular City*, Basingstoke: Macmillan.

Craib, I. (1998) *Experiencing Identity*, London: Sage.

Crosby, A.W. (1986) *Ecological Imperialism: The Biological Expansion of Europe, 900–1900*, Cambridge: Canto, Cambridge University Press.

Cross, M. and Keith, M. (eds) (1993) *Racism, the City and the State*, London: Routledge.

Curtis, L. (1971) *Apes and Angels: The Irishman in Victorian Caricature*, Newton Abbot: David & Charles.

Curtis, L. (1984) *Nothing but the same old Story*, London: Information on Ireland.

Daniels, J. (1997) *White Lies: Race, Class, Gender, and Sexuality in White Supremacist Discourse*, London: Routledge.

Davis, A. (1981) *Women, Race and Class*, London: The Women's Press.

Davis, A. and Gordon, A. (1998) 'Globalism and the Prison Industrial Complex: An Interview with Angela Davis', in *Race and Class*, 40, 2–3: 145–58.

Davis, J.F. (1991) *Who is Black? One Nation's Definition*, University Park: Pennsylvania State University Press.

Davis, M. (1990) *City of Quartz: Excavating the Future of Los Angeles*, London: Verso.

Davis, M. (1998) *Ecology of Fear: Los Angeles and the Imagination of Disaster*, New York: Vintage Books.

Dent, G. (ed.) (1992) *Black Popular Culture*, Seattle: Bay Press.

Diamond, J. (1998) *Guns, Germs and Steel: A Short History of Everybody for the Last 13,000 Years*, London: Vintage.

Diawara, M. (1993) *Black American Cinema*, London: Routledge.

Dines, G. and Humez, J. (eds) (1995) *Gender, Race and Class in Media: A Text Reader*, London: Sage.

Dinnerstein, L. (1994) *Antisemitism in America*, Oxford: Oxford University Press.

Dorfman, A. and Mattelart, A. (1971) *How to Read Donald Duck: Imperialist Ideology in the Disney Comic*, New York: International General.

Douglas, O. (1999) 'Same Family', *Pride*, September: 16–20.

Dreze, J. and Sen, A. (1990) *The Political Economy of Hunger, volume 1: Entitlement and Well-Being*, Oxford: Clarendon Press.

Dyer, J. (1998) *Harvest of Rage: Why Oklahoma City is only the Beginning*, Boulder, Col.: Westview Press.

Dyer, R. (1997) *White*, London: Routledge.

Dyer, R. (1998) 'White', *Screen*, 28, 4: 44–64.

Dyson, T. (1996) *Population and Food: Global Trends and Future Prospects*, London: Routledge.

Edgell, S. (1993) *Class*, London: Routledge.

Edwards, J. (1998) 'The Need for a "Bit of History": Place and Past in English History', in N. Lovell (ed.) *Locality and Belonging*, London: Routledge, pp. 146–67.

Eide, A., Eide, W.B., Goonatilake, S., Gusson, J. and Omawale (1984) *Food as a Human Right*, Tokyo: United Nations University.

Eisenstein, Z. (1996) *Hatreds: Racialized and Sexualized Conflicts in the 21st Century*, London: Routledge.

Elbow, S. (1995) *Doing Time 9 to 5*, Madison, Wisc.: Isthmus.

Engelhardt, T. (1995) *The End of Victory: Culture, Cold War America and the Disillusioning of a Generation*, Amherst: University of Massachusetts Press.

Engelsted, D. and Bird, J. (1992) *Nation to Nation: Aboriginal Sovereignty and the Future of Canada*, Concord, Ontario: Anansi Press.

Fanon, F. (1967)*The Wretched of the Earth*, Harmondsworth: Penguin.

Fanon, F. (1968) *Black Skin, White Masks*, London: MacGibbon & Kee.

Feagin, J.R. and Vera, H. (1995) *White Racism*, London: Routledge.

Featherstone, M. (1995) *Undoing Culture: Globalization, Postmodernism and Identity*, London: Sage.

Fenton, S. (1999) *Ethnicity: Racism, Class and Culture*, London: Macmillan.

Fiske, J. (1994) *Media Matters: Everyday Culture and Political Change*, St Paul: University of Minnesota Press.

Forbes, J. (1993) *Africans and Native Americans: The Language of Race and the Evolution of Red-Black Peoples*, Urbana and Chicago: University of Illinois Press.

Foucault, M. (1971) *Madness and Civilization: A History of Insanity in the Age of Reason*, London: Tavistock.

Foucault, M. (1972) *The Archaeology of Knowledge*, London: Tavistock.

Foucault, M. (1979) *Discipline and Punish*, Harmondsworth: Penguin.

Frankenberg, R. (1993) *The Social Construction of Whiteness: White Women, Race Matters*, London: Routledge.

Frye, M. (1995) 'White Woman Feminist', in L. Bell and D. Blumenfeld (eds) *Overcoming Racism and Sexism*, Lanham, Md.: Rowman & Littlefield, pp. 113–34.

Fryer, P. (1984) *Staying Power: The History of Black People in Britain*, London: Pluto.

Funderburg, L. (1994) *Black, White, Other: Biracial Americans talk about Race and Identity*, New York: William Morrow.

Gabriel, J. (1994) *Racism, Culture, Markets*, London: Routledge.

Gabriel, J. (1998) *Whitewash*, London: Routledge.

George, S. (1986) *How the Other Half Dies: The Real Reasons for World Hunger*, London: Penguin.

Gibson, J. (1994) *Warrior Dreams: Violence and Manhood in Post-Vietnam America*, New York: Hill & Wang.

Giddens, A. (1991) *The Consequences of Modernity*, Cambridge: Polity.

Giddens, A. (1992) *The Transformation of Intimacy: Sexuality, Love and Eroticism in Modern Societies*, Cambridge: Polity.

Gill, A. (1995) *Ruling Passions: Sex, Race and Empire*, London: BBC Books.

Gilman, S. (1991) *The Jew's Body*, London: Routledge.

Gilroy, P. (1987) *There Ain't No Black in the Union Jack*, London: Hutchinson.

Gilroy, P. (1990) 'The End of Anti-Racism', *New Community*, 17, 1: 71–83.

Gilroy, P. (1993a) *The Black Atlantic: Modernity and Double Consciousness*, London: Verso.

Gilroy, P. (1993b) *Small Acts: Thoughts on the Politics of Black Cultures*, London: Serpent's Tail.

Giroux, H.A. (1994) *Disturbing Pleasures: Learning Popular Culture*, New York and London: Routledge.

Giroux, H.A. (1996) *Fugitive Cultures: Race, Violence and Youth*, New York and London: Routledge.

Goldberg, D. (1993) *Racist Culture: Philosophy and the Politics of Meaning*, Oxford: Blackwell.

Gooding-Williams, R. (ed.) (1993) *Reading Rodney King Reading Urban Uprising*, London: Routledge.

Goodman, D. and Redclift, M. (1991) *Refashioning Nature: Food, Ecology and Culture*, London: Routledge.

Goodwin, J.-A. (1994) 'The New Apartheid', *Guardian Weekend*, Saturday, 2 July: 6–11.

Gossett, T. (1965) *Race: The History of an Idea in America*, New York: Schocken.
Grace, H. *et al.* (1997) *Home/World: Space, Community and Marginality in Sydney's West*, Annandale, NSW: Pluto Press.
Gray, A. (1992) *Video Playtime: The Gendering of a Leisure Technology*, London: Routledge.
Greenblatt, S. (1991) *Marvelous Possessions: The Wonder of the New World*, Oxford: Clarendon Press.
Grewal, S., Kay, J., Landor, L., Lewis, G. and Parmar, P. (1988) *Charting the Journey: Writings by Black and Third World Women*, London: Sheba.
Grigg, D. (1985, 1993) *The World Food Problem*, Oxford: Blackwell.
Guicherd, C. (1999) 'International Law and the War in Kosovo', *Survival, International Institute for Strategic Studies*, summer: 19–34.
Guillaumin, C. (1988) 'Race and Nature: The System of Marks', *Feminist Issues*, 25–43.
Gutman, R. and Rieff, D. (1999) *Crimes of War: What the Public Should Know*, New York and London: W.W. Norton.
Hage, G. (1998a) 'At Home in the Entrails of the West', in H. Grace, G. Hage, L. Johnson, J. Langsworth and M. Symonds (eds) *Home/World: Space, Community and Marginality in Sydney's West*, Annandale, NSW: Pluto, pp. 99–153.
Hage, G. (1998b) *White Nation: Fantasies of White Supremacy in a Multicultural Society*, Annandale, NSW: Pluto.
Hall, S. (1981) 'The Whites of their Eyes: Racist Ideologies and the Media', in G. Bridges and R. Brunt (eds) *Silver Linings*, London: Lawrence & Wishart, pp. 28–52.
Hall, S. (1988) 'New Ethnicities', in K. Mercer *Black Film: British Cinema*, BFI/ICA Document 7, London: 27–31.
Hall, S. (1990) 'Cultural Identity and Diaspora', in J. Rutherford (ed.) *Identity: Community, Culture Difference*, London: Lawrence & Wishart, pp. 222–37.
Hall, S. (1991a) 'The Local and the Global: Globalization and Ethnicity', in A.D. King (ed.) *Culture Globalization and the World System: Contemporary Conditions and the Representation of Identity*, Basingstoke: Macmillan, pp. 19–39.
Hall, S. (1991b) 'Old and New Identities, Old and New Ethnicities', in A. King (ed.) *Culture Globalization and the World System*, Basingstoke: Macmillan, pp. 41–68.
Hall, S. (1992a) 'New Ethnicities', in J. Donald and A. Rattansi (eds) *Race, Culture and Difference*, London: Sage, pp. 252–9.
Hall, S. (1992b) 'What is this "Black" in Popular Culture?', in G. Dent (ed.) *Black Popular Culture*, Seattle: Bay Press, pp. 21–33.
Hall, S. (1995) 'New Cultures for Old', in D. Massey and P. Jess (eds) *A Place in the World? Places, Cultures and Globalization*, Milton Keynes: Open University/Oxford University Press, pp. 175–213.
Hall, S., Critcher, C., Jefferson, T., Clarke, J. and Roberts, B. (1978) *Policing the Crisis*, London and Basingstoke: Macmillan.
Hamnett, C. (1995a), in D. Massey and P. Jess (eds) *A Place in the World? Places, Cultures and Globalization*, Milton Keynes: Open University/Oxford University Press.
Hamnett, C. (1995b) 'Controlling Space: Global Cities', in J. Allen and C. Hamnett (eds) *A Shrinking World? Global Unevenness and Inequality*, Milton Keynes: Open University/Oxford University Press.
Hartigan, J.R. (1999) *Racial Situations: Class Predicaments of Whiteness in Detroit*, New Jersey: Princeton University Press.
Harvey, D. (1989) *The Condition of Postmodernity*, Oxford: Blackwell.
Harvey, D. (1996) *Justice, Nature and the Geography of Difference*, Oxford: Blackwell.

Haste, C. (1992) *Rules of Desire*, London: Pimlico.

Hazlehurst, K.M. (1995) *Legal Pluralism and the Colonial Legacy*, Aldershot: Avebury.

Heelas, P. (1998) *Religion, Modernity and Postmodernity*, Oxford: Blackwell.

Herman, E. and Chomsky, N. (1994) *Manufacturing Consent: The Political Economy of the Mass Media*, London: Verso.

Herrnstein, R. and Murray, C. (1994) *The Bell Curve: Intelligence and Class Structure in American Life*, New York: Free Press.

Hesse, B. (1997) 'White Governmentality: Urbanism, Nationalism, Racism', in S. Westwood and J. Williams *Imagining Cities: Scripts, Signs, Memory*, London: Routledge, pp. 86–103.

Hester, M., Kelly, L. and Radford, J. (eds) (1996) *Women, Violence and Male Power*, Buckingham: Open University Press.

Hewitt, R. (1986) *White Talk Black Talk: Inter-social Friendship and Communication amongst Adolescents*, Cambridge: Cambridge University Press.

Hickman, M. (1995a) 'Deconstructing Whiteness: Irish Women in Britain', *Feminist Review*, 50 (summer): 5–19.

Hickman, M. (1995b) *Religion, Class and Identity: The State, the Catholic Church and the Education of the Irish in Britain*, Aldershot: Avebury.

Hickman, M. and Walter, B. (1997) *Discrimination and the Irish Community in Britain: A Report of Research undertaken for the Commission for Racial Equality*, London: CRE.

Hill, M. (ed.) (1998) *Whiteness: A Critical Reader*, New York: New York University Press.

Hillyard, P. (1993) *Suspect Community*, London: Pluto.

Holcomb, B. (1993) 'Revisioning Place: De- and Re-constructing the Image of the Industrial City', in A. Oncu and P. Weyland (eds) *Space, Culture and Power: New Identities in Globalizing Cities*, London: Zed Books, pp. 133–43.

Holm, H.-H. and Sorensen, G. (1995) *Whose World Order? Uneven Globalization and the End of the Cold War*, Boulder, Col.: Westview Press.

Holmes, C. (1979) *Anti-Semitism in British Society 1876–1939*, London: Arnold.

Hoogvelt, A. (1997) *Globalisation and the Postcolonial World*, Basingstoke: Macmillan.

hooks, b. (1982) *Ain't I a Woman? Black Women and Feminism*, London: Pluto Press.

Hughes, R. (1993) *Culture of Complaint: The Fraying of America*, Oxford: Oxford University Press.

Ifekwunigwe, J.O. (1999) *Scattered Belongings: Cultural Paradoxes of 'Race', Nation and Gender*, London and New York: Routledge.

Ignatiev, N. (1995) *How the Irish became White*, London: Routledge.

Ignatiev, N. and Garvey, J. (eds) (1996) *Race Traitor*, London and New York: Routledge.

Jacobs, J. (1996) *Edge of Empire: Postcolonialism and the City*, London: Routledge.

James, S.M. and Busia, A.P.A. (1993) *Theorizing Black Feminisms: The Visionary Pragmatism of Black Women*, London and New York: Routledge.

Jameson, F. and Miyoshi, M. (1998) *The Cultures of Globalization*, Durham, NC and London: Duke University Press.

Jamieson, K.H. (1992) *Dirty Politics: Deception, Distraction and Democracy*, Oxford: Oxford University Press.

Jayawardena, K. (1995) *The White Woman's Other Burden*, New York and London: Routledge.

Jenson, J., Hagen, E. and Reddy, C. (1988) *Feminization of the Labour Force*, Cambridge: Polity.

Jordan, G. and Weedon, C. (1995) *Cultural Politics: Class, Gender, Race and the Postmodern World*, Oxford: Blackwell.

Jordan, J. (1995) 'In the Land of White Supremacy', *The Progressive*, 18 June: 21.

Kabbani, R. (1994) *Imperial Fictions: Europe's Myths of the Orient*, London: Pandora.

Kaldor, M. (1999) *New and Old Wars: Organized Violence in a Global Era*, Cambridge: Polity.

Kaplan, E.A. (1997) *Looking for the Other: Feminism, Film, and the Imperial Gaze*, New York and London: Routledge.

Kearns, G. and Philo, C. (1993) *Selling Places: The City as Cultural Capital: Past and Present*, Oxford: Pergamon.

Kellner, D. (1995) *Media Culture: Cultural Studies, Identity and Politics between the Modern and the Postmodern*, London: Routledge.

Kennedy, P. (1994) *Preparing for the Twenty-First Century*, London: Fontana.

Kiely, R. and Marfleet, P. (eds) (1998) *Globalisation and the Third World*, London: Routledge.

Kiernan, V.G. (1972) *The Lords of Human Kind: European Attitudes towards the Outside World*, Harmondsworth: Penguin.

Kincheloe, J. and Steinberg, S.R. (1998) 'Addressing the Crisis of Whiteness: Reconfiguring White Identity in a Pedagogy of Whiteness', in J. Kincheloe, S.R. Steinberg, N.M. Rodriguez and R.E. Chennault (eds) *White Reign: Deploying Whiteness in America*, New York: St Martin's Griffin, pp. 3–30.

Kincheloe, J., Steinberg, S.R., Rodriguez, N.M. and Chennault, R.E. (eds) (1998) *White Reign: Deploying Whiteness in America*, New York: St Martin's Griffin.

King, R. (1995) 'Migrations, Globalization and Place', in D. Massey and P. Jess (eds) *A Place in the World? Places, Cultures and Globalization*, Milton Keynes: Open University/Oxford University Press, pp. 5–44.

Klein, N. (2000) *No Logo*, London: Flamingo.

Koistinen, P.A.C. (1980) *The Military-Industrial Complex: A Historical Perspective*, New York: Praeger.

Kovel, J. (1988) *White Racism: A Psychohistory*, London: Free Association Books.

Kundnani, A. (1998/9) 'Where Do You Want to Go Today? The Rise of Information Capital', *Race and Class*, 40, 2/3: 49–72.

Kureishi, H. (1997) *The Buddha of Suburbia*, London: Faber & Faber.

Kurtz, L. (1995) *Gods in the Global Village: The World's Religions in Sociological Perspective*, London: Pine Forge Press.

Kushner, T. (1989) *The Persistence of Prejudice: Antisemitism in British Society during the Second World War*, Manchester: Manchester University Press.

LaFeber, W. (2000) *Michael Jordan and Global Capitalism*, New York: W.W. Norton.

Lappe, F.M. and Collins, J. (1988) *World Hunger: Twelve Myths*, New York: Grove Press.

Lash, S. and Urry, J. (1987) *The End of Organised Capitalism*, Cambridge: Polity.

Lash, S. and Urry, J. (1994) *Economies of Signs and Space*, London: Sage.

Latouche, S. (1996) *The Westernization of the World*, Cambridge: Polity.

Lazarus, N. (1999) 'The Prose of Insurgency: Sivanandan and Marxist Theory', *Race and Class*, 41, 1–2 (July–December): 35–48.

Lee, G. (1996) *Troubadours, Trumpeters, Troubled Makers: Lyricism, Nationalism and Hybridity in China and its Others*, Durham, NC: Duke University Press.

Lentin, R. (1997) *Gender and Catastrophe*, London: Zed Books.

Levidow, L. (1996) 'Simulating Mother Nature, Industrializing Agriculture', in G. Robertson *et al.*, *Futurenatural: Nature, Science, Culture*, London: Routledge, pp. 55–71.

Lewis, G. (1996) *Gendering Orientalism: Race, Femininity and Representation*, London: Routledge.

Lichtenstein, A. (1996) *Twice the Work of Free Labor: The Political Economy of Convict Labor in the New South*, London: Verso.

Liebes, T. and Katz, E. (1986) 'Patterns of Involvement in Television Fiction: A Comparative Analyisis', *European Journal of Communication*, 1, 2: 151–71.

Lovell, N. (1998) *Locality and Belonging*, London: Routledge.

Lury, C. (1996) *Consumer Culture*, Cambridge: Polity.

McClintock, A. (1995) *Imperial Leather: Race, Gender and Sexuality in the Colonial Encounter*, London: Routledge.

McGuire, M. (2000) *Raising the Profile*, London: London Guildhall University, Centre for Social and Evaluation Research (unpublished report).

McMichael, A.J. (1993) *Planetary Overload: Global Environmental Change and the Health of the Human Species*, Cambridge: Cambridge University Press.

Macpherson, W. (1999) *The Stephen Lawrence Enquiry*, Report of an Enquiry by Sir William Macpherson of Cluny, London: The Stationery Office.

Manning, M. (1990) 'The Kids are Lippy', *New Society and Statesman*, 16 February: 12–13.

Martin, H.-P. and Schumann, H. (1997) *The Global Trap: Globalization and the Assault on Democracy and Prosperity*, London and New York: Zed Books.

Massey, D. (1995) 'The Conceptualisation of Place', in D. Massey and P. Jess (eds) *A Place in the World? Places, Cultures and Globalization*, Milton Keynes: Open University/Oxford University Press, pp. 45–85.

Massey, D.S. and Denton, N.A. (1993) *American Apartheid: Segregation and the Making of the Underclass*, Cambridge, Mass. and London: Harvard University Press.

Massey, D. and Jess, P. (1995) 'Places and Culture in an Uneven World', in D. Massey and P. Jess (eds) *A Place in the World? Places, Cultures and Globalization*, Milton Keynes: Open University/Oxford University Press, pp. 215–239.

Massey, D. and Jess, P. (eds) (1995) *A Place in the World? Places, Cultures and Globalization*, Milton Keynes: Open University/Oxford University Press.

Maynard, M. and Purvis, J. (1995) *(Hetero)Sexual Politics*, London: Taylor & Francis.

Médecins sans Frontières (1997) *World in Crisis: The Politics of Survival at the End of the Twentieth Century*, London: Routledge.

Mehmet, O. (1995) *Westernizing the Third World: The Eurocentricity of Economic Development Theories*, London: Routledge.

Melman, S. (1974) *The Permanent War Economy: American Capitalism in Decline*, New York: Touchstone.

Mercer, K. (1994) *Welcome to the Jungle: New Positions in Black Cultural Studies*, London: Routledge.

Mies, M. and Shiva, V. (1993) *Ecofeminism*, London: Zed Books.

Miles, R. (1982) *Racism and Migrant Labour*, London: Routledge & Kegan Paul.

Miles, R. (1984) 'Marxism versus the "Sociology of Race Relations"?', *Ethnic and Racial Studies*, 7, 2: 217–37.

Miles, R. (1993) *Racism after 'Race Relations'*, London: Routledge.

Miller, D. (1995) *Acknowledging Consumption: A Review of New Studies*, London: Routledge.

Mingione, E. (1996) *Urban Poverty and the Underclass*, Oxford: Blackwell.

Minh-Ha, T.T. (1991) *When the Moon Waxes Red: Representation, Gender and Cultural Politics*, New York and London: Routledge.

Mirza, H.S. (ed.) (1997) *Black British Feminism: A Reader*, London: Routledge.

Modood, T. and Acland, T. (1998) *Race and Higher Education*, London: Policy Studies Institute.

Modood, T., Berthoud, R., Lakey, J., Smith, P., Virdee, S. and Beishon, S. (1997) *Ethnic Minorities in Britain: Diversity and Disadvantage*, London: Policy Studies Institute.

Mohanty, C., Russo, A. and Torres, L. (1991) *Third World Women and the Politics of Feminism*, Bloomington and Indianapolis: Indiana University Press.

Moraga, C. and Anzaldua, G. (1981) *This Bridge called My Back: Writings by Radical Women of Color*, New York: Kitchen Table, Women of Color Press.

Morley, D. and Robins, K. (1995) *Spaces of Identity: Global Media, Electronic Landscapes and Cultural Boundaries*, London: Routledge.

Morris, L. (1994) *Dangerous Classes: The Underclass and Social Citizenship*, London: Routledge.

Morrison, T. (1992) *Playing in the Dark: Whiteness and the Literary Imagination*, London: Harvard University Press.

Murray, C. (1994) *Underclass: The Crisis Deepens*, London: IEA Health and Welfare Unit.

Myers, N. (1996) *Reconstructing the Black Past: Blacks in Britain, 1780–1830*, London and Portland, Oregon: Frank Cass.

Nakashima, C. (1996) 'Voices from the Movement: Approaches to Multiraciality', in M. Root, *The Multi Racial Experience: Racial Borders as the New Frontier*, London: Sage.

Nixon, S. (1996) *Hard Looks: Masculinities, Spectatorship and Contemporary Consumption*, London: UCL Press.

Oboler, S. (1995) *Ethnic Labels, Latino Lives: Identity and the Politics of (Re)Presentation in the United States*, Minneapolis: University of Minnesota Press.

O'Connell-Davidson, J. (1998) *Prostitution, Power and Freedom*, Ann Arbor: University of Michigan Press.

Ohmae, K. (1995) *The End of the Nation State: The Rise of Regional Economies*, London: HarperCollins.

Oliver, M.L. and Shapiro, T.M. (1995) *Black Wealth, White Wealth: A New Perspective on Racial Inequality*, New York and London: Routledge.

Omawale (1984) 'Introduction', in A. Eide *et al.*, *Food as a Human Right*, Tokyo: United Nations University.

Oncu, A. and Weyland, P. (eds) (1997) *Space, Culture and Power: New Identities in Globalizing Cities*, London: Zed Books.

Ong, P. and Blumenberg, E. (1996) 'Income and Racial Inequality in Los Angeles', in A.J. Scott and E.W. Soja (eds) *The City: Los Angeles and Urban Theory at the End of the Twentieth Century*, London: University of California Press, pp. 311–35.

Parker, D. (1995) *Through Different Eyes: The Cultural Identities of Young Chinese People in Britain*, Aldershot: Avebury.

Parker, D. and Song, M. (eds) (2001) *Rethinking Mixed Race*, London: Pluto.

Perlmann, J. (1997) *Reflecting the Changing Face of America: Multiracials, Racial Classification, and American Intermarriage*, Public Policy Series of the Jerome Levy Economics Institute of Bard College.

Pfeil, F. (1995) *White Guys: Studies in Postmodern Domination and Difference*, London: Verso.

Phoenix, A. and Owen, C. (1996) 'From Miscegenation to Hybridity: Mixed Relationships and Mixed Parentage in Profile', in B. Bernstein and J. Brannen (eds) *Children, Research and Policy*, London: Taylor & Francis.

Pieterse, J. (1992) *White on Black: Images of Africa and Blacks in Western Popular Culture*, London: Yale University Press.

Pieterse, J.N. (1998) *World Orders in the Making: Humanitarian Intervention and Beyond*, Basingstoke: Macmillan.

Plant, S. (1999) *Writing on Drugs*, London: Faber & Faber.

Pratt, M.L. (1992) *Imperial Eyes: Travel Writing and Transculturation*, London: Routledge.

Pritchard, S. (1998) *Indigenous Peoples: The United Nations and Human Rights*, London: Zed Books.

Radway, J. (1984) *Reading the Romance*, Chapel Hill: University of North Carolina Press.

Rampton, B. (1989) 'Some Unofficial Perspectives on Bilingualism and Education for All', *Language Issues*, 3, 2: 27–32.

Regan, P. (1994) *Organizing Societies for War*, London: Praeger.

Renvoize, J. (1993) *Innocence Destroyed: A Study of Child Sexual Abuse*, London: Routledge.

Rex, J. and Moore, R. (1967) *Race, Community and Conflict: A Study of Sparkbrook*, London: Oxford University Press.

Reynolds, T. (1997) '(Mis)representing the Black (Super)woman', in Heidi Safia Mirza (ed.) *Black British Feminism: A Reader*, London: Routledge, pp. 97–112.

Rhodes, C. and Nabi, N. (1992) 'Brick Lane: Village Economy in the Shadow of the City', in L. Budd and S. Whimster (eds) *Global Finance and Urban Living*, London: Routledge, pp. 333–52.

Rich, P. (1996) *Race and Empire in British Politics*, Cambridge: Cambridge University Press.

Riggins, S. (1992) *Ethnic Minority Media: An International Perspective*, London: Sage.

Ritzer, G. (1993) *The McDonaldization of Society*, Thousand Oaks, Cal.: Pine Forge.

Roberts, A. (1999) 'NATO's "Humanitarian War" over Kosovo', *Survival, International Institute for Strategic Studies*, 41, 3 (autumn): 102–23.

Robinson, C.J. (1983) *Black Marxism: The Making of the Black Radical Tradition*, London: Zed Books.

Rodney, W. (1972) *How Europe Undeveloped Africa*, London: Bogle L'Ouverture.

Rodriguez, C.E. (1997) *Latin Looks: Images of Latinas and Latinos in the U.S. Media*, Boulder, Col.: Westview Press.

Rodriguez, N. (1998) 'Emptying the Content of Whiteness: Toward an Understanding of the Relations between Whiteness and Pedagogy', in J. Kincheloe, S.R. Steinberg, N.M. Rodriguez and RE.. Chennault (eds) *White Reign: Deploying Whiteness in America*, New York: St Martin's Griffin, pp. 31–62.

Roediger, D. (1991)*The Wages of Whiteness: Race and the Making of the American Working Class*, London: Verso.

Roediger, D. (1994) *Towards the Abolition of Whiteness: Essays on Race, Politics and Working Class History*, London: Verso.

Root, M. (1992) *Racially Mixed People in America*, London: Sage.

Root, M. (1996) *The Multi Racial Experience: Racial Borders as the New Frontier*, London: Sage.

Russell, A.M. (1988) *The Biotechnology Revolution: An International Perspective*, Brighton: Wheatsheaf Books.

Said, E. (1978) *Orientalism*, London: Penguin.

Said, E. (1993) *Culture and Imperialism*, London: Chatto & Windus.

Sartre, J.-P. (1962) *Anti-Semite and Jew*, New York: Grove Press.

Sarup, M. (1996) *Identity, Culture and the Postmodern World*, Edinburgh: Edinburgh University Press.

Sassen, S. (1994) *Cities in a World Economy*, Thousand Oaks, Ca.: Pine Forge.

Sassen, S. (1998) *Globalization and its Discontents: Essays on the New Mobility of People and Money*, New York: New Press.

Sawday, J. (1995) *The Body Emblazoned: Dissection and the Body in Renaissance Culture*, London: Routledge.

Segal, L. (1990) *Slow Motion: Changing Masculinities, Changing Men*, London: Virago.

Semali, L. (1998) 'Perspectives on the Curriculum of Whiteness', in J. Kincheloe, S.R. Steinberg, N.M. Rodriguez and R.E. Chennault (eds) *White Reign: Deploying Whiteness in America*, New York: St Martin's Griffin, pp. 177–92.

Sen, A. (1984) *Resources, Values and Development*, Cambridge, Mass.: Harvard University Press.

Sherwood, M. (1994) *Pastor Daniels Ekarte and the African Churches Mission*, London: The Savannah Press.

Shiva, V. (1989) *Staying Alive: Women, Ecology and Development*, London: Zed Books.

Shiva, V. (1998) *Biopiracy: The Plunder of Nature and Knowledge*, Totnes, Devon: Green Books in association with the Gaia Foundation.

Shiva, V. and Ramprasad, V. (1993) *Cultivating Diversity: Biodiversity, Conservation and the Politics of the Seed*, Dehra Dun: Research Foundation for Science, Technology and Natural Resource Policy.

Shohat, E. and Stam, R. (1994) *Unthinking Eurocentrism: Multiculturalism and the Media*, London: Routledge.

Sibley, D. (1995) *Geographies of Exclusion*, London: Routledge.

Simpson, M. (1994) *Male Impersonators: Men Performing Masculinity*, London: Cassell.

Singer, L. (1993) *Erotic Welfare: Sexual Theory and Politics in the Age of Epidemic*, London: Routledge.

Sivanandan, A. (1982) *A Different Hunger: Writings on Black Resistance*, London: Pluto.

Sivanandan, A. (1990) *Communities of Resistance: Writings on Black Struggles for Socialism*, London: Verso.

Sleeter, C. (1996) 'White Silence, White Solidarity', in N. Ignatiev and J. Garvey (eds) *Race Traitor*, London and New York: Routledge, pp. 257–65.

Small, S. (1991) 'Racialised Relations in Liverpool: A Contemporary Anomaly', *New Community*, 11, 4: 511–37.

Small, S. (1994a) *Racialized Barriers: The Black Experience in the United States and England in the 1980s*, London and New York: Routledge.

Small, S. (1994b) 'Racial Group Boundaries and Identities: People of "Mixed-Race" in Slavery across the Americas', *Slavery and Abolition*.

Small, S. (1994c) 'Concepts and Terminology in Representations of the Atlantic Slave Trade', *Museum Ethnographers Journal*, 6 (December): 7–21.

Small, S. (1999) 'The Contours of Racialization: Structures, Representations and Resistance in the United States', in R.D. Torres, L.F. Mirón and J.X. Inda (eds) *Race, Identity and Citizenship: A Reader*, Malden, Mass. and Oxford: Blackwell.

Small, S. (2001a) 'Racisms and Racialized Hostility at the Start of the New Millennium', in D.T. Goldberg and J. Solomos (eds) *Blackwell Companion to Race and Ethnic Studies*, Oxford: Blackwell.

Small, S. (2001b) *The Matrix of Miscegenation: Blacks of Mixed Origins under Slavery in the Caribbean and the United States*, New York and London: New York University Press.

Smith, B. (1983) *Home Girls: A Black Feminist Anthology*, New York: Kitchen Table, Women of Color Press.

Smith, N. (1996) *The New Urban Frontier: Gentrification and the Revanchist City*, London: Routledge.

Smoodin, E. (1994) *Disney Discourse: Producing the Magic Kingdom*, New York: Routledge.

Soja, E. (1996) *Los Angeles 1965–1992: From Crisis-generated Restructuring to Restructuring-generated Crisis*, in A.J. Scott and E.W. Soja (eds) *The City: Los Angeles and Urban Theory at the End of the Twentieth Century*, London: University of California Press.

Solomos, J. and Back, L. (1996) *Racism and Society*, Basingstoke and London: Macmillan.

Southall Black Sisters (1990) *Against the Grain: A Celebration of Survival and Struggle*, Southall, Middlesex: Southall Black Sisters.

Spencer, J.M. (1997) *The New Colored People: The Mixed Race Movement in America*, New York: New York University Press.

Spickard, P. (1989) *Mixed Blood: Intermarriage and Ethnic Identity in Twentieth Century America*, Madison: University of Wisconsin Press.

Spillers, H.J. (1987) 'Mama's Baby, Papa's Maybe: An American Grammar Book', *Diacritics*, 17, 2 (summer): 65–81.

Spivak, G.C. (1987) *In Other Worlds*, New York and London: Methuen.

Stannard, D.E. (1992) *American Holocaust: The Conquest of the New World*, New York and Oxford: Oxford University Press.

Stevens, S. (1997) *Conservation through Cultural Survival, Indigenous Peoples and Protected Areas*, Washington, D.C.: Island Press.

Stevenson, N. (1995) *Understanding Media Cultures: Social Theory and Mass Communication*, London: Sage.

Stone, L. (1979) *The Family, Sex and Marriage in England 1500–1800*, London: Penguin.

Stone, L. (1993) *Broken Lives: Separation and Divorce in England 1660–1857*, Oxford: Oxford University Press.

Sundquist, E. (1996) *The Dubois Reader*, Oxford: Oxford University Press.

Taylor, J. (1998) *Body Horror: Photojournalism, Catastrophe and War*, Manchester: Manchester University Press.

Taylor, S. (1993) *A Land of Dreams: A Study of Jewish and Caribbean Migrant Communities in England*, London: Routledge.

Taylor, W. (2000) *This Bright Field: A Travel Book in One Place*, London: Methuen.

Thompson, E.P. (1985) *Star Wars*, Harmondsworth: Penguin.

Thompson, J. (1995) *The Media and Modernity*, Cambridge: Polity.

Tirman, J. (1984) *The Militarization of High Technology*, Cambridge, Mass.: Ballinger.

Tizard, B. and Phoenix, A. (1993) *Black, White or Mixed Race?*, London: Routledge.

Tomlinson, J. (1991) *Cultural Imperialism: A Critical Introduction*, London: Pinter.

Torres, R.D., Mirón, L.F. and Inda, J.X. (eds) (1999) *Race, Identity and Citizenship: A Reader*, Malden, Mass. and Oxford: Blackwell.

Torres, S. (1998) *Living Color: Race and Television in the United States*, Durham, NC and London: Duke University Press.

Trachtenberg, J (1993) *The Devil and the Jews: The Mediaeval Conception of the Jew and its Relation to Modern Antisemitism*, Philadelphia: The Jewish Publication Society.

Trexler, R.C. (1995) *Sex and Conquest: Gendered Violence, Political Order, and the European Conquest of the Americas*, Ithaca, NY: Cornell University Press.

Tucker, B. and Mitchell-Kernan, C. (eds) (1995) *The Decline in Marriage among African Americans: Causes, Consequences and Policy Implications*, New York: Russell Sage Foundation.

Twine, F.W. (1999) 'Bearing Blackness in Britain: The Meaning of Racial Difference for White Birth Mothers of African-Descent Children', *Social Identities*, 5, 2 (June): 185–210.

USA Today, Monday, 3 November 1997: 1 and 2.

Vidal, J. (1999) 'The Seeds of Wrath', *Guardian*, London: 19 June.

Virilio, P. and Lotringer, S. (1997) *Pure War*, New York: Semiotexte.

Walby, S. (1997) *Gender Transformations*, London and New York: Routledge.

Waldinger, R., Aldrich, A., Ward, R. and associates (1990) *Ethnic Entrepeneurs: Immigrant Business in Industrial Societies*, London: Sage.

Wallace, M. (1990) *Invisibility Blues*, London: Verso.

Walvin, J. (1973) *Black and White: The Negro and English Society*, London: Allen Lane.

Ware, V. (1992) *Beyond the Pale: White Women, Racism and History*, London: Verso.

Waters, M. (1995) *Globalization*, London: Routledge.

Weekes, D. (1997) 'Shades of Blackness: Young Black Female Constructions of Beauty', in H.S. Mirza (ed.) *Black British Feminism: A Reader*, London and New York: Routledge, pp. 113–26.

Whelan, W.J. and Black, S. (1982) *From Genetic Experimentation to Biotechnology: The Critical Transition*, Chichester and New York: John Wiley & Sons.

Whimster, S. and McGuire, M. (forthcoming) 'Rescuing Urban Ecology: The Case of Spitalfields', in L. Short (ed.) *Thinkglobal*, World Wildlife Fund UK and Cumbria College of Art and Design.

Whitten Jr., N.E. and Torres, A. (eds) (1992) *Blackness in Latin America and the Caribbean: Social Dynamics and Cultural Transformations: volume 2: Eastern South America and the Caribbean*, Bloomington and Indianapolis: Indiana University Press.

Wiegman, R. (1995) *American Anatomies: Theorizing Race and Gender*, Durham, NC and London: Duke University Press.

Williams, E. (1964) *Capitalism and Slavery*, London: André Deutsch.

Williams, P. (1997) *The Genealogy of Race: Towards a Theory of Grace*, Reith Lectures, London: BBC.

Williams, R. (1983) *Keywords*, London: Fontana.

Williamson, J.W. (1995) *New People: Miscegenation and Mulattoes in the United States*, Baton Rouge: Louisiana State University Press.

Williamson J. (1995) *Hillbillyland*, London: University of North Carolina Press.

Wilson, A. (1978) *Finding a Voice: Asian Women in Britain*, London: Virago.

Winant, H. (1994) 'Racial Formation and Hegemony: Global and Local Developments', in A. Rattansi and S. Westwood (eds) *Racism, Modernity and Identity: On the Western Front*, Cambridge: Polity, pp. 266–89.

Wood, E.M. (1986) *The Retreat from Class: A New 'True' Socialism*, London: Verso.

Wright, E.O. (1985) *Classes*, London: Verso.

Wright, E.O. (1997) *Class Counts: Comparative Studies in Class Analysis*, Cambridge: Cambridge University Press.

Young, E.M. (1997) *World Hunger*, London: Routledge.

Young, L. (1996) *Fear of the Dark: 'Race', Gender and Sexuality in the Cinema*, London: Routledge.

Young, R. (1990) *White Mythologies: Writing History and the West*, London: Routledge.

Young, R.C. (1995) *Colonial Desire: Hybridity in Theory, Culture and Race*, London: Routledge.

Zack, N. (1993) *Race and Mixed Race*, Philadelphia: Temple University Press.

Zack, N. (1997) *Race/Sex: Their Sameness, Difference and Interplay*, London: Routledge.

Zizek, S. (1997) *The Plague of Fantasies*, London: Routledge

Index